Virtual Gender

Fantasies of Subjectivity and Embodiment

Mary Ann O'Farrell and Lynne Vallone, Editors

Ann Arbor

The University of Michigan Press

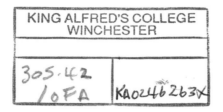
Copyright © by the University of Michigan 1999
All rights reserved
Published in the United States of America by
The University of Michigan Press
Manufactured in the United States of America
⊚ Printed on acid-free paper

2002   2001   2000   1999   4   3   2   1

A CIP catalog record for this book is available from the British Library.

Library of Congress Cataloging-in-Publication Data

Virtual gender : fantasies of subjectivity and embodiment / edited
    by Mary Ann O'Farrell and Lynne Vallone.
        p.   cm.
    "The essays in this volume were developed in response to issues
    considered at the 1996 Virtual Gender conference sponsored by the
    Interdisciplinary Group for Historical Literary Study (now the
    Center for Humanities Research) at Texas A&M University"—
    Includes bibliographical references and index.
    ISBN 0-472-09708-3 (cloth)
    ISBN 0-472-06708-7 (paper)
        1. Sex role.   2. Gender identity.   3. Body, Human—Social aspects.
    4. Women in popular culture.   5. Women in literature.   6. Gender
    identity in literature.   7. Feminist criticism.   8. Feminist theory.
    I. O'Farrell, Mary Ann.   II. Vallone, Lynne.
    HQ1075 .V57   1999
    305.3—dc21   99-6685
                                                                      CIP

Virtual Gender

Acknowledgments

The essays in this volume were developed in response to issues considered at the 1996 Virtual Gender conference sponsored by the Interdisciplinary Group for Historical Literary Study (now the Center for Humanities Research) at Texas A&M University. We thank conference directors Margaret J. M. Ezell and Pamela R. Matthews for producing the occasion for a constantly stimulating exchange of ideas. We would also like to thank Larry J. Reynolds, former director of IGHLS, for his leadership and encouragement. We are grateful to Larry, Margaret, and Pam for setting us on the rewarding task of editing this volume. J. Lawrence Mitchell, head of the department of English, and Woodrow Jones Jr., dean of the College of Liberal Arts, have been consistently supportive of the Interdisciplinary Group's efforts. As subsequent directors of the Group, Jeffrey N. Cox and James M. Rosenheim have provided significant assistance in the production of this volume. Patricia Brooke and Claire Carly have been invaluable editorial assistants. As always, Howard Marchitello, Pamela Matthews, and David McWhirter have been generous friends and readers. Members of the Interdisciplinary Group have been models of collegiality and congeniality and sources of the best intellectual challenge.

Contents

Introduction

Mary Ann O'Farrell and Lynne Vallone

Where is the body in fantasy? What are the consequences of fantasy for real and imagined bodies? How is gender inflected when fantasy separates it from its embeddedness in sex? Such questions suggest that the charged fantasies that become culture and ideology derive their charge in part from a complex relation to the body. The merely apparent virtuality of gender fantasy engages irresistibly the material body—whether understanding it as something to escape, something from which fantastic scenarios derive, or that on which fantasies inscribe themselves. And yet the establishment of a sex/gender distinction has elided the question of embodiment's relation to gender. But, as Robyn Warhol argues in this volume, "recent feminist theory enables us to see gender not so much as an entity in opposition to sex but, rather, as a process, a performance, an effect of cultural patterning." It is the work of the essays in this volume to restore and to explore the question of gender's relation to embodiment by balancing on the sex/gender divide—by investigating, that is, the profitable confusions through which bodies and gender have been understood and articulated. Such topics as transgender discourse, for example, as Bernice Hausman notes, "can demonstrate to feminism problems that exist in its own theoretical frameworks, as these are stretched to their breaking point by transgender theorists."

Critics of cyberculture have already been most engaged in considering the body's relation to gender: for them understanding cyberculture has meant debating the place of the body in a virtual realm, and articulating that place has meant confronting questions of gender. As a "wonderful *plot device*," virtual reality encourages experimental narratives of a subjectivity that exceeds the limitations of embodiment.[1] In this volume Kay Schaffer examines the ways in which "an oppositional politics" can be "conjoined with explorations of alternate sexual modalities and postmodern subjectivities." Virtual reality fantasies in which particular bodies are remade in virtual space (as ungendered or differently gendered, as disembodied, as more or less powerful and more or less vulnerable) are predicated on the central fantasy that the body can be transcended. But, if virtual fantasies sometimes involve playing with virtual fire, it is because virtual reality promises the lived body safe passage in that virtual world. As N. Katherine Hayles has noted, however, "Far from being left behind when we enter cyber-space, our bodies are no less actively involved in the construction of virtuality than in the construction of real life."[2] The components of the virtual body, that is, derive from a construction and an aesthetic of gender already found in the world (what Charlotte Canning describes as "the physical and material 'mess and clutter' of 'carr[ying]' history in the body"), and the world has long been operating with a notion that might profitably be named virtuality.

The debate between an idea of the virtual world as a site for alternative gender constructions and a concept of it as just another place where such conventions are replicated derives from prior and long-standing fantasies about gender. Notions about the significance of gender for behavior, aesthetics, and ethics have often been formulated in those genres and works we understand as literally "fantastic": in Singer's "Yentl," in *As You Like It*, in Ovidian metamorphoses and animal-groom folktales, in the Flies and Blobs and Things of cheesy 1950s cinema, in Barrie's Peter Pan no less than Mary Martin's, and in Wilde's picture of Dorian Gray. But gender fantasy has had as significant a place in the political realm—if a less acknowledged one—as in the literary and cinematic.

Our volume *Virtual Gender* offers a way of identifying and naming the persistent cultural desire for an imaginative space in which to "put on" alternative gender identities while examining as well the equally persistent and consequent critique of that desire. The body in gender fantasy may serve as platform or anchor, as ploy or foil, as impediment or toy. The essays in this volume tap the energies that circulate within and without this imaginative space (and within and without the imaginative body) from Queen Elizabeth I's assumption of a masculine prerogative to the performance of online identities. Reading literature, politics, performance, and cybertexts as well as cultural iconography and cultural criticism, the essays themselves debate the politics of gender fantasy, taking as their central figure for this imaginative space the notion of "virtuality." Collectively, the essays theorize virtuality, using the concept to examine cyber-art, for example, but also to extend virtuality beyond cyberspace to a consideration of print discourses. The term *virtual gender,* then, refers for these essays to the core set of issues at stake for subjectivity and embodiment in gender fantasy.

Exploiting the complicated and phantasmatic relationship between gender and the body for their profit in shaping the body politic and the cultural imaginary, some women have been able strategically to use gender's fluidity in order to offset gender's constraints. Elizabeth I is iconographically useful in this regard. Writing of the ways in which "a definite ascription of sovereignty combines with . . . indeterminacy regarding the . . . pertinence of a female monarch's gender," Janel Mueller notes that this indeterminacy, which we might call virtual gender, "emerges as a primary constituent of the rhetoric of Elizabeth's public self-representations." Elizabeth creates a fantasy of a masculine monarchy for her subjects and is able to exploit this fantasy from her unique position as female monarch. A similar indeterminacy facilitates the "elliptical expression of erotic feeling" in early modern English women's writing, according to Harriette Andreadis, who suggests that "a silencing of the relations between women had not yet taken place because the sexual borderlands demarcating transgression had yet to be defined." And early modern air travel, writes Sidonie Smith, generates a kind of fantastic virtual realm in which, while "the subject of mobility finds herself implicated in the cultural constructions of femininity as constitutive constraint, she discovers the mobilities and elasticities in those constraints."

But, if virtual gender names utopian gender fantasies, it can as easily refer to the imposition of cultural fantasies on material bodies. "When we talk of a national body politic," writes Carroll Smith-Rosenberg, "we are talking of *virtual reality*—the willing suspension of disbelief, the projection of an image upon the screen of public discourse, the acceptance of that projection as virtual, meaning functional, meaning real in the sense of really accepted and acted upon." If, as Helen Thompson suggests, the attention paid to the uterus by the 1784 French Royal Commission investigating Mesmerism "has less to do with the sex it would fix" than with the meanings attributable to bodies in the public sphere, it is nevertheless true that the discursive bodies produced in anti-Mesmerist discourse resemble too closely the physical bodies of French women in ecstasy. The women of Federalist America—more acted upon than acting in the "male rhetorical violence" of the new republic's periodical literature—are represented, Smith-Rosenberg argues, "as the political subject's negative others, and consequently as unfit, flawed members of the body politic." For Thompson's Mesmerist women, no less than for Smith-Rosenberg's Federalist women, discursive constructions of gender are "functional, . . . acted upon."

Working in different fields and speaking across disciplinary boundaries, contributors to this collection consider the claims of futurity and history; the status of embodiment; the origins of gender; gender politics; the pains of subjectivity; the uses of utopian fantasy; technological advancements and information technology; the experience of gendered communities; and the role of gender in global politics. By examining the contours of virtual gender, we are able to see both its difficult contradictions and the consistency of its dreams.

We have organized the ten essays, which share an interest in the gender politics of performing and embodying identity, into sections about gender fantasy and the public sphere, gender fantasy in imaginative space, and gender fantasy's inescapable physicality. Collectively, the essays write a history of embodiment's relation to gender as a discursive formulation, articulating the tensions involved in understanding gender as inevitably embodied yet fantasizing, sometimes, the body's release from the constraints imposed by gender and culture. The essays in part 1, "Subjectivities in the Public Sphere," examine the means by which gender is negotiated in the public spaces of twentieth-century cultural iconography (Smith), of early modern culture (Mueller), and of print (Thompson). The essays in part 2, "Engendering Virtuality," consider the implications of embracing the liberatory potential of fantastic space for gender play. Considering online bulletin boards (Warhol), performance (Canning), early modern Sapphic rhetoric (Andreadis), and cyberfeminist installations (Schaffer), these essays explore the subversive pleasures of imagination for the creation of gender identities. The essays in part 3, "Embodied Identities," together constitute a powerful reminder of the body and its exigencies. The crucial demands of real bodies (Hausman) and real politics (Smith-Rosenberg and Benhabib), this section indicates, have everything to do with the formation of the political subject, which has compelling consequences for lived experience.

Our collection conjoins its considerations of gender identity with a complex sense of cyberculture's reconceptualizations of subjectivity through the notion of virtuality. In doing so, this volume is able to link a contemporary interest in futurity and virtuality with an interest in history and gender play, and the essays debate the role of gender in literature, politics, cyberculture, history, sexuality, and public space. Virtual gender, the essays suggest, is best thought out in an interdisciplinary context. The juxtaposition of virtuality with reality, of body with fantasy, and of history with imagination generates a fruitful dialogue among essays in queer theory, popular culture, American studies, women's studies, performance, Australian cyber-art, early modern studies, and global politics.

Sidonie Smith's essay "Virtually Modern Amelia: Mobility, Flight, and the Discontents of Identity" initiates our contributors' discussions of the real work of virtual gender with just such productive juxtaposition. Smith's examination of Amelia Earhart's role in the cultural imagination locates

Earhart's adventurous "celebrity femininity" in the context of the notion of an "itinerant masculinity" that has previously understood itself in opposition to a fictively stationary womanhood. Considering Earhart's actions as aviator—as well as considering her account of those actions in her travel narrative—Smith offers a complex reading of the contradictory means by which women (as actors, as consumers, as ideas) revise avant-garde modernism and reveal its self-reflexive ambivalences.

Perhaps there is no body position more public than that of the sovereign. In "Virtue and Virtuality: Gender in the Self-Representations of Queen Elizabeth I" Janel Mueller argues that Queen Elizabeth's public gender identity was neither fixed nor immutable. The development of Elizabeth's "virtual gender" can be traced through the political speeches of self-account she made throughout her reign; these self-accountings justified her actions as a female monarch in full possession of her royal prerogative and power.

Helen Thompson's essay "Gender, or the King's Secret: Franz Anton Mesmer's Magnetic Public Sphere" investigates the role of gender in the practice of Mesmerism and the public scrutiny that evolved from it through secret and official royal commission reports as well as in illustrations of Mesmeric episodes. Devoted to describing and analyzing the "effects of Mesmerism upon the physiognomic and moral constitution of women," the secret report focuses on the "mobile nerves" and lively imaginations of women in general that account for the public and synchronous behaviors of Mesmer's female patients. Within and without the female body in Mesmeric "crisis," Thompson argues, the tensions and confusions of "publicity"— both theatrical and rational—are played out.

In "The Inevitable Virtuality of Gender: Performing Femininity on an Electronic Bulletin Board for Soap Opera Fans" Robyn Warhol listens to cyber-chat about soap operas as a way of considering technologies of gender. The Internet, Warhol maintains, makes it possible to attend to the always-virtual status of gender by separating "individual subjects' gender performances from the perceived sex of their bodies." Members of the online soap community—regardless of their sex—perform a discursive femininity brought online from the off-line context that informs soap opera as a cultural institution and soap viewing as a feminized habit and choice.

Charlotte Canning's essay "Remembering and Forgetting: Feminist Autobiography in Performance" describes the intersection of "memory, autobiography and identity" in the performance pieces *Sally's Rape* (1991) by Robbie McCauley and *Milk of Amnesia / Leche de Amnesia* (1994) by Carmelita Tropicana. Using the strategies of feminist autobiography, these two artists play out the struggle over racial, sexual, and gender identities in the context of American slavery and Cuban colonization and exile. Through their performances of "feminist truth-telling," Canning suggests, McCauley and Tropicana—and their audiences—are brought to resist forgetting and to perform change.

Sensitive to the problematic "back-projection" by means of which it is tempting for contemporary students of queer cultural history to read the evidences of premodern same-sex erotics, Harriette Andreadis considers what it means to discover and to examine past structures and practices without imposing on them the tenets of late-twentieth-century identity politics. Doing so, Andreadis's essay "Theorizing Early Modern Lesbianisms: Invisible Borders, Ambiguous Demarcations" considers the virtuality of sexual subject positions that have not yet been defined and reconstructs erotic friendships between "respectable" women in the early modern period, permissible because articulation has not yet made them available for policing.

Taking as its subject the cyberfeminist computer art installation and game All New Gen, Kay Schaffer's essay "The Game Girls of VNS Matrix: Challenging Gendered Identities in Cyberspace" considers the status of the political work undertaken as part of the game's experiments with sexual and gender identities. Though mindful of those institutions and structures that might recontain its best disruptive efforts, Schaffer celebrates the possibilities for virtual fantasy afforded by the VNS Matrix's game: if feminist cyber-art has not yet refashioned the world in its perverse image, it nevertheless makes it possible to articulate reimagined worlds and refigured identities through the complex oscillations involved in virtual gender play.

Considering the powerful virtual reality that constitutes the national body politic, Carroll Smith-Rosenberg's essay "Constituting Nations / Violently Excluding Women: The First Contract with America" examines the ways in which American national fantasy depends upon ridiculing women and excising them from that body. Bringing her examination of the feminist critique of liberalism to bear upon research into the representation of women in political debates about the Federal Constitution, Smith-Rosenberg finds that a developing male political identity strengthened itself by converting anxieties about women's imagined threats to the emerging nation into a compensatory sense of women as ridiculous, false, and unsuitable for participation in the public realm.

In her essay "Virtual Sex, Real Gender: Body and Identity in Transgender Discourse" Bernice Hausman spotlights the notion that gender is "virtual," as Warhol and others maintain. Through her interrogation of transgender theory and discourse, Hausman exposes the place of the body in the formation of identity and argues that identity cannot be understood as entirely distinct from the lived experience of the "real" body, whether differently or conventionally gendered. Facing up to gender's embodiment, Hausman suggests, can be a point of departure for the rectification of real-world gender discrimination.

In her essay "Sexual Difference and Collective Identities: The New Constellation" Seyla Benhabib engages a retrospective analysis of identity debates within feminism over the last two decades, coupled with an awareness of the insights and dangers inaugurated by "the new global constellation." By toggling back and forth between global political considerations and the concerns of feminist theory, Benhabib outlines a viable model for continuing to think about identities in the context of a radical democratic politics.

Benhabib's essay directs us toward the material contexts in which the stakes of virtual gender are realized. Benhabib recognizes "a new awareness afoot—a recognition of interdependence among women of different classes, cultures, and sexual orientations." For Carmelita Tropicana and for Queen Elizabeth, for us, there is always something at risk as well as in play in the realms of gender fantasy and something to be won as well as lost in virtual gender's implementation in the world of embodied subjectivities.

NOTES

1. Marc Laidlaw, "Virtual Surreality: Our New Romance with Plot Devices," in *Flame Wars: The Discourse of Cyberculture*, ed. Mark Dery (Durham and London: Duke University Press, 1994), 92.

2. N. Katherine Hayles, "Embodied Virtuality: Or How to Put Bodies Back into the Picture," *Immersed in Technology: Art and Virtual Environments*, ed. Mary Anne Moser and Douglas MacLeod (Cambridge, Mass., and London: MIT Press, 1996), 1.

PART 1. Subjectivities in the Public Sphere

Virtually Modern Amelia
Mobility, Flight, and the Discontents of Identity

Sidonie Smith

> Woman's place is in the home, but failing that the airodome.
>   —Lady Heath, qtd. in Susan Ware, *Still Missing*

> Men flyers have given the impression that aeroplaning is very
> perilous work, something an ordinary mortal should not
> dream of attempting but when I saw how easy men flyers
> handle their machines I said I could fly. Flying is a fine,
> dignified sport for women, it is healthy, and stimulates the
> mind.
>   —Harriet Quimby, "How I Made My First Big Flight
>   Abroad," *Fly* (June 1912)

> This new sport is comparable to no other. It is, in my opin-
> ion, one of the most intoxicating forms of sport, and will, I
> am sure, become one of the most popular. Many of us will
> perish before then, but that prospect will not dismay the
> braver spirits. In devoting themselves to the new cause, those
> who have the true aviator's soul will find in their struggle
> with the atmosphere a rich compensation for the risks they
> run. It is so delicious to fly like a bird.
>   —Marie Marvingt, *Colliers*, 30 September 1911

Mobilities and Virtual Gender

The anthropologist Victor Turner argues that the journey—as event, personal experience, and cultural symbol—creates, secures, and reproduces
communal meanings. Integral to the repertoire of meanings attached to
journeying in the West have been the meanings attached to itinerant masculinity and sessile femininity. Eric J. Leed enforces the constitutive

masculinity of travel when he argues that, "from the time of Gilgamesh," journeying has served as "the medium of traditional male immortalities," enabling men to imagine escape from death with the "crossing" of space and the "record[ing]" of adventures "in bricks, books, and stories." He even labels this travel, which provides men the opportunity to achieve notable distinction in futurity through differentiating experience far from home, "spermatic" travel.[1]

What Judith Butler describes as "the domain of socially instituted norms"[2] functions to "force" the domestication of women through protocols of proper femininity that tether women to home and to a requisite sessility that has nothing to do with futurity. "Not only is her place at home," writes Karen R. Lawrence, "but she in effect is home itself, for the female body is traditionally associated with earth, shelter, enclosure."[3] As Meaghan Morris observes, this "stifling home" has been precisely "the place from which the voyage begins and to which, in the end it returns."[4] Thus, the domain of socially instituted norms, as it tethers feminine subjectivity to sessility, confinement, convention, and servitude, forces the masculinization of the traveler, he who boldly negotiates unfamiliar and "undomesticated" spaces. Ever in the process of becoming men, travelers affirm normative masculinity through purposes, activities, behaviors, dispositions, perspectives, bodily movements, and through the narratives of travel returned to the sending culture. We cannot separate Odysseus from his travels nor Aeneas nor the Knights of the Round Table nor Columbus nor Captain Cook nor Boswell nor Byron nor Loti nor, closer to our own times, Jack Kerouac. Nor can we separate them from the narratives of their travels.

Their narratives can be read as journey myths "project[ing]," as Richard Slotkin suggests of myths generally, "models of good and heroic behavior that reinforce the values of ideology, and affirm as good the distribution of authority and power that ideology rationalizes."[5] But of course the purposes, activities, behaviors, dispositions, and perspectives determinative of itinerant masculinity and its myths in the West have changed over time. Specific kinds of travel have constituted specific kinds of traveling subjects: pilgrimage the medieval supplicant; exploration the survivalist; settlement the new capitalist entrepreneur; scientific exploration the "enlightened" observer; the grand tour the aristocratic/bourgeois gentleman, missionary landing the subject of "progress"; exotic flight the romantic rebel. And these travelers have returned with narratives that link mobilities to subjects and those subjects to particular worldings. Yet, however various the subject of travel (and his narratives), as an active and mobile subject—one who stands in awe, supplicates, survives, conquers, claims, penetrates, surveys, colonizes, studies, catalogs, organizes, civilizes, critiques, celebrates, absorbs, goes "native"—"the traveler" has remained endurably "masculine" and his claim on futurity endurably gendered.

At the end of the twentieth century the traveler can no longer be assured of earning any distinction in conventional mobility, since the realm of the formerly adventurous and individualizing has been saturated with other travelers, including large numbers of women travelers and large numbers of working-class and petit bourgeois travelers. (Nor can the traveler be assured that the home from which he sets out is sustained through any dependable sessility of domesticated women.) For some devotees of adventurous travel the onslaught of mass tourism has effected a "feminization" of travel. This is the implicit argument with which Leed concludes *The Mind of the Traveler* when he identifies in our cultural zeitgeist a "pervasive feeling" that "*real* travel," which he describes as "outward bound, hard, dangerous, and individualizing," is impossible due to the shrinkage of the globe into "one world," increasingly accessible to the many. Its very accessibility "foreclos[es] the possibility of escape" and thus the possibilities of "extending the male persona in time and space."[6] Real travel has become virtually impossible.

Technologies of Motion

New technologies of motion—locomotive, plane, automobile. Tourism. Masses of women travelers. These are not coincidental effects of modernity. Mass tourism in the West emerged at the same time that large numbers of middle-class women began to leave that stifling home for points foreign, increasingly as a result of the emergence of faster, safer, and more comfortable technologies of motion.

The distinguishing logic of itinerant masculinity has always had to do with the relationship of men to their animals or men to their machines of motion, that is, to emergent technologies of motion. Think, for instance, of Odysseus' vessels, communities of men bound together in an ethos of camaraderie. Or of the sometimes too intimate enclosed carriage of the grand tourist. Or of the horse crossing vast expanses of land. Or of the slow and often exhausting trek by foot across deserts or mountains or ice or tundra. Or of the automobiles of a Jack Kerouac. Each of these modes of motion is identified with "masculine" qualities. The sailing ship requires brute strength, sophisticated knowledge of navigation, courage, resilience. Travel by foot requires endurance and the capacity to defend oneself from possible attack. Horsemanship requires strength and skill. And it requires, to be effective with speed and rugged terrain, a straddling posture. Travel by foot requires stamina and a willingness to "get dirty." Travel by car involves speed and the danger that comes with sheer mechanical force, the power of four hundred horses.

The mechanics of motion before the nineteenth century—foot, horse, coach, sailing ship—were relatively slow, exposed, and oftentimes undependable means of travel. As the narrator of Marguerite Duras's novel *The Lover* recalls wistfully, "people were used to those slow human speeds on both land and sea, to those delays, those waitings on the wind or fair weather, to those expectations of shipwreck, sun and death."[7] The modes of motion were also exposed to the elements, to danger, and to the dirt of the ground. In Europe and in metropolitan centers in the Americas "respectable" female travelers (of the aristocratic and later the emerging bourgeois classes) were expected to keep their feet off the ground of travel. They might ride a horse, sidesaddle. But they usually rode in conveyances that prevented their feet from touching land.[8] If they traveled by foot they might cross-dress as a man in order to protect themselves from attacks on their bodies.

But the experiences of travel changed forever in the nineteenth century with the technological advances of the industrial revolution. In the 1840s the new steam engine harnessed tremendous forces only recently imaginable. With its steam-streamered signature, the railway changed the course of modernity, moving large numbers of people and goods across difficult terrain on a dependable schedule at relatively moderate expense. The luxury liner and the steam locomotive also provided the physical safety of protected enclosures and relatively comfortable passage at increased speeds. Within a half-century a succession of new forms of transportation, the bicycle, the airplane, and the automobile, further increased the safety, the comfort, the reach, the speed, the availability of transportation. With these new technologies came reorientations to time and to space, dramatic cultural shifts gaining momentum between the 1880s and World War I.

If, as Kristin Ross reminds us, "modern social relations are . . . always mediated by objects,"[9] then the social relations of travel and travel narrating are mediated by objects such as the locomotive, the airplane, the automobile. Each of the technologies that transport bodies through space organizes motion in ways that affect the temporal and spatial dynamics of travel, the perceptual relationship between the traveler and both landscape and humanscape, the experiential response of travelers to movement, the terms of liminality characteristic of border crossings, and the meanings travelers make of travel. Moreover, there are histories to technologies, to their development, design, deployment, transformation, to their rise and fall. And these histories intricately interpenetrate other histories, histories of feminisms and colonialism, for instance, or histories of knowledge production and subject formation.

The powerful engines that propelled vehicles through space at unimaginable speeds were increasingly pervasive symbols of modernity, audible from far distances. The grinding sound of locomotive engines, the drone of airplane wings, the honking of unruly automobiles, became the background noise of what Virginia Scharff calls "motorized modernity,"[10] announcing at every interval of the day the humming achievements of powerful economic forces and imperial ventures, announcing that the future had arrived. Products of increasingly sophisticated science and engineering, they were engines of dramatic change, extending the capabilities of human beings— taking them faster, farther, with more protection (and sometimes more danger) across the consecutive social spaces of cities, nations, of continents, of the globe itself.

As they permeated everyday life, these transportation technologies affected the organization of the social space through which vehicles and their passengers passed. If deployment of these technologies has rearranged the organization of "home," of countries, communities, and housing, their pervasiveness has restructured human perception and consciousness. Certainly, they have ratcheted up the speed with which individuals are bombarded with sensual data and impressions. Hurling through space, the traveler becomes conscious of constantly changing sounds, sights, smells, visual and spatial environments. And time, too, has been transformed through the technologies of modernity. For instance, the reach of the locomotive and the need to coordinate its movements as well as the instantaneity of telegraph communication required the imposition of World Standard Time, the organization of time sense that emanated from Europe and its imperial prerogatives and ceaselessly marks the segments of days in cultures across the globe.

Yet the speed with which the locomotive and the airplane ply space encourages in travelers an imaginative and private sense of time through the complex blurring of notions of past, present, and future.[11] Thus, the mechanics of motion generates dynamic tensions affecting the way the traveler experiences the "private" as opposed to the public or social movement of time. Stephen Kern elaborates certain implications of this transformed experience of time when he notes that the new technology "speeded up the tempo of current existence and transformed the memory of years past, the stuff of everybody's identity, into something slow."[12]

Throughout the reorganization of space, sense, perception, and consciousness produced in and produced by modern motion technologies, "the domain of socially instituted norms" persist. As Virginia Scharff says of the emergence of "motorized modernity," "the critical cultural categories of masculinity and femininity penetrated, applied to, and organized" the world of emergent technologies.[13] Invention, design, and production of machines were masculine endeavors. The thrusting power identified with machines such as the steam engine was decidedly phallic power. On the one hand, the new technologies of the airplane and the automobile were taken up avidly, promising as they did to affect a rejuvenated masculinity, a point to which I return. Flight and automobile travel promised new means of putting individualizing and defining adventure back into travel. On the other, new designs that sought to make machines and their traveling ensemble more comfortable were described as feminizing designs. The sleeping car. The automatic transmission. These were changes catering to the disabling characteristics of dependent femininity (even as they were embraced by male travelers). And, so, the world the machines transformed has been permeated by the same protocols of masculinity and femininity that characterize the travel the machines have made possible. As the editors of this volume suggest, the realm of the new technologies becomes "just another place where [gender] conventions are replicated."[14]

If the cultural preoccupation with mobility has been one of the defining conditions of modernity, the cultural logic of mobility has endured as a defining masculinist logic, stipulating normative conventions of sessile femininity as it projects normative scenarios of masculinity. This is not to say that it can be reduced to any universal expression of masculinity, since, as elaborated earlier, versions of masculinity are plural, their mobilization culturally and historically specific. Moreover, within culturally and historically specific locations "disparate versions of masculinity," as Judy Wajcman cautions, "reflect class division, as well as ethnic and generational differences."[15] Nonetheless, a masculinist logic sets men in motion through undomesticated spaces.

And, so, when a woman moves deliberately through undomesticated space she necessarily negotiates this cultural logic of defining mobility, whether or not she considers travel an enabling force in her struggle with women's cultural construction in subordination.[16] Yet mobility is undefining as well, in the sense that it puts under pressure the sedimented habits and identities attached to specific homes. Transportation into diverse spaces shifts the terms of self-locating within personal, familial, and communal environments. As Frances Bartkowski notes, to be mobile, to be in transit, is to enter a liminal zone characterized by the oscillation between the emptying of identity and the filling of identity.[17] As the editors of *Travelers' Tales* argue, "travel is corrosive" of the certitudes of subjects in transit.[18] In various senses of the word the traveler unbecomes a certain kind of woman as she voyages, literally and virtually, through new social spaces.

Through the narrative of her travels the traveler re/presents the motivations for, the itinerary, the destinations, the duress, the imaginative extension, and the achievement of travel. The narrator constitutes as un/defining, that is, the travel she seems merely to be reporting. As she does so she engages the terms of her negotiation of the liminal terrain between becoming and unbecoming the subject of ambivalent masculinity/femininity. As she does so, she rethinks travel through and away from its masculinist assumptions. For even as the subject of mobility finds herself implicated in the cultural constructions of femininity as constitutive constraint, she discovers the mobilities and elasticities in those constraints.

If identity functions as a perceptual point of transition, neither fixed nor entirely unfixed, through which the provisional meaning of travel materializes and fractures, the specific vehicle of motion, with its power to organize space, perception, consciousness, and encounter affects the identifications and misidentifications of travel. The mode of motion, whether locomotion, flight, automobility, or foot, is itself defining of the logic of mobility. Thus, technologies of motion have everything to do with the ways in which traveling women use mobility to achieve un/defining identity effects.

Redefining Masculinity a l'aire

Let's take flight as a case in point. At the end of the nineteenth century technologies of motion—the locomotive, the automobile, and the bicycle—remained earthbound, terrestrial technologies. With its inelegance and its routine obedience the locomotive had become a somewhat prosaic, an autochthonous beast. Certainly, there was still the excitement of acceleration, the brute power of its persistent motion, and the promise of speed and the terror of accident. But there was no take-off, no ascent. Of course, the balloon had offered sporadic occasions for the earthbound to rise and drift through the air. But the maneuverability of the balloon, always tenuous, depended more upon air currents than the technological acumen of the balloonist. Maneuverability was extremely limited. Thus, for all intents and purposes, technologies of motion remained earthbound.

All that changed with Kitty Hawk. At Kitty Hawk the Wright brothers lifted their heavier-than-air flying machine off the ground and held it suspended in air for those few fleet seconds. In trial flights and the subsequent demonstration events in Paris, the airplane and its pilot seemed to lift every spectator into another register of being. Dreams of flight that had preoccupied human beings for centuries, informing their myths, their imaginations, their science of observation, and their mechanical inventions, materialized in midair. Spectators, reporters, pilots themselves, proclaimed the end of the old order and the dawn of the new, one in which humans would defy the laws of gravity to conquer even the skies.

"As a semimagical instrument of ascent," suggests Lawrence Goldstein, "the flying machine offered to its apostles a form of *transport* in both familiar senses of that word. It provided a mobile and beatific vision of a new heaven and a new earth."[19] The radical disruption of gravitational pull evidenced in the ascent of the new machine signaled a radical rupture with the degenerate and constraining ground of the past and the inauguration of a new dispensation. Human beings were no longer earthbound; they were heaven bound. The modern century had taken off in a vehicle assembled out of nuts, bolts, cloth, sheet metal, and rubber tires.

Kitty Hawk and successor flights in the early decades of the twentieth century captured the imaginations of people on both sides of the Atlantic Ocean. Hundreds of thousands of people flocked to air races, where they accorded the new aviators overnight celebrity, lavishing them with money and homage for their daring aerial exploits. Wright, Blériot, Santos-Dumont, Farman, Latham, Lefevre, Chavez, Conneau. And the aces, Garros, Boelcke, Immelmann, Richthofen, Guynemer, Baracca. These were celebrity names in the early decades of aviation. Later, of course, there would be Lindbergh. Flight delivered the pilot from the clutches of chthonic groundedness, a groundedness that was historical and cultural as well as material. Thus, the aviator became a new type of hero—thoroughly modern and modernist man.

In the early reports of Orville Wright's 1909 exhibition flight in Paris the typology of the air pilot with Wright as progenitor was fixed through such defining characteristics as self-reliance, loneliness, insouciance, spirituality, dedication, indifference to the masses on the ground.[20] This myth of exceptionalist individuality stretched the distance between the hero and the common grounded mortal caught in the nets of bourgeois respectability or industrial dehumanization. Flight secured the metaphorical elevation of the new hero over the masses, whose aspirations to escape the earth he carried with him into the heavens. His was mythical transport.

The aviator's escape was represented as a gendered trajectory in which the new hero shed his complacent attachment to the enervating past and rose toward a revolutionary future.[21] Modernist poets and intellectuals, such as the futurist poet F. T. Marinetti, fervently embraced this renewed masculinization of the skies through aerial ascent from "mother" earth. Dedicating his 1909 play, *Poupées électriques: drama en trois actes* (*Electric Puppets*), to Orville Wright, Marinetti described the aviator as a man "who knew how to raise our migrating hearts higher than the captivating mouths of women."[22] Groundedness Marinetti identified with the moist, warm, malleable, seductive, devouring, and emasculating orifices of women. Mother earth and her female minions kept men too attached to the ground, to the baser realm of instinct and desire. Wright would take them up and away from such terrestrial snares, delivering them to a purified, lighter-than-air masculinity. Soaring heavenward, the aviator evaded the ground-edness identified with umbilical cords and an intolerable sessility. Then, too, soaring heavenward, he transcended the sexual anarchy on the ground, product of the crisis in gender identity so pervasive in the first decades of the twentieth century.[23] The aviator-hero was one potent answer to the crisis of masculinity below.

Aviator and machine were at one, soaring high above those on the ground in a dazzling display of aerial virility. Defying the laws of gravity, embracing the risk of the modern, the early aviators and air aces flirted with death with every ascent, a flirtation that became the value-added to the adventure of flight, the potential cost of escape from enervating sessility. That risk of the modern evidenced an audacious disregard for the dangers of sheer mortality.[24] Celebrating the élan and ethos of the aviator, the poet D'Annunzio announced that "danger seemed the axis of the sublime life."[25] This same D'Annunzio climbed into the cockpit during an air race in Italy in order to experience flight firsthand, thereby aligning himself with the "celestial helmsman" triumphant over nature, space, and time. D'Annun-zio's was a fervidly masculinist ethos. But his futurist ethos was a product of the general ethos of the time. In Vienna Sigmund Freud pondered the sym-bolic identification of flying machines and the penis, noting "the remarkable characteristic of the male organ which enables it to rise up in defiance of the laws of gravity."[26]

The new hero achieved his transcendence as he mastered "the cold, inhu-man machines that the nineteenth century had bequeathed" and "trans-form[ed] them into resplendent art and myth."[27] Unlike the machines that displaced man, controlled him, dwarfed him, airplanes enhanced the reach of his mastery. A prosthetic extension of the male form, the airplane func-tioned as a symbolic object through which masculinity could be restored. Here was technological, rational, thoroughly modern masculinity for an age awed by new technologies yet concerned about the ways in which those technologies contributed to the disciplining of individuals and the emasculation of men through systems of mass production. Magnified by mechanical form rather than diminished by it, men could be men rather than the "cautious, timid, and obedient workers" Michael S. Kimmel describes as the efficient products of those systems.[28] The "aces" of World War I "exemplified more purely than any other figure of their time what it meant to be a man."[29] Alone in the sky, fighting to the death, in control of the new machine, meeting his adversary man to man, dependent upon his own ingenuity in maneuvering his machine, the ace epitomized heroic motorized masculinity. Below him the masses of common soldiers huddled impotently in trenches, suffering the emasculating effects of fatigue, nerves, hysteria, shell shock, during the long intolerable wait at the lines.

Far below, in other global locations, the stunned members of the "backward" races, awestruck before the magic of new technology, gazed heavenward in fear and trembling, recognizing their own impotence before the remarkable power of aerial masculinity. Or so cartoons and posters serving the airline industry implied in their representations of colonial domination. For the invention and increasing sophistication of the airplane, just like the invention of the locomotive and the deployment of the railway system in the nineteenth century, reaffirmed for the West the superiority of its heroes and its cultural achievements. In official and popular discourses around aviation, the airplane immediately became the newest symbol of a triumphant modernity. With this radically new technology, according to early proponents of aviation, man would be able to "conquer" the air—that next (colonial) frontier. "The conquest of the air" was the metaphor commonly invoked to proclaim the benefits of the new technology. It was a phrase, as Robert Wohl notes, "designed to appeal to a young generation whose fathers and older brothers had only recently completed the conquest of the globe. The new empire to be subjugated lay in the sky."[30] Thus, proponents of aviation, hard-pressed to make the case for the utility of flight in the everyday lives of citizens, directed attention to the utility of aviation for national and imperial spread and for communal dreams of supremacy. If former frontiers of masculinist domination had closed to a new generation of men of fierce ambitions, the sky offered another domain for the demonstration of superiority.[31]

With its promise and delivery of a regenerative masculinity, flight rejuvenated an only apparently spent modernity. But aerial masculinity went further, linking technological and perceptual logics, and transforming the aviator into what artists and intellectuals of the early twentieth century described as a "poet of the air." For aerial subjectivity introduced a radically new way of perceiving the world.[32]

In flight, as earlier in railway travel, the aviator discovered speed without rootedness. Buoyant with speed, the airborne subject experienced the rush of lifting into (an illusory) immateriality. With ascent the scope of space and distance the eye could take in expanded exponentially. Incarcerated in a flying eye socket, severed from connections to things earthly, the aviator became a focalizing point of panoramic vision, producing for himself an order that took in vast space, an order from above rather than an order from eye level. No longer a sojourner in proximate space, he produced for himself as well perception independent of local roots and cultural contingency. Details of changing vistas blurred because distance made the ground and objects on the ground less individuated. Figures on the ground shrunk until they vanished into insignificance. Whole villages and single buildings, mountains and fields, all diminished in size until they compressed into two-dimensionality. Far below, the world appeared as a vast project of still fixedness. Increased distance between the aerial subject and the ground thus flattened out, abstracted, the world outside. A panoramic, abstracted, impersonal reality became the new reality of flight.[33]

Embracing a durable, if temporary, isolation, an individualism á l'aire, the aerial subject could imagine himself an omniscient subject, mastering space from above, rescuing distance from time and time from distance. The early aviators embraced flight for the kind of subjectivity it delivered to them. Enveloped in their cockpits, an interiority nested inside a mechanical interiority, they looked down and pondered the dynamic relationship of ground to flight. And they maneuvered through this space between ground and "I" by means of the mechanical prosthesis that was the plane itself, an extension of the body but not the body. The aviator thus became an early avatar of what Donna Haraway calls the cyborg subject, part human, part machine, a new kind of perceiving subject in a new kind of body, a virtual body freed from the constraints of an earthbound embodiment.

Aviator Narratives

To reproduce the myth-history of the aviator as new man, there had to be narratives by the aviators as well as poems, paintings, newspaper accounts, and promotional materials produced by the emergent aviation industry. Aviators themselves recognized the profitability—in monetary and celebrity terms—of writing about their experiences as air pilots. And so, by the late

1910s a new genre of aviation narrative had taken shape with its own conventions: dramatic stories of life-threatening incidents; commentaries on the land and people passed over; autobiographical information about the context of the flight; a record of emotional responses in flight; and the description of reception upon landing.[34] As the aviators produced the narratives through which they could secure their celebrity and profit from their status as new men, the narratives themselves produced the aviator as a certain kind of mythic hero.

Aviator narratives immediately became popular in the emerging film industry. In fact, the technologies of aviation and of the motion picture were contemporaneous developments, and they soon became mutually informing technologies. The history of aviation films begins in 1912 with Elvira Notari's Italian movie *The Heroism of an Aviator in Tripoli*. Soon after came the French film *Marriage by Aeroplane* in January 1914; *An Aerial Revenge* (1915); *Dizzy Heights and Daring Hearts* (1915); and *The Great Air Robbery* (1919).[35] In many of these early films the thrill and suspense of the filmic narrative centered on the dangers faced by the aviators, the central focus of the aviator narratives themselves. Yet joined to this plot of danger was a romance plot, integral to the narrative of homecoming. The returning aviator was rewarded for his heroism with a very grounded and grateful woman.[36] The romance plot of the early aviator films positioned women visually where they were understood to be—firmly on the ground in sessile anticipation. If they were involved in any kind of ascent, it was the ascending arc of their heads as they directed their gaze toward the sky. Raising their eyes heavenward, they watched passively with awe and anxiety the fate of the intrepid man in his prosthetic machine.

The conventions of normative femininity "grounded" woman, for she was identified with a femininity tethered to embodiment. The aviator Jean Conneau articulated the relationship of woman to aerial flight when he claimed that "aviation is for adults, alert, vigorous, of robust health, and capable of resisting fatigue. Such organic qualities are rarely found in women, and it's really a pity."[37] Women might be identified as "birds"— recall Torvald's nomination of ideal wife Nora in Ibsen's *A Doll's House*— but they were not expected to fly like a bird, at least not of their own volition, their own technical skill, their own daring. The sky was male territory and its conquest a male prerogative. To enter the cockpit of the airplane required the aviator to be technically skilled, quick to understand the machine, to identify with and through the machine, to be courageous, death defying, and dogged.

Aviator narratives, films, and popular discourses of aviation projected the sky as an imaginary domain uninhabited by women and thus far removed from the crises in gender identity roiling down below. On the ground female sexuality had been released as threat, as had the possibility of female enfranchisement. In the release into risk that accompanied ascent, the aviator seemed to rend the umbilical cord to sexual disorder and degenerate masculinity.[38] He promised a return to an earlier period before the crisis in masculinity, when, according to Kimmel, manly virility was synonymous with the character projected from deep within the rugged and isolated individual. His was the virile integrity of danger and of distance from the masses swarming as so many dots far below. Yet he was indisputably and reassuringly modern, since his was sure mastery of the powerful engines of modernity.

Women of the Air

But, as all such imaginary territories of identity, the sky proved to be about as unstable a domain of modernist masculinity as the ground below. For the gendered terms of social relations on the ground were contradictory and fiercely contested. Thus, while women may have been unwanted as compatriots in the conquest of the air, while they may have found it difficult to find men willing to give them flying lessons or to work with them on fashioning their machines, they became aviators. The increasing influence of motorized modernity created desires in women for speed and distance. In a time of purposeful, if cacophonous and competing, feminisms women quickly realized the value of technical expertise. They forged their own relationships to the new technology. They imagined themselves leaving the earth below as well. "It is so delicious to fly like a bird," enthuses Marie Marvingt in 1911, just months after Orville Wright stunned the other developers of flying machines in Paris. Women claimed the exhilarations of flight male aviators claimed— the sense of freedom, the mastery of the machine, the escape from sessility, the danger, and the pleasures of a new vision accessible to the chosen few.[39] They became agents of aerial modernity.

Raymonde de Laroche (of France), Marie Marvingt, Harriet Quimby, Eugenie Shakovskaya, and later Mathilde Moisant, Ruth Law, Bessie Coleman, Katherine Stinson, Marjorie Stinson, Amelia Earhart, and Anne Morrow Lindbergh. (And before them had come the aeronauts or balloonists— Madame Blanchard, chief of air service for Napoleon, Elisa Garnerin, Margaret Graham.) Women found ways to get lessons, even if they had to disguise themselves to do so. Raymonde de Larouche was the first woman to earn a license (in France). On August 1, 1911, Quimby earned the distinction of being the first American woman to earn her pilot's license. Even the African American Bessie Coleman found a way to get the training she needed to do stunt flying, although she had to go to France because no schools were open to African Americans in the United States. Despite these obstacles, Coleman was the first woman to earn an international pilot's license. Although commercial aviation was closed to women, women in the 1910s and 1920s found jobs as stunt pilots. They found ways to buy their own machines. They found sponsors for their attempts to break records. They found records to break, such as the long-distance record Ruth Law set in 1916. And they found ways to distinguish their new identities through dress. In the air these women became avatars of modern woman, comfortable with powerful and dangerous machinery.[40] Whatever their expressed political views, theirs was a tacit motorized feminism.

Thus, the age of aviation introduced a new spectacle of femininity. Mastery of this radical mode of mobility shifted the defining logic of identity. Flight transported the modern woman to an imaginary domain through which to negotiate the constitutive constraints of normative femininity and its discontents through familiarity with modern technology and with that familiarity escape, if only temporarily, from sessile femininity. And with the new woman of the air came new cultural narratives through which the "aviatrix" was made visible as a particular type of modern woman and through which cultural anxieties about gender identity and about sexual anarchy in the skies were played out.

Virtually "Earhart"

Up in the air the female aviators of the late 1920s and 1930s "put on" alternative gender identities. In their narratives of flight they negotiated, in distinct ways, the cultural anxieties that attended their exceptional feats and the virtual masculinity identified with their technological proficiency and their familiarity with the dangerous zone of flight. It is to one of these narratives, Amelia Earhart's first aviator narrative, that I turn to explore how the woman of flight imagined the future of the skies as a virtual space for women.

Earhart wrote two narratives of flight—*20 Hrs. 40 Min. Our Flight in the Friendship, The American Girl, First across the Atlantic by Air, Tells Her Story* (1928) and *The Fun of It* (1932). *20 Hours* capitalizes on her celebrity status after the flight of the *Friendship* on June 18, 1928. Its production and publication was, from our point of view, startlingly swift. She finished writing the narrative on August 25, barely two months after the flight. The published book hit the bookstores two weeks later, on September 10.[41] The speed with which her narrative reached the mass public testifies to the utility of narrative in the marketing of celebrity. Her publisher, Putnam, recognized what a salable commodity Earhart had become. If the flight of the *Friendship* made Earhart's name a household word in Europe and the United States, her narrative of that flight could play a critical role in catalyzing the public's romance with "Amelia." Soon there would be other commercial venues of celebrity, a line of clothes and a line of airline luggage, speaking tours, and advertisements for products such as Lucky Strikes. But first there had to be narrative.

Earhart's complex relationship to celebrity femininity is captured in the reflexive passage with which she concludes her narrative. Here she invokes the metaphor of the text as plane.

> Finally the little book is done, such as it is. Tomorrow I am free to fly.
>
> Now, I have checked over, from first to last, this manuscript of mine. Frankly, I'm far from confidant of its air-worthiness, and don't know how to rate its literary horse-power or estimate its cruising radius and climbing ability. Confidentially, it may never even make the take-off.
>
> If a crash comes, at least there'll be no fatalities. No one can see more comedy in the disaster than the author herself. Especially because even the writing of the book, like so much else of the flight and its aftermath, has had its humor—some of it publishable! (280–81)

The tone here is one of tongue-in-cheek apologetics. In pointing to her vulnerability as a writer and her competence as an aviator, Earhart reaffirms her knowledge of planes, the locus of her credibility as author, but she also reveals how critical the book is to her achievement of celebrity, in a way second only to flight itself.

Earhart's book becomes a metaphorical plane, a form of transport technology carrying flight into the everyday life of her readers and transporting "Amelia Earhart" through the world as a popular icon. In order to maintain her public identity as aviator she must fly; and in order to fly she must raise money; and to raise money she must remain a public icon. Thus, her return home through narrative must be a return to publicity. The female aviator must become and remain a public spectacle in order to maintain her celebrity. Having lifted off the ground and put on an alternative gender identity—the very grounds of her celebrity—Earhart can only remain aloft through the imperative of visibility politics.

The photographs, title, and opening testimonial Putnam editors attached to *20 Hours* function as framing devices that "package" Earhart as a particular kind of celebrity. Scholars of the Hollywood "star" system have argued that the celebrity figure "gives a form of embodiment to the mass subject,"[42] fleshing out for the consuming masses imaginary selves and imaginary lives through which they can fantasize future selves. For such an embodiment visibility is essential. Thus the obligatory photographs incorporated into the text. Identifying Earhart with the engine of the modernity, the airplane, and with a monumental event, the flight across the Atlantic, the photos collectively present the spectacle of the exceptionalist individual—with a particular style of flesh. Free of fleshly excess, hers is a taut body designed functionally for mobility, a virtually weightless body that appears to have severed the relationship of femininity and sessility. Mannish, even boyish, the "slim, exercised, and active feminine body" of the aviatrix signifies, according to Barbara Green, "a pared-down modernism and machine-age aesthetic."[43] In these photos Amelia is made visible and proximate through a visual iconography associated with athletic femininity. Slim, boyish, open-faced, hers is a gender-blended embodiment of heroic modernism. This emblem of modernity offers the public, especially young girls, a way of fantasizing themselves as thoroughly modern young women without having to mark themselves as too visibly masculinized.

The title and testimonial work to familiarize the exceptional young woman as well. The epithet the long title attaches to this thoroughly modern subject of flight is "the American girl." *American* designates Earhart's role as emblem of the national modern, sign of America's advanced status in the community of modern nations. Thus, Earhart's achievement can be recuperated not as transgressively masculine but as part and parcel of the national agenda of "progress." The more familiar appellation *girl* defuses cultural anxieties about female exceptionalism by containing the aviatrix within normative repertoires of "girl" femininity. Earhart is the girl next door who has dedicated herself to serving others, not pursuing her own self-interests. This is the message offered in the introductory testimony by Marion Perkins, head worker at Denison House, Boston's second oldest settlement house (11–17). According to Perkins, the daring young woman who has poached on the domain of aerial masculinity is really social worker and educator, a familiar of the traditionally feminine sphere of work, a familiar of traditionally feminine values.

Supplements to Earhart's narrative, the framing devices of photos, title, and testimony render the exceptional aviator, the woman of the skies, simultaneously a modern and traditional young woman, a young woman of the future and a woman of the past. To the degree that the technical feats of the modern young woman in the flying machine are celebrated and mediated by traditional norms of femininity, she becomes a figure at once remote and familiar. Such remoteness in familiarity, such familiarity in remoteness, is critical to the making of the celebrity status of the female aviator.

The narrative that Earhart offers her reader does similar kinds of work but with far more complex effects. On one level *20 Hours* unfolds according to the formulaic logic of aerial adventure. The aviator opens with a brief autobiographical sketch of her childhood and young adulthood; she describes her training as a pilot; she describes how she was chosen to make the trip; she chronicles the long tortuous delay in Trepassey, Newfoundland, the indolence from the wait, the abortive attempts at take-off, the isolation; she describes the flight itself and, of course, the reception in England. This is the standard fare of masculinist aviation narratives, designed to foreground the character traits of the indomitable hero, "his" mastery of the new technology, and the exceptional, because dangerous, feat of adventurous flight. In effect, this is the story that must be told—the defining fable of aerial mobility. It provides the aviator with a characterological portrait and an action script of agency. But there's a young woman rather than a man in the cockpit of the narrative, a young woman negotiating the strange celebrity that attends her fortuitous adventure in the domain of aerial masculinity. And to that negotiation she brings familiar moves. That is, through discursive strategies coded as appropriately feminine Earhart represents herself as less than truly heroic, less than virtually masculine.

For one, she reframes her achievements as modest rather than risky. In the foreword she is diffident, self-denigrating. Admitting her inability to write "a work," she expresses hope that the book catches the "fun" of flying and "that some of the charm and romance of old ships may be seen to cling similarly to the ships of the air" (9). Suddenly catapulted into fame, "America's girl" presents herself as flying for the fun of it rather than for some serious purposes as men do. And she signals that, as a woman of somewhat comfortable means, she does not have to fly to make a living. Thus, she offers indirect assurance to her reader that she is not seriously competing with men for mastery of the skies nor challenging the identification of the aviator as new man.

America's girl also anchors her professional identity in the sphere of social and educational work rather than the sphere of adventure. She describes her early interest in nursing and in settlement work as well as her job at Denison House. Later, in recalling her activities in London after the flight, she tells of her tour of Toynbee Hall, the London settlement house that served as a model for such houses in the United States. In this way

Earhart implies that her values have not changed with her entry into the world of aviation, that she remains a young woman dedicated to serving others, that her values are tethered securely to the ground of conventional gender arrangements.

The logic of serving comes through as well in her detailed report of the flight across the Atlantic. Here she enacts her role as educator when she uses the logbook as a teaching tool. Incorporating passages copied directly from the logbook as the narrative spine of the journey, Earhart interprets, for the uninitiated reader, the nitty-gritty details of flight—how the plane was organized, where the gas tanks were located, how she spent her time, what the crew ate. "The gastronomic adventures of trans-oceanic flying really deserve a record of their own," she writes facetiously. "Ham sandwiches seemed to predominate en route" (141). These are the small domestic details of flight. She uses the occasion as well to inform her reader about the technicalities of flight. "People are so likely to think of planes as frail craft that I draw attention to this entry," she writes: "Friendship weighs 6,000 pounds empty, and on the flight she carried about her own weight again" (176). She explains how, against common sense, the higher you fly the safer you are. In this attention to the quotidian Earhart familiarizes her reader with the world of aviation, makes the world of flight more common and less fantastic.

Rather than concluding the narrative of her historic flight with the self-aggrandizing description of the hero's welcome she received in London, Earhart diverts attention away from herself as heroic protagonist in two ways. First, as a missionary for aviation, she addresses larger issues having to do with the state of aviation (especially with women as passengers and aviators). In "Aviation Invites" Earhart prognosticates that aviation will and can become part of everyday life and proclaims the experience of flight to be "matter-of-fact" (216). When she translates the technology of flight through the technology of automobility, using the experience of driving to capture for her female reader the experience of flight (220), she brings airborne subjectivity back down to earth. She also dismisses her reader's fear by poking fun at those who express fear of flying: "I know a woman who was determined to die of heart failure if she made a flight. She isn't logical, for she rolls lazily through life encased in 100 lbs of extra avoirdupois, which surely adds a greater strain on her heart—besides not giving it any fun, at all" (218). Ultimately, Earhart makes the airplane over into an everyday item of consumption. "It is the modern note in transportation," she declares, "comparable to the electric refrigerator, vacuum devices and all the other leisure-making appliances of the household. Aviation is another time-saver ready to be utilized" (237–38). Likened to a vacuum cleaner, the plane becomes just another household commodity. By implication the aviator becomes a kind of aerial housewife going about routine domestic duties. She takes sessility into the skies.

Second, in her final chapter Earhart assesses her notoriety as "a public character" but with a lightness and humor that undermines any lionizing self-promotion (281). She catalogs the mail she receives, including several examples of strange and humorous correspondence, offers of marriage, letters condemning her sponsorship of a particular brand of cigarettes, silly photos, poetry (289). An editorial diminishing her contribution to the flight is sent her by someone who underlines certain passages in it, such as "*her presence added no more to the achievement than if the passenger had been a sheep.*" To this Earhart responds whimsically with a parenthetical comment: "This is the zoological last straw! After two weeks of mutton at Trepassey I'm sure the boys would not have endured the proximity of a sheep as cargo on the Friendship" (292). She notes the editorial that asserts that she had little to do on the flight and that her notoriety came only from the fact that she was a woman. She reproduces the long joke she receives about Amelia Earhart as a stereotypical "back seat driver" (295–301). In a text designed to insure her celebrity status, Earhart simultaneously establishes her celebrity credentials and pokes fun at herself as a celebrity, brings herself back down to earth.

The airplane lifts Earhart out of the repertoires of femininity on the ground, and doing so introduces into the skies the gender blending that threatens heteronormative social arrangements on the ground. But the narrative of her flight reattaches Earhart to certain repertoires of femininity. The antiheroic rhetoric of domesticity, the logic of service, the missionary purpose, the self-deflating humor, these are discursive features through which Earhart positions herself as a traditional American girl espousing an ethics of domesticity.[44] Through such presentational features she neutralizes the identification of the female aviator as threateningly masculine, as out of place in the imaginative space of masculine mobility. But, in representing herself as less than truly heroic, she also affects a transformation of the imaginary domain of flight itself. As it joins traditional repertoires of femininity to the modern spectacle of aviation, therefore, Earhart's narrative undoes, even as it reproduces, certain defining features of aviator narratives. With the invocation of the word *fun* in reference to aviation and its recurrence in the title of her 1932 sequel, *The Fun of It,* Earhart shifts the associative register for imagining aviation from "danger" to "fun."

Emptying the sky of much of its danger, this female aviator severs the identification of flight with a masculinity of risk. The "intrepid birdman" of an earlier era of flight has become the proper girl next door. Then, instead of romanticizing the journey and distancing herself from her grounded readers, she educates her reader, sharing her knowledge with them in a voice of intimate engagement. In educating the mass public, and specifically women, about the quotidian details of the spectacular "event," Earhart encourages a familiarity with flight that is potentially empowering for women. She also reimagines flight as a domestic drama, a drama through which the uncommon aviator is brought back down to earth. Familiarizing flight and deflating the heroic difference of the aviator, Earhart redefines the relationship of women to this engine of modernity. As she does so, she demystifies flight as a domain of aerial masculinity and the aviator as a remote and uncommon subject.

Critically, this demystification of the domain of aerial masculinity through the figure of the ladylike young woman (Earhart was dubbed, remember, "Lady Lindy") was part of a larger cultural transformation. With her historic flight across the Atlantic in 1927 Amelia Earhart was drawn into "the selling of aviation." In order to domesticate aviation and to facilitate the development of commercial aviation, to make the skies a safe and comfortable space for consumers of air transport, the earlier representation of flight as daring, dangerous, remote, fantastic, and romantic had to be displaced by another kind of representation. Flight had to be remade as practical rather than exotic so that masses of people, formerly so many dots on the ground, could rise up into the air. The intrepid birdman image had to be displaced. And the woman aviators were enlisted by the airline industry to do the work of transformation. As Joseph J. Corn acknowledges, it was the cultural stereotype of women aviators as "frail, timid, unathletic, and unmechanical" that opened opportunities for women aviators in the later 1920s and 1930s. "Who could better supplant the masculine, athletic image of fearless, superhuman aviators and allay peoples anxieties about flight."[45] In the years from 1927 to 1940 women were hired to demonstrate planes and to sell them. They were funded to enter races and undertake promotional flights. Their celebrity was sustained by the industry that needed them to launch the new age of aviation.

As an agent for the airline industry and for the cause of flight more generally, Earhart appeals to conventional gender stereotypes when she talks of women as customers. "As [women] become an important factor in passenger revenue," she predicts in "Women in Aviation," "their requirements will be increasingly studied and met" (238). She assures her readers that the airline industry will make over the spaces of aviation (airplane, airport) as attractive and suitable places for women. They will become comfortable, safe, clean, "feminized" sites. Yet, when Earhart discusses women as pilots, she discards the discourses of gendered differences and assigned spheres. She recognizes the difficulty women have in getting the requisite training since they do not have access to the armed services, where many men learn to fly (240). Nor do they have easy access to other training opportunities. But, having nodded to their disadvantages in gaining access to aviation, she proceeds to describe for her readers how they excel in the kinds of skills required of the aviator, the risks encountered, the safety factors. In the course of doing so, she casually dismisses arguments against women's participation in aviation based on some essential incapacity for technical challenge and constitutional aversion to danger. Individual women can make their way and claim a legitimate place in aviation on their own individual merits. Promoting women as aviators in this way, Earhart claims a continued place for women in the domain of aerial masculinity. Or, rather, she redefines the domain of aerial subjectivity as neither male nor female, as virtually genderless. In this instance hers is an invasive female agency motivated by the politics of exceptionalist individualism. Here, at this particular point in her narrative, Earhart halts the logic of domestication.[46]

Earhart's narrative plays in most aspects to the cultural consumption of exceptionalist individualism. That consumption is requisite for her celebrity. Her "female" readership will consume her story because of her status as aviator. But the text is also addressed to women as domestic consumers and designed to facilitate the inevitable domestication of flight by making the mass of women more comfortable with the idea of flight. This transformation of aviation from an arena of exceptionalist individualism to the domain of consumerism portends the inevitable demise of the mythic hero of the air and the celebrity the text is meant to sustain. As those masses reimagine themselves as aerial subjects, this thoroughly modern arena of exceptionalist individualism vanishes. The vacuumization of flight disrupts the logic of aerial heroism.

The Conclusion to an Era

Even as the proponents of avant-garde modernism hailed the aviator as new man and flight as a medium of stylistic innovation, in popular modernisms—films, celebrity publicity, aviator narratives—the figure of the "bird woman" became a site around which modernist themes and the ambivalences of modernity circulated. In multiple ways Amelia Earhart, like Anne Morrow Lindbergh and Beryl Markham after her, negotiated the anxieties of modern social relations generated by the airplane and the transformation of the world inaugurated at Kitty Hawk. Entering the imaginary domain of aerial masculinity, she became an agent of modernity, affirming her right to a future in the skies. Through familiarity with this most modern of modern technologies she escaped, at least momentarily, the domestication of women through protocols of proper femininity and released herself from defining sessility. Yet she encountered in her aerial exploits and the celebrity that they bestowed on her the phantasm of the "lady flier" and all the cultural iconography attached to her—from her sleek, boyish figure to her perceived incompetence to her radical threat. The Amelia Earhart of the narrative was thus a virtual effect of the celebrity status achieved by the early aviatrixes and the cultural meanings their penetration of the skies generated in the fantasies of the mass of mortals huddled on the ground.

The period of the celebrated female aviator was a short-lived one, spanning 1927 to 1940. For that brief stretch of years celebrity was made possible by the agency of the individual aviators who entered the small planes maneuvering through the skies, the imperatives of an airline industry intent on expansion, and the spectacular event—the air race, the high-altitude test, the first flight across country, continent, or ocean. In addition to aviator, industry, event, and machine, it was made possible as well by the myth of progress, with its imperialist design. Thus, the lady flier became an emblem of the most modern of women, an emblem of the futurity of Western womanhood. But, of course, these aviators were doing other cultural work than merely representing Western womanhood. If the masses of people, formerly so many dots on the ground, were to rise up into the air, the sky had to be made "safe" for less heroic consumers. And the women aviators, by affirming for the masses that flight was safe and comfortable, that it didn't require exceptional heroics, that even young women could feel comfortable up there in the skies, played their role in the transformation of aviation to big business. They made compelling advertising copy.

Agent or advertising copy. The palpable tensions in Earhart's very popular aviator narrative encompass without fully resolving the problems of celebrity feminism in an age of rising consumer culture. Amelia Earhart is at once an active agent of aerial modernity, an avatar of the national modern, and the commodified agent for a more conservative agenda, the domestication of flight in service to big business. It is precisely the event as remarkable that assigns Earhart her elevated status. But her role as spokeswoman for the emerging commercial aviation industry means that she has to empty the event of its extraordinary and dangerous dimension. America's girl, whose winsome image was broadly reproduced—in her own narrative, in advertisements, on newsreels—participates in the dismantling of this frontier of defining heroism.

So Earhart's identity is itself placed in transit by this modernist mode of travel and the contradictory logics of her narrative of flight. Out of expediency and a wily disingenuousness, Earhart traverses values from masculinist exceptionalism to domestic consumerism and the acceptable feminism of her modern admirers. They in turn consume her fantastic aerial identity.

The end of the 1930s marked the end of the era of small aircraft and the individualist heroism associated with flight. World War II and the rise of commercial aviation would bring bigger planes, larger crews, and routine flights. With this transformation to commercial aviation women found little access to jobs as pilots. Soon the figure of the confident lady air pilot was displaced by the figure of the smiling stewardess.[47] (It would be decades before Sally Ride would gain celebrity by blasting off into the future at Cape Canaveral.)

But the figure of Amelia Earhart has persisted in the cultural imaginary since she ended up paying the ultimate price of the risk of flight—and undermining her message to potential consumers about flight's safety. With her disappearance over the Pacific Ocean in 1937 Earhart became a virtual emblem of gender-blended exceptionalist heroism. Because Lady Lindy left us without the body of evidence, without the body as evidence of a fixable death, her phantasm continues to haunt the imaginary spaces of the vast Pacific Ocean. Amelia Earhart continues to fly forever high above the ground and the grounds of a fictively stationary womanhood. And down below, on the ground, new books written about her and new documentaries made of her life and new theories of her disappearance continue to be consumed with unabated interest.

If, to reprise the claim of Ross, "modern social relations are . . . always mediated by objects," then virtually modern Amelia remains unimaginable without the prosthetic airplane against which she was so often photographed and in which she disappeared. Her untimely death guaranteed that she would forever be one with the airplane that brought her celebrity. In this sense the cultural memory of Amelia Earhart testifies to the persistence of virtual—and virtually masculine—heroism.

NOTES

1. Eric J. Leed, *The Mind of the Traveler* (New York: Basic Books, 1991), 286. For a fascinating tracking of the etymological roots of the words for travel in Indo-European languages, see esp. 5–14.

2. Judith Butler, *Bodies That Matter: On the Discursive Limits of "Sex"* (New York: Routledge, 1994), 182.

3. Karen R. Lawrence, *Penelope Voyages: Women and Travel in the British Literary Tradition* (Ithaca: Cornell University Press, 1994), 1.

4. Meaghan Morris, "At the Henry Parkes Motel," *Cultural Studies* 2 (1988): 12.

5. Richard Slotkin, *Regeneration through Violence: The Mythology of the American Frontier, 1600–1860* (Middletown: Wesleyan University Press, 1973), 507.

6. Leed, *Mind,* 286.

7. Marguerite Duras, *The Lover,* trans. Barbara Bray (New York: Harper Collins, 1986), 115.

8. See Annegret Peltz, *Reisen Durch die Eigene Fremde: Reiseliteratur von Frauen Als Autobiographische Schriften* (Koln: Bohlau, 1993).

9. Kristin Ross, *Fast Cars, Clean Bodies: Decolonization and the Reordering of French Culture* (Cambridge: MIT Press, 1995), 5.

10. Virginia Scharff, *Taking the Wheel: Women and the Coming of the Motor Age* (Albuquerque: University of New Mexico Press, 1991), 165.

11. For a fascinating analysis of the interrelationships of new technologies, cultural practices, artistic movements, and notions of human consciousness between 1880 and the end of World War I, see Stephen Kern, *The Culture of Time and Space, 1880–1918* (Cambridge: Harvard University Press, 1983).

12. Kern, *Culture of Time and Space,* 129.

13. Scharff, *Taking the Wheel,* 165.

14. Mary Ann O'Farrell and Lynne Vallone, eds., *Virtual Gender: Fantasies of Subjectivity and Embodiment* (Ann Arbor: University of Michigan Press, 1999), 2.

15. Judy Wajcman, *Feminism Confronts Technology* (University Park: Pennsylvania State University Press, 1991), 143.

16. See Chantal Mouffe, "Feminism, Citizenship, and Radical Democratic Politics," in *Feminists Theorize the Political,* ed. Judith Butler and Joan W. Scott (New York: Routledge, 1992), 382.

17. Frances Bartkowski, *Travelers, Immigrants, Inmates: Essays in Estrangement* (Minneapolis: University of Minnesota Press, 1995), esp. xiii–xxviii.

18. George Robertson, Melinda Mash, Lisa Ticknew, Jon Bird, Barry Curtis, and Tim Putnam, eds., *Travellers' Tales: Narratives of Home and Displacement* (New York: Routledge, 1994), 5.

19. Lawrence Goldstein, *The Flying Machine and Modern Literature* (Bloomington: Indiana University Press, 1986), 5–6.

20. Robert Wohl, *A Passion for Wings: Aviation and the Western Imagination* (New Haven: Yale University Press, 1994), 27.

21. Wohl, *Passion,* 268.

22. F. T. Marinetti, *Poupées électriques: drame en trois actes* (Paris: E. Sansot, 1909), 36.

23. See Lyn Pykett, *Engendering Fictions: The English Novel in the Early Twentieth Century* (London: E. Arnold, 1995), 19.

24. Wohl, *Passion*, 255–56.

25. D'Annunzio, *Forse che si forse che no* (Milan: Treves, 1910), 68. Quoted in Wohl, *Passion*, 122.

26. See Gillian Beer, "The Island and the Aeroplane: The Case of Virginia Woolf," in *Nation and Narration*, ed. Homi K. Bhabha (New York: Routledge, 1990), 265. See esp. Beer's note 2.

27. Wohl, *Passion*, 29.

28. Michael S. Kimmel, "Consuming Manhood: The Feminization of American Culture and the Recreation of the Male Body, 1832–1920," *Michigan Quarterly Review* 23.1 (1996): 7–36.

29. Wohl, *Passion*, 282.

30. Wohl, *Passion*, 69.

31. The conquest of the air not only signified the thrust into new spaces available for "colonization." It also had very profound effects for the consolidation of colonial empires. Aviation was recognized early on as an invaluable means to maintain and to expand colonial control. Colonies could be more efficiently mapped, organized, and administered with the help of the airplane and its "magical" powers. Moreover, since planes would "diminish the importance of distance" (Wohl, *Passion*, 81), they would facilitate not only the internal unification of colonies but also the exchange between the colonies and the metropolitan centers of Europe. Then, too, airplanes offered another opportunity for the Western powers to assert their dominance and to stun their colonial subjects with the dazzling display of their obvious superiority. For some enthusiasts this magical machine without legs or attachment to earth promised to dazzle the more "primitive" colonial subjects, for whom it would become a kind of god from the sky. Finally, the ability of the airplane to reach inaccessible locations, and to transport people to such locations, was another reason they were seen as important to colonial control and warfare.

Technological mastery of the skies (and time) became associated not only with the advancement over the colonized peoples of the world but over the enemies of national progress as well. The nationalist dreams of colonial and imperial spread were fed by the recognition of the importance of aviation to modern warfare. The conquest of the air would ensure victory in the skies overhead, signifying the superior might of one nation over its enemies. Early in aviation history novelists and poets as well as the aviators themselves, and their publicists and supporters, recognized this linkage, as is evidenced by the appearance of H. G. Wells's prescient visions of aerial combat in *The War in the Air* (1908).

32. Wohl, *Passion*, 272.

33. This abstracted mode of seeing linked the aviators in the air to certain avant-garde artists on the ground. Identifying with the future that flight augured, with its energy, vibrancy, promise of unboundedness, the painter Delaunay, for instance, used the airplane as a generative image in his canvases. Delaunay's propellers slash the space of the canvas, shattering color into patches of vibrating light, rearranging and redefining the space of representation in ways analogical to the ways in which flight redefined the aviator's relation to physical space. And Wohl suggests that for the Russian formalist Malevich "flight became a metaphor for the transformation of

consciousness, its liberation from the constraints of normal day-to-day existence, and the redefinition of time and space" (Wohl, *Passion*, 161).

34. Wohl, *Passion*, 271.

35. Stephen Pendo, *Aviation in the Cinema* (Metuchen: Scarecrow Press, 1985), 10.

36. Wohl, *Passion*, 278.

37. Qtd. in Wohl, *Passion*, 282n. 87.

38. See Kimmel, "Consuming Manhood," 16.

39. Wohl, *Passion*, 256–57.

40. Yet their history has been all but erased, except for the story of Amelia Earhart, the aviator who garnered the most publicity.

41. Ware, *Still Missing: Amelia Earhart and the Search for Modern Feminism* (New York: Norton, 1993), 108.

42. Miriam Hanson, "The Mass Production of the Senses: Classical Cinema as Popular Modernism," paper delivered at the University of Michigan, Program for the Comparative Study of Social Transformations, 26 March 1997.

43. Barbara Green, *Spectacular Confessions: Autobiography, Performative Activism, and the Sites of Suffrage, 1905–1938* (New York: St. Martin's, 1997), 23.

44. As Joseph J. Corn suggests, the women aviators of the late 1920s and 1930s "self-consciously conformed to feminine norms for the cause of flight" ("Making Flying 'Thinkable': Women Pilots and the Selling of Aviation," *American Quarterly* 31.4 [1979]: 566. They designed proper feminine attire for the airplane; they identified themselves with the realm of domesticity; they socialized while on tour and during races.

45. Corn, "Making Flying 'Thinkable,' " 559.

46. Susan Ware sees this contradiction in discursive strategies as integral to Earhart's modern feminism. "In order to get women into the air as passengers," Ware notes, "she was forced to rely on traditional gender stereotypes that exaggerated the differences between women and men. This strategy was a very different approach from that of hers for getting women into the air as pilots, which downplayed such differences" (71).

47. Corn, "Making Flying 'Thinkable,' " 570–71.

Virtue and Virtuality
Gender in the Self-Representations of Queen Elizabeth I

Janel Mueller

That persons and texts are social constructions has been the guiding premise of recent work on the complexities of gender in period representations of Elizabeth I. Some critics have emphasized the theatricality of the Queen's public interactions with her subjects, imputing manipulativeness if not outright duplicity to her.[1] Louis Montrose has argued, by contrast, that textual representations of Elizabeth become sites of contestation where the author as the Queen's political subject seeks to exercise control over the Queen as his poetic subject, the issue being the signifying power of her image.[2] Montrose's essays offer a perspective on representation as a species of mutual struggle that studies by Susan Frye, Julia M. Walker, and Nanette Salomen apply to genres as diverse as civic pageantry, epic encomium, and portrait painting.[3] A similar outlook informs Philippa Berry's diagnosis of the cultural anxieties attaching to Elizabeth's virgin queenship, Carole Levin's analyses of the cultural semiotics of rumors and anecdotes about the Queen, and Helen Hackett's tracing of the contradictions in elite and popular figurations of her.[4]

So potent has the assumption been—that social construction is defined by what a subject necessarily undergoes or cognizantly submits to—that the Queen's own agency in self-representation has drawn far less notice.[5] Allison Heisch and Frances Teague have properly called for closer attention to our records of what Elizabeth said in public about herself.[6] Since 1993 I have been collaborating on an edition of Elizabeth's speeches, selected letters, verse, and prayers from their earliest and most reliable manuscript sources, of which a number are in the Queen's own hand.[7] Surviving drafts or revisions in Elizabeth's hand show extensive changes, which could equally well have occurred after delivery as beforehand. There is no way of telling which, and the heaviness of revision encourages the presumption of both. I have proposed elsewhere that Elizabeth be considered the first reader—that is, the first interpreter—of the texts of her public speeches, and Leah Marcus has independently reached a similar conclusion.[8]

Paying special regard to her handling of the factor of gender, the present essay examines Elizabeth's self-representations on public occasions for which we have written texts, in English, all but one of these—the Tilbury speech—being addresses to Parliament. I augment this material with several letters written to James VI of Scotland in the Queen's own hand. Before turning to these materials, I want to make my own premises clear. I recognize the thoroughly rhetorical character of these texts; I do not claim access to any unmediated truth of Elizabeth's mind or heart. Yet I am not disposed to rule out detectable patterns of her own desire as enacted in her self-representations. What I am concerned to establish, in the first place, is that the long-term agency she exercises is projecting, withholding, defending, or asserting definitive features of her public identity where gender and monarchy were perceived (by her and her subjects alike) to converge. This case study confirms that the social construction of gender can receive crucial input from the subject being constructed and that the input is considerable in the historically specific and admittedly out-of-the-ordinary instance of Elizabeth I. In the second place I hope that my account of what Elizabeth evidently understood by "virtual gender" will provide a chapter in the yet-to-be-written prehistory of this term as defined by Mary Ann O'Farrell and Lynne Vallone to name gender fantasy beyond as well as within contemporary cyberculture.

Given her historical reputation for mercuriality, indirection, and delay as well as the emphasis in current critical emphasis on the contestatory aspects of her contemporaries' representations of her, one might expect her own self-representations to manifest great variety, even inconsistency, through the long course of her reign. There are marked differences of occasion and political concern surrounding the public speeches, and in a few cases—her speeches on the Parliamentary petition to execute Mary Queen of Scots and the so-called Golden Speech—the records of what Elizabeth said differ both in their fullness and in the order of their contents. But if allowance is made for the discursive register in which she is working—in particular, whether it is religious or secular—the most striking feature of her public reflections on herself is their deep, dynamic consistency. In regard to herself Elizabeth regularly treats gender—by which I mean the social expectations, place, role(s), and attributes ascribed to an individual on the basis of biological sex—as virtual, that is as one among several prospective or potential sources of confirmation for the rightness of her rule. Unless she is speaking in a sustained way of her relation to God, she does not readily treat her feminine gender as a determinant of what she must do or be. My purpose in the following discussion is to make intelligible the dynamics and inner logic of how Elizabeth represents herself as England's sovereign, her evasions as well as her engagements with gender identity as she pursues her characteristic public mode of self-accounting.

In England masculinity was a nearly unbroken norm for monarchy; until the mid-sixteenth century there had been only the brief, precarious reign of Queen Matilda during a struggle over the Crown in the twelfth century.[9] It was intrinsically problematic for Elizabeth that she was a female sovereign. Constance Jordan has identified the paired notions that undergird Elizabeth's self-understanding and self-representation throughout her reign. Neither of these is peculiar to the Queen; both, in fact, became staples of the thought of Tudor England. One notion holds that female sovereignty is an exceptional consequence of God's will exercised in two overlapping domains: in divine-right monarchy (God ordains specific persons to rule as his earthly representatives) and in general and particular providence (God directs the courses of nations and of individuals' lives). As Jordan puts it, "In sixteenth-century political thought, gynecocracy is . . . justified by appeals to providence and divine right."[10] Another notion figures the relation of ruler and ruled as that of the sovereign's two bodies: the one a body natural, marked by biological sex and for eventual mortality; the other a body politic, the institution of monarchy and its attendant powers incorporated in the natural bodies of successive occupants of the English throne.[11]

Elizabeth's reign had been immediately preceded by her sister Mary's. In its 1554 Act Concerning Regal Power, Parliament had declared that, although "the most ancient statutes of this realm being made by Kings then reigning . . . only attribute and refer all prerogative . . . unto the name of King," yet

> the law of this realm is and ever hath been and ought to be understood, that the kingly or regal office of the realm, and all dignities, prerogative royal, power, preeminences, privileges, authorities, and jurisdictions thereunto annexed, united, or belonging, being invested either in male or female, are and be and ought to be as fully, wholly, absolutely, and entirely deemed, judged, accepted, invested, and taken in the one as in the other; so that what and whensoever statute or law doth limit and appoint that the King of this realm may or shall have, execute, and do anything as King. . . . The same the Queen (being supreme Governess, possessor, and inheritor to the imperial

Crown of this realm as our said Sovereign Lady the Queen most justly presently is) may by the same authority and power likewise have, exercise, execute . . . and do, to all intents, constructions, and purposes, without doubt, ambiguity, scruple, or question.[12]

The primary aim of this act is to specify, in identical terms, the rights of a legitimate monarch of either sex to authority and power. Yet the system of hereditary monarchy contained a deep gender bias: any legitimate male offspring of a regnant monarch would inherit the throne before any legitimate female offspring would. Demonstrably, maleness was superior to femaleness as an attribute of sovereignty. Hence, as Carole Levin has noted, the gender implications of these identical rights remain uncertain: "It may mean that politically [a queen] is a man or that she is a woman who can take on male rights. She may be both woman and man in one, both king and queen together, a male body politic in concept while a female body natural in practice. . . . The act does seem to suggest an aura of monarchy that goes beyond traditional representations of power as only male."[13] Similar observations hold regarding the unspecificity of gender implications in the operations of divine right and providentialism that put a queen, by God's will, on the throne. A definite ascription of sovereignty combines with indefiniteness, unspecificity, regarding the social realization of a queen regnant's gender. I call this odd construct the "virtual gender" of Elizabeth I. *Virtual* here signifies that she has full potentiality to perform feminine roles as a wife and mother but also registers that she may, as sovereign, opt to leave these feminine roles unactualized, concentrating instead on the office, qualities, and roles of a monarch.

I have found virtual gender to be a primary component of the rhetoric of Elizabeth's public self-representations, which she repeatedly casts in the form of a stocktaking.[14] Highly sensitive to the temporal and qualitative aspects of Elizabeth's rule, they address a set series of questions, clearly implied if not always explicitly posed. Typically the questions run in this fashion: Who was I before I came to rule? How have I come to rule England? What qualities do I need to rule England well? When (or if) I manifest these qualities, what kind of ruler am I? What is my relation to my subjects and theirs to me?

Elizabeth develops one major line of answers from her earliest Parliamentary speeches onward. This is to argue that, as God put her on the throne, so he will see to the necessities and the modalities of her rule. Continued grounding in providentialism and divine right shows in her responses to her set of implicit questions and the gender issues that they address. The preponderant note of Elizabeth's speeches to the Parliaments of 1559, 1563, and 1566 is her primary regard to God's service rather than to human expectations, as before when she was "a privat woman," so now that she is a "prince."[15] Her speech to the Commons on February 10, 1559, adverts repeatedly to her single state in terms—"this kynde of life," this "trade of life," "this mynde"—that cast it as her God-given calling and preserve a notable unspecificity of gender in her first-person references:

> From my yeares of understanding syth I first had consideracion of myself to be borne a servitor of almightie god, I happelie chose this kynde of life, in which I yet lyve. Which I assure yow for myne owne parte, hath hitherto best contented my self and I truste hath bene moost acceptable to god. . . . With which trade of life I am so throughlie acquainted, that I truste, God who hath hitherto therin preserved and led me by the hand, will not nowe of his goodnes suffer me to goe alone. . . . It may please god to enclyne my harte to an other kynd of life. . . . It might please almightie god to contynew me still in this mynde, to lyve out of the state of mariage."[16]

Elizabeth's successive public self-accountings seek to dispel the assumption that God's will for her obliges her as Queen to actualize the roles of wife and mother. She holds that her feminine gender should remain virtual—that is, there is no imperative for her to marry and bear an heir to the throne or otherwise specify the line of succession—as her Parliaments of 1559, 1563, and 1566 so strongly and repeatedly urged her to do. Engaging most forthrightly with the prescriptive force of gender expectations in her February 10, 1559, speech to the Commons, Elizabeth warned that bearing a child would not necessarily insure the security of her throne and the good order of the kingdom. Such weighty national concerns should not be left to the imponderable outcomes of sexual reproduction but to the cognizant joint provision of God and Elizabeth (in the merest adumbration of the nonbiological succession, which would bring James VI of Scotland to the English throne after her death in 1603). In her words, "good provision by his [God's] healpe may be made in convenient tyme, wherby the realme shall not remayne destitute of an heire that may be a fitt governor, and peraventure more beneficiall to the realme then such offspring as may come of me. For although I be never so carefull of your well doinge and mynde ever so to be, yet may my issue growe out of kynde, and become perhappes ungracious."[17]

As Elizabeth saw her primary imperative, she was to devote herself to the well-being, the wise, just, moderate "care" (a favorite word), of her people of England. Thus she declares in her speech of February 10, 1559: "I will never . . . conclud any thing that shalbe prejudiciall to the realme. For the weale, good and safetie wherof I will never shune to spend my life."[18] In her speech of November 5, 1566, at her highest rhetorical pitch, the Queen expostulates to the Parliamentary delegation regarding her record of caring rule: "Was I not borne in the Realme? were my parents borne in anye Foreyne Contrey? ys there any cause I sholde alyenatte my selfe from beynge carefull over this Contrey? ys not my kyngdome here? whom have I opressede? whom have I enrychede to others harme? what turmoyle have I made in the comon wealthe that I shold be suspected to have no regarde to the same? Howe have I governyde syns my Reygne? . . . I need not to use many woordes, for my deeds doo try me."[19] Her gender, she maintains, is irrelevant to the exercise of her peaceful, prosperous rule. Again and again she constitutes her people and herself in a reciprocal relation: she bears them all her "good will," increasingly her love and care, and they bear her their "service," increasingly, their love and care. This benevolent, affective bond is what Elizabeth seeks to establish as the norm of who she is as sovereign of England and what her relations are to her subjects throughout her reign. It is her grand refrain.

If Elizabeth shunts aside the social and biological imperatives that Parliament and her Privy Council aim to impose on her, what is the name of the kind of ruler she is? It is easy to see what her own preferences in nomenclature are. She most often styles herself prince and her rule or throne princely, in what, at this period, sustains its gender-neutral sense: the derivation of *prince* from Latin *princeps,* a noun of so-called common—or indifferently masculine or feminine—gender.[20] In a series of seven speeches or parts of messages from 1559 to 1566, she condescends only once, or perhaps twice (for two manuscript versions differ on just this point), to reassure her subjects by invoking her actual gender as a more rhetorically potent virtual gender whereby she figures as the mother of her country.[21] Her uncertain use of it is demonstrated by its absence from the otherwise superior text of her February 10, 1559, speech and its presence in a version from an anonymous Parliamentary journal.[22] The certain instance occurs in Elizabeth's speech of January 10, 1563, to the Commons, which responds to their plea for her "most honorable and motherly carefulness" with these words: "I assure yow all that though after my death yow may have many stepdames, yet shall yow never have any a more mother, then I meane to be unto yow all."[23]

Where Elizabeth chose at rare points in this earlier period to use gender-specific terminology, her own decided preference was to style herself a virgin queen, although, as Sir John Neale noted, her contemporaries did not really understand such terminology.[24] Her first Parliamentary speech of 1559 concludes with this epitaph upon herself: "In the end this shalbe for me sufficient that a marble stone shall declare, that a Quene having raigned such a time lyved and dyed a virgin."[25] Overall, however, the fraught atmosphere in Parliament from 1559 to 1566—when she was between twenty-five and thirty-four years of age—did not encourage her to conflate her actual gender and actual status in the composed figure of virgin queenship. There are recurrent flarings of indignation and insecurity in these speeches, precisely at points where Elizabeth finds the men of Parliament preempting her actual status, her regal authority, by insisting on the imperatives, as they conceive them, of her actual gender for her. To the extent that these men try to compel her to wifehood and motherhood, they threaten her sovereignty.

In a fragmentary draft of the opening of her speech of November 5, 1566, in her own handwriting, Elizabeth castigates the Parliamentary delegation who have come "ny a traiterous trik" in pressing her marriage like "brideles [bridleless] colts" who "do not know ther ridars hand Whom bit of kingely rain did never snafle yet," punning angrily on "rein" and "reign."[26] In her fuller speech of the same day she returns to the authoritarian images by which she figures the palpable offense against her body politic, reproving "unbrydelyd persons whose heds were never snaffled by the ryder" and exclaiming, "A straunge thynge that the foote sholde dyrecte the hede in so weyghtye a cawse, which cawse hathe bynne so dylligentlye weyede by us." But the deepest sense of infringement and insubordination registered in this speech comes, shockingly, as Elizabeth's imagining of her own deposition. In projecting this unspeakable outcome, she reverses her otherwise consistent practice in other speeches of this period; she both actualizes and emphasizes the gender specificity of her self-references: "Thowghe I be a woman, yet I have as good a corage answerable to my place as evere my father hadde. I am your anoynted Queene. I wyll never be by vyolence constreyned to doo any thynge. I thanke god I am in deede indued with suche qualytyes, that yf I were turned owte of the Realme in my pettycote, I were hable to lyve in any place of Chrystendom."[27]

At this notable juncture the speech of November 5, 1566, attests both the incompleteness and the vulnerability of Elizabeth's political and rhetorical project to recede into virtual gender by rendering actual gender irrelevant to her successful exercise of her prerogative. Under what is as yet only rhetorical compulsion from her subjects, she is brought to acknowledge that love is not the only virtue of the heart that a ruler must manifest; courage is also necessary. The imagined deposition scene singles out courage as the virtue needed when confronting the limits or the forcible termination of one's sovereign authority. Courage emerges as secular, political, and strategic; it is not a theological source of empowerment. It also uniquely elicits gender anxiety from Elizabeth the Queen.

She is sure that the legitimacy of her rule consists with her gender: "I am your anoynted Queene." She is also sure that the courage to assert her authority can consist with her feminine gender: "Thowghe I be a woman, yet I have as good a corage answerable to my place as evere my father hadde." She does not, however, stipulate what actions would confirm her possession of courage. She is manifestly anxious about what she would do to defend her authority if she had to go beyond merely claiming and asserting it. If Elizabeth fully possesses courage answerable to her place, then why the specter of being turned out of the realm in her petticoat, able to live in any place of Christendom? This seems to be a scenario of usurpation and exile, one spelling her political and military defeat or incapacity. (The assertion of the capacity she would have in such circumstances is unspecific; "I were hable to lyve in any place of Chrystendom" includes, perhaps, her independence of mind, her scholarly pursuits, and her fluency in several European vernaculars as well as Latin and Greek.)[28]

So questions multiply in and around this passage. Could courage be a feminine trait of Elizabeth's as a monarch, or is it a virile concomitant of the "vyolence" that she has forsworn as an aspect of her policy—and perhaps could not practice effectually anyway? Under the most perilous circumstances can a queen exercise sovereignty as successfully as a king? At this juncture the Virgin Queen faces but does not answer these questions. Not until the Armada crisis two decades later will she surmount the gender anxieties that she attaches to the question of maintaining her sovereign authority under the imminent threat of physical violence to her person and office.

Nearly a decade separates the first group of Elizabeth's Parliamentary speeches from her next recorded address. In her March 15, 1576, speech in the House of Lords, her lengthening record of self-expending rule and her sense of God's special guidance and protection as the enabling condition of her rule yield representations of a lofty, gender-neutral identity for herself in her relation with other human beings. Only in relation to God does she actualize her feminine gender and claim special status for her royal virginity. Like the Blessed Virgin Mary and other holy women of Scripture, she styles herself God's handmaid: "As for those rare and speciall benefittes which many yeares have followed and accumpanied my happie Reigne, I attribute them to God alone, the prince of Rule, and counte my self no better then his handmayde. . . . Theis Seaventene yeares and more, God hath bothe prospered and protected you with good successe under my direction.

And I nothing doubt but the same maynteyninge hande will guyde youe still and bringe you to the ripenes of perfection."[29]

The systematic convergence of this theological language with gender-specific self-reference permits a generalization: femininity (the soul's traditional gender in Christianity) is the position that Elizabeth acknowledges as normative for her in relation to God. Here, indeed, she projects herself as being so entirely the compliant handmaid of God that there is no distinguishing between her hand and his in the final sentence of the quoted passage.[30] When she focuses in a secular register on her relation to her people or to other sovereigns, however, she goes the route of unspecificity that I have been calling virtual gender, stressing her conviction of its irrelevance for wise and virtuous rule. Even in this 1576 speech, in which she is outspoken about her femininity and her role as God's handmaid, she subjects other aspects of her self-gendering to understatement and indirection. What, then, does she impute to herself as God's handmaid? Is Elizabeth laying claim to sacred virginity, a status that Helen Hackett shows panegyrists to be regularly ascribing to the Queen from the later 1570s onward?[31]

Elizabeth does claim virginity and reaffirm her unconditional preference for it, stating in effect that her life would be no Cinderella story even if she were Cinderella. She evokes a milkmaid as a counterfactual image of a private female self, one sufficiently lowly to make life choices free of constraint because they are not seen to matter one way or the other: "If I were a milkmaide with a paile on myne Arme, whereby my private person mighte be litle sett by, I woulde not forsake my single state to matche my self with the greatest monarche." Elizabeth would remain the Lord's handmaid, even if she were the milkmaid that she is not.[32] But she has not finished her relational self-accounting. This Lord's handmaid is equally and utterly the servant of England's well-being. In her words, "For your behoof there is no waye so difficulte that maye touche my private, which I coulde not well content my self to take: And in this case as willingly to spoile my self quite of my self, as yf I shoulde put of my upper garmente when it wearies me, yf the presente state might not thereby be encumbred."[33]

For the good of England, Elizabeth merges into the public weal any personal self she might have and does so as matter-of-factly as she would take off one of her heavily brocaded and jeweled gowns of state. She in effect works an innovation in Tudor political theory, producing the Queen's one body, the body politic, which has subsumed all else of her.[34] Her life in and as this body politic is, however, as full of affect as a body natural, replete with the mutual love between subjects and sovereign in which, from first to last, she constitutes her life and identity as England's sovereign:

One speciall favour I must needes confesse I have just cause to vaunt of, that whereas varietie and Love of chaunge is ever so rife in Servuntes to ther Masters, children to theire parentes, and in private frendes one to another, as that for one yeare or perhappes for twoe they can content themselves to houlde theire course upprighte, yet after by mistruste or doubte of worse they are dissevered and in tyme waxe wearye of theire wonted likinge. Yet still I finde that assured zeale amonge my faithfull Subjectes (to my speciall comforte) which was first declared to my great encouragement.

Can a prince that of necessitie must discontent a numbre to delight and please a few (because the greatest parte is ofte not the best inclined) continue so longe tyme without greate offence, much mislike or common grudge? Or happs it often that princes Accions are conceived in so good parte and favorablie interpreted? No, no my Lordes, howe greate my fortune is in this respect, I were ingrate if I should not acknowledge.[35]

The question unanswered earlier duly returns. What is this singular condition of Elizabeth's, evoked in her 1576 speech in conjoint terms of intimacy with God and trustful, safe familiarity with her subjects? It is an exalted state, one undergirded by the singleness of life, that makes possible her unstinting devotion of herself in the civil and religious domains simultaneously. It is the safest possible state for her and her people. The experiential prospect of violence, and the virtue that it necessitates, courage, have no place in this 1576 speech. Is hers, then, the state of sacred virginity that was represented at this period as conferring not just physical safety but immortality?[36] On such a criterion Elizabeth's self-representation does not qualify as sacred virginity, for she closes the speech with explicit reflections on her own mortality (and the contest over the succession that her death might precipitate): "I knowe I am but mortall . . . and so the whilest prepare my self to welcomme death when soever it shall please god to send it: . . . But let good heede be taken that in reachinge to farre after future good, you perrill not the presente, or by dispute beginne to quarrell and fall by dispute together by the eares before it be decided, who shall weare my Crowne."[37] I take Elizabeth here to be containing—by demystifying—the furthest reaches of the transcendent associations that she had attached to herself in her relations with God through much of this speech. Elizabeth's body politic may effectually subsume her body natural in the day-to-day modality of self-expending rule, but in the last analysis—at the extremity of life and at the limits of her sovereign authority—there will be the Queen's two bodies. Her death, she wryly notes, will confirm that truth.

This lofty, above-the-fray perspective on her self-representation alters sharply, however, in the two 1586 speeches replying to the Parliamentary petition urging the execution of Mary Queen of Scots, who had been found guilty of capital offenses against Elizabeth's life and crown. (The ever-more-deadly animosity between the two queens had an eighteen-year prior history. In 1568, after being forcibly ejected from her realm, Mary had sought political asylum in England. Elizabeth's initially well-disposed reception turned into restrictive confinement as Mary plotted with English and Continental Catholics in an unending series of intrigues to put her on the throne of England.) The first of these speeches, which survives in one version with corrections in Elizabeth's handwriting, develops a striking equivalence between herself and Mary Queen of Scots. Elizabeth has had to confront the fact "that one not different in sex, of like estate and my neare kinne, sholde be fallen into so great a Crime . . . my life hath ben full daungerouslie sought, and death contrived." Elizabeth has tried by secret communication to get Mary to confess her wrongs and repent, just as if "we were but as two milke maides, with pailes upon oure armes, or that there were no more dependency upon us, but myne owne life were onlie in danger, and not the whole estate of youre religion and well doings." But Mary as Queen has admitted to no more of a milkmaid's private identity than Elizabeth did in 1576 or will do here. That hypothetical private construction proves a failure and an illusion. Both Mary and Elizabeth are defined by their sovereign status, their political and religious opposition, and their mutually exclusionary predicaments: it is the one life or the other. In having to confront the present as, in effect, an ultimatum to her, Elizabeth in her first Parliamentary speech of 1586 develops her second scenario of violent death, which, like that of her expulsion from her kingdom in her 1566 speech, unfolds in highly gender-specific terms:

> Former remembrances, my present feeling, and future expectacion of evills, I say, have made me think an evil is much the better the less while it dureth, and . . . taught mee to bear with a better mind these treasons, then is common to my sexe, yea with a better hart perhaps, then is in some menn. . . . I thus conceived, that had theire purposes taken effect, I sholde not have founde the blow, before I had felt it, nor though my perill sholde have bene great, my paine shold have bene but small and shorte, wherein as I wold be loth to dye, so bloodie a death, so dowbt I not but God wold have geven me grace to be prepared for such a chanche.[38]

The judicial imperative of executing Mary Queen of Scots is the first of two crises that compel Elizabeth to articulate, with gender-specific attributes, her understanding of herself as meriting the throne of England. Her earlier confident pronouncements on the virtuality of gender, its irrelevance to virtuous and successful rule, do not suffice at such a perilous juncture. In the copy of her second speech in answer to the Parliamentary petition for

Mary's execution, delivered November 24, 1586, and likewise bearing revisions in her own hand, Elizabeth protests her inexorable present predicament with more vehemence than she has used in any other public speech:

> Sins now it is resolved, that my suretie cannot be established, without a Princess['s] head, I have just cause to complaine that I who have in my tyme pardoned so manie rebells, winked at so manie treasons, and either not produced them, or altogether slipt them over with silence, shold now be forced to this proceeding against such a person. I have besids during my reigne seene . . . manie opprobrious bookes and pamphlets against me, my realme, and state, accusing me to be a tyrant. . . . What will theie not now say, when it shall be spread, that for the safetie of her life a maiden Quene could be content, to spill the blood even of her owne kinswoman. I maie therefore full well complaine, that anie man shold thinke me given to crewelties, whereof I am so guiltless and Innocent, as I shold slander God, if I shold saie he gave me so vile a mynd: Yea I protest I am so farre from it, that for myne owne life, I wold not touche her.[39]

In her distress Elizabeth retreats to her most cherished self-representation in gendered terms, that of "a maiden Quene," here one as "guiltless and Innocent" as maids are conventionally thought to be. Elsewhere in this speech, however, she styles herself in the gender-neutral terminology of a "prince." And now, resuming her mode of self-accounting, Elizabeth pronounces on her philosophy of ethical sovereignty for the first time in her writing. She gives her view of the qualities requisite to a ruler—three out of the four she names are Plato's cardinal political virtues—and she also specifies what she considers to be their linkages with gender:

> I was not simplie trained up, nor in my yewth spent my tyme altogether idly, and yet when I came to the crowne, then entred I first into the scole of experience: bethinking my self of those things that best fitted a kinge, Justice, temper, Magnanimite, Judgment; for I found it most requisite that a Prince shold be endued with Justice, that he shold be adorned with temperance, I conceaved magnanimite to beseeme a royall estate possessed by whatsoever sex, and that it was necessarie that such a person shold be of Judgment. . . . And for the two first this may I truly say: among my subjects I never knew a difference of person wheare right was one, nor never to my knowledge preferrd for faict what I thought not fitt for worth. . . . For the two latter I wyll not boast. . . . But this dare I boldly affirme: my verdict went ever with the truth of my knowledg.[40]

Elizabeth had studied the Greek text of Plato with her tutor Roger Ascham.[41] Here she alludes to book 4 of the *Republic*, in which, at 427e, it is agreed that the state, if rightly founded, will be good in the full sense of the word—that is, wise, courageous, temperate, and just—and, at 441e–442e, wisdom, courage, temperance, and justice are specified as the attributes of the just man.[42] Significantly, Elizabeth omits courage from her otherwise Platonic quartet of the cardinal political virtues. In its place, she says, she conceived "magnanimite to beseeme a royall estate possessed by whatsoever sex." Her explanation seems to bespeak uncertainty whether "a royal estate possessed by whatsover sex" could attain the virtue of courage. In fact, a look at etymologies that Elizabeth would have known shows that the gender trouble attaching to Greek *andreia*, the term for *courage* in these *Republic* passages, is real. Its root meaning is manliness (from *andros*); its most constant classical association is with a fighting spirit on the battlefield, the steadiness to risk death and kill, even though the word comes to acquire a more general meaning of "courage." A Latin analogue, *virtus* (from *vir*, a man), poses a similar problem in equating "virtue" with "force."[43] Evidently Elizabeth thought that sustaining her claim to be a body fit to govern England would require her, a female, to replace the Platonic cardinal political virtue of courage with "magnanimitie."

Elizabeth's substitution is sufficiently drastic to have no Platonic source. Aristotle defines Greek *megalopsychia* (Latin *magnanimitas*) in the *Nicomachean Ethics* at 1123b and following. The sense of this virtue is more literally rendered in English as "great-spiritedness" or "great-souledness."[44] Aristotle praises it as "the crowning beauty of the virtues," a lofty pride and self-esteem that reach "moral nobility" through concern for one's honor and dishonor.[45] It testifies to the tenacious hold of gender difference on even the independent and innovative mind of Elizabeth that the virtue she substitutes for the seemingly non-gender-neutral *courage* also proves to be non-gender-neutral in an important way. As O'Farrell and Vallone pertinently remark in the introduction to this volume: "The components of the virtual body, that is, derive from a construction and an aesthetic of gender already found in the world."[46] The feminine sense of great-souled concern for one's honor is an impeccably respectable sexual reputation. The masculine sense of great-souled concern for one's honor is unblemished public esteem. Elizabeth says that she "conceaved magnanimitie to beseeme a royall estate possessed by whatsoever sex." Consistent with her earlier claims to virtual gender, Elizabeth as sovereign could well have conceived of herself as being great-souled in both a feminine and a masculine sense. Perhaps, indeed, this dually gendered concern for honor as impeccable sexual reputation and unblemished public esteem is what she fundamentally means by virgin queenship.

It also testifies to the residual hold of conventional gender roles on the mind of Elizabeth that, as late as 1586, she can ascribe to a monarch of either sex a lofty pride and self-esteem focused chiefly on honor and dishonor yet cannot ascribe to a monarch of either sex courage understood as the shedding of an enemy's blood in battle. This second speech of 1586 ends with Elizabeth's "answer answerless" to the question of whether she will proceed judicially to Mary's beheading. She entreats the men of Parliament: "Excuse my doubtfullnes, and take in good part my aunswer aunswerles: wherein I attribute not so much to my owne Judgment, but that I think . . . if I shold say, I wold not doe what yoe request, it might peradventure be more then I thought, and to say I wold do it, might perhaps breed perill of that youe labor to preserve"—namely, her own life and crown.[47] In the gender-specific vocabulary that she selectively employs at points when she is under pressure, Elizabeth may be in a kingly seat or a kingly estate, but she cannot say of herself that she is a "king" in the full Platonic sense of possessing the four cardinal political virtues. Courage equated with the taking of an enemy's life is not an attribute to which she ever explicitly lays claim in the self-representations of her Parliamentary speeches.

The catalytic conditions for Elizabeth's acquisition of courage thus defined begin to take shape in the letters that she and Mary's son, James VI of Scotland, exchanged in the weeks prior to Mary's beheading in February 1587. Throughout this correspondence Elizabeth addresses James as an alter ego, a prince who is no stranger to mortal peril, who can be trusted (under urging) to find an enemy in his own mother and the truest of friends in herself. In a letter of late January she expostulates to James: "See whither I kipe the Serpent that poisons me . . . by saving of her life. . . . Do I not make my selfe, trowe ye, a goodly pray . . . ? Transfigure your selfe into my state and Suppose What you aught to do, and therafter Way [weigh] my life, and reject the Care of murdar, and shun all baites that may untie our Amities, and let all men Knowe, that Princes Knowe best their owne lawes."[48] In an early February letter Elizabeth next starkly opposes her bloodshedding and Mary's, asserting for the first time the necessity of the latter. She appeals to James as a princely alter ego: "I doute not but your wisdome wil excuse my nide, and waite my necessitie, and not accuse me ether of malice or of hate. . . . make Account I pray you of my firme frindeship, love and Care, of which you may make sure Accownt . . . , from wiche My deare brother let no sinistar whisperars, nor busy troblars of Princis states persuade you to leave."[49]

But Elizabeth's letter of February 14, 1587, breaks the news of Mary's execution to James in the quite different terms of "that miserable accident, which (far contrary to my meaninge) hath befalen." Directly thereafter she reverts to her characteristic mode of self-accounting, thus bringing the substance of this letter to James in line with that of her Parliamentary speeches. "I besech yow that . . . yow will beleave me, that yf I had bid [commanded] aught I wold have bid [stuck] by yt. I am not so bace minded that feare of any livinge creature or prince should make me afrayde, to do that were just or, done, to denye the same." Elizabeth here makes a triple denial of fear— fear of any living creature or prince, fear of doing justice, fear of admitting that she had done justice—in the matter of Mary Queen of Scots. Then, in her very next sentence, she analogizes between herself and a king: "I am not of so bace a linage, nor cary so vile a minde; but as not to disguise, fits most a kinge, so will I never dissemble my actions but cawse them shewe even as I ment them. Thus assuringe your self of me that, as I knowe this was deserved, yet yf I had ment yt I would never laye yt on others shoulders."[50]

What is this triple lack of fear to see and acknowledge justice done? Has Elizabeth contrived to claim the political virtue of courage by implication while denying her own intent and agency? It appears that she thinks she has acted as "fits most a kinge" and done just this. Significantly, however, James's reply to this letter places her words and actions, as well as his own reaction, not in the domain of courage but in the moral category corresponding to Elizabeth's *magnanimitie,* a great-souled concern for one's honor. He responds thus: "Quhairas by your lettir . . . ye purge youre self of yore unhappy fact . . . with youre many and solemne attestationis of youre innocentie, I darr not uronge you so farre as not to judge honorablie of youre unspotted pairt thairin, so . . . I uishe that youre honorable behavioure in all tymes heir after may fully persuade the quhole uorlde of the same."[51]

Thus it is that Elizabeth must be said to first unambiguously claim possession of the virtue of courage in her speech to the English troops at Tilbury camp on August 9, 1588, during the period of anxious uncertainty following the storm-racked dispersal of the Armada, the supposedly invincible expeditionary force of Spanish galleons and troops that had failed in its intended invasion of England on July 27. Not only do the historical circumstances of this speech make the political connection between Mary's execution and the sending of the Armada to punish Elizabeth, but the moral connection between Platonic courage and Aristotelian magnanimity is traced by Elizabeth in the speech itself:

I am com amounge you att this tym . . . , being resolved in the middst and heate of the battle to Live and Dye amoungst you all, to Lay down for my god, and for my Kyngdom and for my people myn honor and my blood even in the dust. I know I have the body butt of a weake and feble woman, butt I have the harte and stomack of a Kinge, and of a Kinge of England too. And take foule scorn that Parma or any prince of Europe should dare to invade the borders of my realm: to the which rather then any dishonour shall grow by mee, I myself will venter my royall blood, I myself will be your generall, judge, and rewarder of your vertue in the feild.[52]

That she speaks and acts in an overtly military context alters to some degree every element that had long been of defining importance in Elizabeth's self-representations. Her self-expending care that has doubly bound her to God and to her people no longer conforms to the model of Christlike self-sacrifice but is now that of a warrior risking both life and reputation to repel an enemy aggressor. Her *megalopsychia,* or magnanimity, appears in her "foule scorn that . . . any prince of Europe should dare to invade the borders of my realm."[53] Her *andreia,* or manliness of battle courage, appears in her resolve "in the middst and heate of the battle to Live and Dye . . . , to Lay down . . . myn honor and my blood even in the dust."

Most significantly, Elizabeth at Tilbury sets aside her former insistence on the irrelevance of gender to good and successful rule. She claims to possess, not a courage as answerable to her place as ever her father had (the analogical formulation in her 1566 Parliamentary speech) but, in a direct self-predication, the heart and stomach of a king of England. The heart was both the seat of courage—hence the English etymology by way of Anglo-French *cor* and *corage*—and the seat of royal identity, commanding special regard to where a monarch's heart was buried. Specifically at this period, the stomach was the organ of violent, high-spirited deeds performed under a marked negative animus.[54] At Tilbury Elizabeth's great-souledness becomes "stomach" because of the crucial convergence, which she registers, of her "heart," or courage. What might remain her understanding of the virtuality of her gender in a long reign of peace—the irrelevance of being a woman to her record as a ruler—must now, in the context of war and its different standards for a ruler's competency, be actualized as a kind of super-gender, at least in the mode of public performance.[55] At this point of supreme crisis Elizabeth conflates masculine and feminine gender in her woman's body with its king's heart and stomach (see fig. 1). Then, as general, judge, and rewarder of virtues in the field, she puts her androgynized anatomy into immediate action.[56]

A final paradox involving virtue and virtuality waits in the wings, however. Once Elizabeth had represented herself as King-and-Queen and laid claim to the full Platonic quartet of political virtues, then and then only, it

Fig. 1. Elizabeth I as the embodied Primum Mobile of the geocentric universe; courage (*fortitudo*) is the virtue of her fifth sphere, that of Mars. Frontispiece of John Case's *Sphaera Civitatis* (Oxford, 1588). (Reproduced by permission of the British Library.)

appears, could the factor of gender become truly irrelevant—in the sense of indifferent—to her representations of her sovereignty. In her final trio of Parliamentary speeches the shifting play of gender references is conspicuous. In her April 9, 1593, speech at the closing of Parliament, Elizabeth imputes military courage and masculinity to herself in warring against the King of Spain but otherwise styles herself in gender-neutral or conventionally feminine terms as she conducts her predictable self-accounting. The pertinent stretch merits extended quotation because this speech is relatively little known:

> This Kingdome hath had many noble and victorious princes. I will not compare with any of them in wisdome, fortitude and other vertues (but saving the dutye of a chylde that is not to compare with her father) in love, care, sincerity and justice I will compare with any prince that ever you had or ever shall have. It may be thought simplicitie in me that all this tyme of my raigne have not sought to advance my territories and enlarged my dominions. For both opportunity hath served me to doe it, and my strength was able to have done it: I acknowledge my womanhood and weaknesse in that respect. But it hathe not bene feare to obtayne or doubt how to keep the thinges so obtayned that hath withholden me from these attempts: only my mynde was never to invade my neighbours nor to usurpe uppon anye: only contented to raigne over my owne and to rule as a juste prince. Yet the Kinge of Spayne doth challenge me to be the beginning of this quarel and the Causer of all the warrs . . . : but in saying that I have wronged him, that I have caused these warres, he doth me the greatest warres that maye be. . . . I feare not all his threateninges, his great preparations and mighty fortes do not scarre me, for though he come against me with a greater force then ever was his invincible navye, I doubt not (god assistinge me, uppon whom I allways trust) but I shall be able to defeate him and utterly overthrowe him. I have a great advantage of him for my cause is just.[57]

Among other evidence of gender lability in this late period, the celebrated "Golden Speech" of November 30, 1601, offers the richest panoply of self-references deployed according to a principle of indifferent access, as Elizabeth speaks of herself now as a king, now as a queen, now as a prince. She begins by acknowledging her thankfulness, as "a lovinge King," to those members of Parliament who have informed her that various appointees of hers have abused her trust and grants of privileges, but have conveyed the information without impugning her prerogative. "They doubt not," she says, "it is lawfull for our kingly state to grant gifts of sundry sortes of whom we make election, either for service done, or merit to be deserved, as being for a King to make choice on whom to bestow benefits." She then pursues her characteristic self-accounting across a full spectrum of gender references:

> You must not beguile your selves or wrong us, to thinke that the glosing lustre of a glistering glory of a Kings title may so extoll us, that we thinke all is lawfull what we list, not caringe what we doe. . . . The vanting boast of a kingly name may deceive . . . such a Prince as cares but for the dignity, nor passes not howe the raines be guided, so he rule. . . . But you are cumbred (I dare assure) with no such Prince, but such a one, as lookes how to give accomt afore another Tribunal seat then this world affords. . . . We thinke our selves most fortunately borne under suche a starre, as we have bene inabled by Gods power to have saved you under our reigne, from forreigne foes, from Tyrants rule, and from your owne ruine, and do confesse, that wee passe not so muche to be a Queene, as to be a Queene of such Subjects, for whom (God is witnesse, without boast or vaunt) we would willingly lose our life, ere see such to perish. . . . So great is my pride in reigning, as she that wisheth no longer to be, then Best and Most would have me so.[58]

The self-accounting in Elizabeth's last Parliamentary speech of December 19, 1601, also treats gender references as matters of indifference while both laying claim to the cardinal political virtues and reviving her oldest claim to be fit to rule her people because of her care and love for them. In a new synthetic move she now defines her "care to benefit" the realm in terms of these cardinal virtues: justice ("my care was ever by procedinge justelie and uprightlie to conserve my peoples love"), wisdom ("I have bene studiouse and industriouse . . . as a carefull head to defend the body"), conjoint great-souledness and courage ("it hath pleased god . . . to make me an instrument of his holy will in deliveringe the state from danger and my self from dishonor"), and temperance ("no prince have bene mor unthankefully requited whose intentione hath bene so harmeless and whose actions so moderat").[59] *Prince* is the staple term of self-reference through most of this speech. Yet, in the very last, valedictory lines of what has been a consistently gender-neutral and gender-muted speech, Elizabeth declares as follows to the members of Parliament regarding her newly stiffened tactics of militancy in Ireland. She suddenly adopts a high degree of gender specificity and just as suddenly moves beyond it in a reference to herself as England's sovereign:

> At this time it will be sufficient to let you know the groundes and motives of the warr to which you contribute, the merit of the princesse for whos sake you contribut: that my care is neither to continewe warr nor conclud a peace but for your good, and that you maie perceve how free your Quene is from givinge any cause of those attemptes that have ben made on hir onless to sav hir people or defind hir state be to be censured. This testimony I wold have

you carry home, for the world to knowe that your soverain is more carefull of your conservation then of hir self, and will daily crave of god that they that wish you best may never wish in vaine.[60]

These final words of her last Parliamentary speech put a surprisingly naturalizing and ordinary-seeming close on Elizabeth's series of public self-representations as England's sovereign. It is appropriate that the last such self-representation she offers is the gender-neutral *your soverain,* for this was the constant standard by which she evaluated and interpreted herself in the course of her reign.

I have argued that the early Elizabeth insisted on the virtuality of her gender as the condition of her sovereignty. She would not fulfill her responsibility and authority through the social and biological roles of wife and mother, only through the affective and metaphorical roles of her country's mother and God's handmaid. The sustaining character of Elizabeth's self-understanding throughout her reign was religious and theological. She could amply configure her life and death in those terms, to which gender was immaterial except as a foil to exalt divine providence and power. Yet the prospect and the eventual necessity of shedding the blood of another queen, a kinswoman, a mortal enemy, compounded with the Armada invasion to spur a later Elizabeth to a new species of self-understanding and self-representation in terms of the (somewhat adapted) Platonic quartet of political virtues. This self-understanding was secular, practical, and in its key component, almost impossibly demanding when it required of her the courage to take her enemy's life. As her rhetorical formulations demonstrate, such courage could not remain virtually gendered or gender neutral for Elizabeth; she could only articulate and claim it as "the heart and stomach of a King."

The gender specificity here is both complicated and mediated by a clear recognition that it applies to Elizabeth's body politic, not to the natural body that her sovereignty had merged with it. Nevertheless, her masculine courage was actual enough: she did execute Mary; she came to resist the invading Spanish at Tilbury; she did speedily try and execute the earl of Essex for his treasonous armed uprising against her in 1601. What remains finally significant, I think, about Elizabeth's manipulations of gender in her public self-representations is the felt imperative that the perils and extremities of her experience during her long reign can be seen to have placed upon her. She would seek justification for her sovereignty in every crucial register of her time and culture because she defined the measure of her rule as omnicompetence. Having found and appropriated such justification, secular as well as sacred, masculine as well as feminine, the late Elizabeth could again be indifferent about the factor of gender in relation to her fitness for her royal office.

But this late indifference, which permits her to range through a whole gamut of gender terms in referring to herself, is quite unlike the indifference voiced early in her reign, when all she could do was insist that her sex would not disqualify her from ruling the realm with entire dedication and the most loving and most positive intentions. As documented mainly by her Parliamentary speeches, she quite self-cognizantly derived her gendered identity from her royal office as she determined, over time, what its conscientious exercise made her out to be—whether prince or queen, princess or king, but always a consummate sovereign of England's people. But these determinations are not merely deterministic; the various names for herself are the readable traces of her political and personal desires. We have, perhaps, been slow to recognize her achievement in this regard because we ordinarily track the determinants of gender identity at more mundane cultural levels than the one she occupied. Elizabeth I may be the first social constructivist of gender who is on record in her own words, as a principal agent of her own public formation.

NOTES

I am grateful to Margaret Ezell and Pamela Matthews for inviting me to speak at the conference on "Virtual Gender" that they organized at Texas A&M University in April 1996. I received helpful comments on my presentation, which consisted of the material on Elizabeth's eventual self-attribution of the masculine virtue of courage, as well as much valuable collegial stimulation (particularly from David Cressy and Mary Ann O'Farrell) and the idea for my title. The members of the Renaissance Workshop at the University of Chicago also have my thanks for their incisive questions and suggestions about this essay. I am additionally grateful for thoughtful written comments from Stephen Bennett, Meiling Hazelton, Joshua Scodel, Jill Niemczyk Smith, and Richard Strier.

1. Stephen Greenblatt, *Renaissance Self-Fashioning* (Chicago: University of Chicago Press, 1980), 165–69; Leonard Tennenhouse, *Power on Display: The Politics of Shakespeare's Genres* (New York: Methuen, 1986); Leah S. Marcus, "Shakespeare's Comic Heroines, Elizabeth I, and the Political Uses of Androgyny," in *Women in the Middle Ages and Renaissance,* ed. Mary Beth Rose (Syracuse: Syracuse University Press, 1986), 135–53; and *Puzzling Shakespeare: Local Reading and Its Discontents* (Berkeley and Los Angeles: University of California Press, 1988).

2. Louis Adrian Montrose, "'Eliza, Queene of Shepheardes' and the Pastoral of Power," *English Literary Renaissance* 10 (1980): 153–62; "Gifts and Reasons: The

Contexts of Peele's *Araygnement of Paris*," *ELH* 47 (1980): 433–61; "Shaping Fantasies: Figurations of Gender and Power in Elizabethan Culture," *Representations* 1.2 (1983): 31–64; "The Elizabethan Subject and the Spenserian Text," in *Literary Theory / Renaissance Texts,* ed. Patricia Parker and David Quint (Baltimore: Johns Hopkins University Press, 1986), 303–40, esp. 320, 332; "*A Midsummer Night's Dream* and the Shaping Fantasies of Elizabethan Culture: Gender, Power, Form," in *Rewriting the Renaissance: The Discourses of Sexual Difference in Early Modern Europe,* ed. Margaret W. Ferguson, Maureen Quilligan, and Nancy J. Vickers (Chicago: University of Chicago Press, 1986), 65–87.

3. Susan Frye, *Elizabeth I: The Competition for Representation* (New York: Oxford University Press, 1993); see also Julia M. Walker, "Spenser's Elizabeth Portrait and the Fiction of Dynastic Epic," *Modern Philology* 90 (1992): 172–99; and Nanette Salomon, "Positioning Women in Visual Convention: The Case of Elizabeth I," in *Attending to Women in Early Modern England,* ed. Betty S. Travitsky and Adele F. Seeff (London: Associated University Presses, 1994), 64–95.

4. Philippa Berry, *Of Chastity and Power: Elizabethan Literature and the Unmarried Queen* (New York: Routledge, 1989); Carole Levin, "*The Heart and Stomach of a King": Elizabeth I and the Politics of Sex and Power* (Philadelphia: University of Pennsylvania Press, 1994), chaps. 4, 5, and 7; Helen Hackett, *Virgin Mother, Maiden Queen: Elizabeth I and the Cult of the Virgin Mary* (New York: St. Martin's Press, 1995).

5. Important pioneering accounts of Elizabeth as self-authoring include Allison Heisch, "Queen Elizabeth I: Parliamentary Rhetoric and the Exercise of Power," *Signs* 1 (1975): 31–55; and Frances Teague, "Queen Elizabeth in Her Speeches," in *Gloriana's Face: Women, Public and Private, in the English Renaissance,* ed. S. P. Cerasano and Marion Wynne-Davies (Detroit: Wayne State University Press, 1992), 63–78. Maria Perry, *The Word of a Prince: A Life of Elizabeth I from Contemporary Documents* (Woodbridge, Suffolk: Boydell Press, 1990), succeeds admirably in writing a biography of Elizabeth in her own words up to the early 1570s but thereafter relies more heavily on contemporaries' reports of the queen's words and actions.

6. Heisch remarks that "the parliamentary speeches permit substantial insight into the ways in which Elizabeth explored and exercised her monarchal power and in which rhetoric may become an instrument of power" ("Queen Elizabeth I," 31). Teague adds: "Elizabeth I sought to shape her public image through her oratory. . . . After a re-evaluation of Queen Elizabeth's speeches, a new image of the Queen will emerge (and I use the word 'image' advisedly). She will be more shrewd than vain, more practical than imperious, more thoughtful than fiery. Above all, she will be a superb user of language" ("Queen Elizabeth in Her Speeches," 63, 75).

7. *Speeches, Letters, Verses, and Prayers of Queen Elizabeth I,* ed. Leah S. Marcus, Janel Mueller, and Mary Beth Rose (Chicago, forthcoming).

8. Janel Mueller, "Textualism, Contextualism, and the Writings of Elizabeth I," in *English Studies and History,* ed. David Robertson, Tampere English Studies, no. 4 (Tampere, Finland: University of Tampere Press, 1994), 11–38; Leah S. Marcus, "Elizabeth and Parliament: Speech, Manuscript, and Print" (paper delivered at the

session on "Manuscript and Print: The Competition, Overlap, and Mutual Influence of the Two Systems of Transmission," MLA Convention, San Diego, December 1994).

9. Levin, "*Heart and Stomach of a King,*" 176n. 14.

10. Constance Jordan, *Renaissance Feminism: Literary Texts and Political Models* (Ithaca: Cornell University Press, 1990), 131; see also 202; as well as Jordan's article, "Representing Political Androgyny: More on the Siena Portrait of Queen Elizabeth I," in *The Renaissance Englishwoman in Print,* ed. Anne M. Haselkorn and Betty S. Travitsky (Amherst: University of Massachusetts Press, 1990), 157–76.

11. The classic exposition is Ernst H. Kantorowicz, *The King's Two Bodies: A Study in Mediaeval Political Theory* (Princeton: Princeton University Press, 1957), which stresses the theological derivation of this political conception; see also Marie Axton, *The Queen's Two Bodies: Drama and the Elizabethan Succession* (London: Royal Historical Society, 1977).

12. 1 Mary, st. 3, c. 1, in J. R. Tanner, *Tudor Constitutional Documents, A.D. 1485–1603* (Cambridge: Cambridge University Press, 1930), 123–24; see also Heisch, "Queen Elizabeth I," 35.

13. Levin, "*Heart and Stomach of a King,*" 121.

14. Laurie J. Shannon identified the centrality of this device in "The Queen's Account" (paper delivered at the session on "The Writings of Elizabeth I," MLA Convention, Chicago, December 1995).

15. British Library, Lansdowne MS 94, art. 15, fol. 30v. This is a draft in the queen's hand, much revised at another sitting with a different pen, in darker ink and smaller writing. Text printed in T. E. Hartley, ed., *Proceedings in the Parliaments of Elizabeth I,* 2 vols. (Leicester: Leicester University Press, 1981), 1:114.

16. British Library, Lansdowne MS 94, art. 14, fol. 29r–v. In its retention of several of Elizabeth's characteristic spellings (e.g., *ennemise, healpe, apon*) this copy in secretary hand reinforces its authority. Text printed in Hartley, *Proceedings,* 1:44–45.

17. British Library, Lansdowne MS 94, art. 14, fol. 29r. Text printed in Hartley, *Proceedings,* 1:45.

18. British Library, Lansdowne MS 94, art. 14, fol. 29r–v. Text printed in Hartley, *Proceedings,* 1:45.

19. Cambridge University Library MS Gg.3.34, fols. 209–14, at 210–11. Text printed in Hartley, *Proceedings,* 1:146.

20. See *Oxford English Dictionary: prince,* 1b. She may use the adjective *kingly* in self-reference, as in "princely seat and kingly throne" (Jan. 28, 1563) or "kingly rein" (fragment of November 5, 1566), but she never refers to herself as "king" in this period. Carole Levin's failure to register that *prince* can be gender neutral at this period lessens the value of her discussion of "Elizabeth as King and Queen" (*Heart and Stomach of a King,* chap. 5, esp. 125).

21. Hackett, *Virgin Mother, Maiden Queen,* 4, 40, 50–52, 74, 77–78, 98, 118–19, 200. The appellation "mother of her country" had first been applied to Mary Tudor.

22. "I wyll never in that mattere conclude anye thynge that shalbe prejudycyall

to the Realme, for the weale and saftye wherof as a good mother of my Contreye will never dhone to spend my life" (Cambridge University Library MS Gg.3.34, fols. 199–201, at 201). Text not printed in Hartley but listed in his census of variants. The otherwise superior version is British Library, Lansdowne MS 94, art. 14.

23. The Commons' petition to the Queen at Whitehall, January 28, 1563, is preserved as PRO, State Papers Domestic, Elizabeth, 12/27/36, fols. 139–142r; quoted phrase from 139v. The queen's answer is the immediately following item: PRO, State Papers Domestic, Elizabeth, 12/27/36, fols. 143r–44r.

24. J. E. Neale, *Elizabeth I and Her Parliaments* (New York: St. Martin's, 1958), 1:33.

25. British Library, Lansdowne MS 94, art. 14, fol. 29r–v. Text printed in Hartley, *Proceedings*, 1:45. Both he and I offset a torn bottom of the page by restoring two readings (such, the *-ed* of *lyved*) from Bodleian Library, Rawlinson MS D723. Cambridge University Library MS Gg.3.32, fol. 201, has this emphatic underscoring: "a quene havynge Reygnede suche a tyme lyvyde and dyede *a vyrgyne.*"

26. PRO, State Papers Domestic, Elizabeth, 12/41/5, fol. 8r–v. Text printed in Hartley, *Proceedings*, 1:145.

27. Cambridge University Library MS Gg.3.34, fols. 209–14. Text printed in Hartley, *Proceedings*, 1:146, 147, 148.

28. See Elizabeth's public Latin oration at Oxford University, September 5, 1566, as preserved in Bodleian, Rawlinson MS D.273, fol. 111r: "Sanè fateor patrem meum diligenter curavisse ut in bonis litteris recte instituerer, atque quidem in multarum linguarum varietate enim versata sum" (Indeed I confess that my father took most diligent care to have me correctly instructed in good letters, and I was even engaged in the variety of many languages [my trans.]). Henry, of course, had seen to his daughter's acquisition of languages as potential accoutrements of diplomacy, not of exile.

29. British Library, Additional MS 33271, fols. 22r–24r. Hartley, *Proceedings*, 1:471–75, prints Northamptonshire Country Record Office, Fitzwilliam of Milton Political MS 177, a closely according version, and Exeter College, Oxford, MS 92, fol. 62r–v, a shorter and much more divergent text.

30. In the tiny multilingual volume (British Library, MS Facsimile 218) in her own hand, dated ca. 1579–82 and known as "Queen Elizabeth's Prayer Book," she also styles herself God's handmaid in both of the prayers composed in English and in the Latin prayer: "Heare the most humble voice of thie handmaide, in this onelie happie, to be so accepted" (sig. 3r); "Lorde God Father everlasting which . . . of thy great mercie, hast chosen me thy servant and handmaid to feede thy people . . . with a faithfull and a true hart: and rule them prudentlie with powre" (sig. 31r); "Da mihi ancillae tuae cor docile" (Give me, thy handmaid, a teachable heart [sig. 22r]). Other locutions in these prayers indicate that Elizabeth prefers to specify her gender as well when she represents herself in her political role, for example, as "a sovereign Princesse over the people of England" (sig. 3v) and herself and the people of her realm, including its Huguenot refugees, as "mere et nourrice de tes chers enfans," "la mere et les enfans que luy as donné . . . au bien de ta povre Eglise" (mother and nurse

of your dear children, the mother and the children whom you have given her . . . for the welfare of your poor Church) in the French prayer (sigs. 10v, 13v). The printed text of this prayer book is *A Book of Devotions Composed by Her Majesty Elizabeth Regina, with Translations by the Reverend Adam Fox D.D. and a Foreword by the Reverend Canon J. P. Hodges* (Gerrards Cross: Colin Smythe, 1970). I interpret Elizabeth's systematic pattern of choice as indicating the normativity of feminine gender for expressing the Christian soul's place and role in its personal address to God.

31. See Hackett, *Virgin Mother, Maiden Queen*, chaps. 4–5, 7.

32. Two contemporary sources indicate that Elizabeth's milkmaid image had autobiographical origins. In rehearsing the dangers and deprivations of her imprisonment in Woodstock Castle by her sister, Queen Mary, in 1554, John Foxe editorializes: "Thus this worthy lady, oppressed with continual sorrow, could not be permitted to have recourse to any friends she had, but still in the hands of her enemies was left desolate. . . . Whereupon no marvel if she, hearing upon a time, out of her garden at Woodstock, a certain milkmaid singing pleasantly, wished herself to be a milkmaid as she was; saying that her case was better, and life more merry than was hers, in that state as she was" (John Foxe, *Acts and Monuments,* ed. Stephen Reed Cattley [London: Seeley, Wardside, and Seeley, 1837], 8:619; this narrative first appeared in Foxe's 1570 editon). Thomas Platter, a German who traveled in England in 1599, relates a quite similar anecdote told by the guide who showed him Woodstock Castle: "It is said of her, that watching the milkmaids milk the cows upon the meadow, she often declared that nothing would give her greater happiness than to be a milkmaid like those whom she saw out on the field, so miserable and perilous was her captive plight" (*Thomas Platter's Travels in England, 1599,* ed. and trans. Clare Williams [London: Jonathan Cape, 1937], 221).

33. British Library, Additional MS 33271, fols. 23v, 24r; see also Hartley, *Proceedings,* 1:472–73.

34. See also Edmund Plowden, "The Case of the Duchy of Lancaster," whose predications lay more stress on the duality-within-unity of the sovereign's bodies: "The King has a Body natural, adorned and invested with the Estate and Dignity royal; and he has not a Body natural distinct and divided by itself from the Office and Dignity royal, but a Body natural and a Body politic together indivisible; and these two Bodies are incorporated in one Person . . . by . . . Consolidation" (qtd. in Kantorowicz, *King's Two Bodies,* 9).

35. British Library, Additional MS 33271, fols. 24r, 22v; see also Hartley, *Proceedings,* 1:471–72.

36. See Hackett's discussion, *Virgin Mother, Maiden Queen,* 115–26, 213–30.

37. British Library, Additional MS 33271, fols. 24r–v; see also Hartley, *Proceedings,* 1:473.

38. British Library, Lansdowne MS 94, Art. 35A, fol. 84v; see also T. E. Hartley, *Proceedings in the Parliaments of Elizabeth I,* vol. 2: *1584–89* (New York: Oxford University Press, 1995), 248–53.

39. British Library, Lansdowne MS 94, art. 35B, fols. 86r–88r; quotation from

86r. Copy in the same small and neat italic as art. 35A, revised scratchily and loosely in Elizabeth's rapid italic; see also Hartley, *Proceedings*, 2:267–68.

40. British Library, Lansdowne MS 94, art. 35B, fol. 87v–88r; see also Hartley, *Proceedings*, 2:268–69. The other, apparently close-to-contemporary report of her second speech on the petition to execute Mary Queen of Scots imposes somewhat clearer schematism on Elizabeth's gendered taxonomy of the political virtues: "I dyd put my self to the scole of experyence, wher I sought to lerne what thynges wer most fytte for a kynge to have, and I found theym to be fower, namely Justice, temperance, mangnanymyte, and Judgemente. . . . Thys may I saye and trulye, that as Salamon, so I above all thynges have desyred wysdome at the handes of God And I thanke hym he hathe given me . . . Judgemente and wytte. . . . As for magnanymyte I wyll profasse yt ever, And for the the course of Justyce I proteste that I never knewe dyfferense of persons, that i never set one before an other but uppon juste cause. . . . And for thempere [temperance] I have had alwayes care" (Cambridge University Library MS Gg.3.34, fols. 312–16; quotation from 314).

41. For testimony on Elizabeth's learning, see Roger Ascham, *The Schoolmaster*, ed. Lawrence V. Ryan (Charlottesville: University of Virginia Press for Folger Shakespeare Library, 1967), xvi–xxi, 56, 80–81, 87.

42. See *The Collected Dialogues of Plato,* ed. Edith Hamilton and Huntington Cairns (Princeton: Princeton University Press, 1963), 669, 684–85.

43. For pertinent discussion, see Hanna Fenichel Pitkin, *Fortune Is a Woman: Gender and Politics in the Thought of Niccolò Machiavelli* (Berkeley: University of California Press, 1984).

44. Quentin Skinner traces to a passing reference in Cicero's *De officiis* the equation of magnanimity with courage (Latin *fortitudo*), which, I would note, must be the warrant for Elizabeth's substitution here ("Ambrogio Lorenzetti: The Artist as Political Philosopher," *Proceedings of the British Academy* 72 [1986]: 28). I owe this reference to my colleague Elissa Weaver.

45. See Aristotle, *Nicomachean Ethics,* ed. and trans. H. Rackham, Loeb Classical Library (Cambridge: Harvard University Press, 1975) bk. 4, chap. 3, sec. 1, 16–19, 212–13, 218–19. Also noteworthy is Sir Thomas Elyot's definition of *magnanimity,* which curiously appears to conflate a masculine quality with a feminine one: "Audacitie with timerositie maketh Magnanimitie" (*The Book of the Governor,* ed. Foster Watson [London: Dent, 1907], 95).

46. Mary Ann O'Farrell and Lynne Vallone, 2.

47. British Library, Lansdowne MS 94, art. 35B, fol. 88r. The meaning, though again not the wording, in Cambridge University Library MS Gg.3.34 at fol. 316, accords closely.

48. Elizabeth I to James VI, January–February 1587. British Library, Additional MS 23240, art. 18, fols. 57r–58r, at fol. 58r. This letter is in the queen's dashed, late italic hand. Printed in *Letters of Queen Elizabeth and King James VI of Scotland,* ed. John Bruce, Camden Society no. 46 (London: J. B. Nichols, 1859), 42–43.

49. Elizabeth I to James VI, early February 1587. British Library, Additional MS 23240, art. 19, fols. 61r–62r, at fol.61v–62r. This letter is also in the queen's late

italic. Printed in Bruce, *Letters of Queen Elizabeth and King James VI of Scotland*, 44–45.

50. Elizabeth I to James VI, February 14, 1587. British Library, Cotton MS Caligula, C.IX, fol. 201 (my transcription). Copy in secretary hand.

51. James VI to Elizabeth I, ca. March 1587. British Library, Additional MS 23240, art. 20, fol. 65. Although this letter in James's hand is unsigned, Bruce does not doubt that it was sent. Printed in Bruce, *Letters of Queen Elizabeth and King James VI of Scotland*, 46. James articulates his vision of a future Great Britain on the occasion of informing Elizabeth of his acceptance of his mother's execution. See also Stephanie H. Jed, *Chaste Thinking: The Rape of Lucretia and the Birth of Humanism* (Bloomington: Indiana University Press, 1989), for discussion of how Livy and later Renaissance humanists viewed the suicide of Lucretia and the revenge murder of Tarquin as founding events for the Roman republic.

52. British Library, Harley MS 6798, art. 18, fol. 87r–v. Copy, relocated and reverified by Leah Marcus; my transcription. The hand is of the earlier seventeenth century, in a seal brown ink, on a single leaf measuring ca. 6 by 8 inches. A quite closely according text is printed in modernizing spelling, without any indication of provenance, by John Nichols, ed., *Progresses and Public Processions of Queen Elizabeth*, 3:xiii–xiv.

53. The gender implications of Elizabeth's *megalopsychia* here are, in fact, more intricate still. Since she is defying an act of invasion of her realm in an age when the confines of her body natural would have been associated with the borders of England in the concept of the sovereign's Two Bodies, her masculine concern for her honor on this occasion defends and protects her feminine concern for her honor. An apposite image is offered by the Ditchley portrait of Elizabeth (1592?), attributed to Marcus Gheeraerts the Younger, which shows her standing on a map of England, her feet set in Oxfordshire, the hem of her full, deep-folded skirt and cape retracing the watercourses of the Severn and the Thames. I owe this comparison to Meiling Hazelton.

54. Significantly, the *OED* cites only sixteenth- and seventeenth-century examples for the three subdivisions of its eighth (and altogether obsolete) meaning of the noun *stomach*: 8a—spirit, courage, valor, bravery; 8b—pride, haughtiness, obstinacy; and 8c—anger, ill-will, vexation.

55. Judith Butler's "performativity of gender" might at first seem an applicable referent here. In her words, "Performativity is . . . not a singular 'act' [of the 'assumption' of sex], for it is always a reiteration of a norm or set of norms, and to the extent that it acquires an act-like status in the present, it conceals or dissumulates the conventions [of 'a regulatory apparatus of heterosexuality'] of which it is a repetition" (*Bodies That Matter: On the Discursive Limits of "Sex"* [New York: Routledge, 1993], 12). But multiple historical specificities in Elizabeth's situation at Tilbury resist assimilation to the emphases on normativity, reiteration, and heterosexuality that define Butler's concept.

56. Winfried Schleiner, "*Divina virago*: Queen Elizabeth as an Amazon," *Studies in Philology* 75 (1978): 163–80, examines the post facto tradition that Elizabeth

had appeared at Tilbury as an armed Amazon in full battle dress. He makes it clear that the only report with contemporary credentials, James Aske's poem, *Elizabetha triumphans* (London, 1588), supplies meager physical details—"our princely Soveraigne / . . . / Most bravely mounted on a stately Steede / With Trunchion in her hand (not us'd thereto)"—while drawing a comparison to "the *Amazonian Queene,*" Penthesilea (quotation from 170).

57. British Library, Cottton MS Titus F.II, fol. 99r; see also T. E. Hartley, ed., *Proceedings in the Parliaments of Elizabeth I,* vol. 3: *1593–1601* (London: Oxford University Press, 1995), 173–74. This speech is reported (uniquely) in a Parliamentary journal compiled by an MP in the House of Commons who does not identify himself.

58. I have chosen to cite the imprint, *Her Majesties Most Princelie Answere, delivered by her selfe at the Court at White-hall, on the last day of November 1601 . . . The same being taken verbatim in wrytinge by A. B. as neere as he could possiblie set yt downe* (London, 1601); PRO, State Papers Domestic, Elizabeth, 122/282/67, fols. 137r–41v, because this could not have been issued without Elizabeth's approval. The several substantively different versions of the Golden Speech include British Library, Stowe MS 362, fols. 168r–72r; BL, Harley MS 787, fols. 127r–28v; and Cambridge University Library, Additional MS 335, fol. 39r–v; see also Hartley, *Proceedings,* 3:292–97, 412–14.

59. British Library, Cotton MS Titus, C.VI, fols. 410r–11r. Copy in a difficult, late-sixteenthth-century secretary hand preserved among the original letters and papers of Henry Howard, earl of Northampton, Lord Privy Seal, warden of the Cinque Ports, and chancellor of Cambridge University.

60. British Library, Cotton MS Titus, C.VI, fol. 411r; see also Hartley, *Proceedings,* 3:281.

Gender, or the King's Secret
Franz Anton Mesmer's Magnetic Public Sphere

Helen Thompson

On April 24, 1784, the Paris journal *Mémoires secrets* announced the appointment of a royal commission to investigate the practices of Mesmerism. Since his arrival in Paris in 1778, Franz Anton Mesmer's spectacular deployments of his invisible magnetic fluid, "magnétisme animal," had become increasingly popular. Indeed, Mesmer's seances placed indecent stress upon the popular: they were frequently disorderly, activated by physical contact, and punctuated by convulsions as participants were magnetized by touch or by extending their limbs into a communal magnetic trough. The revitalizing powers of animal magnetism were both undetectable and inordinately material, induced by the hysterical contiguity of Mesmerist and patients of all classes and both sexes.

In his account of Mesmerism in late-eighteenth-century France, Robert Darnton stresses the ungovernability of science at this time, suggesting that Mesmerism, in occupying an unstable disciplinary space, was open to popular or subversive political appropriation.[1] My own attention, as I read the commission's report, will not initially be turned toward Mesmerism's fit within the volatile climate of the "Enlightenment" but to the zone or organ that occupies an instrumental place in the commissioners' recapitulation of the Mesmeric scene:

> The large number of patients, lined up in many rows around the baquet [wooden magnetic tub, filled with water and iron filings], at once receive magnetism by the following means: iron wands that transmit the baquet's magnetism; a cord entwined around their bodies and their linked thumbs, which communicate the magnetism of their neighbors; and the sound of a piano or a melodic voice resonating in the air. The patients are also magnetized directly, by means of fingers and iron wands held before the face, above or behind the head, and upon the affected parts, always observing the different poles. One works by fixing them with the gaze. But above all, they are

magnetized by touch, by the pressure of fingers upon the hypochondria and the regions of the lower stomach, an application continued for some time, up to several hours.[2]

The "hypochondria" were central to Mesmeric practice, as Darnton states: "Most mesmerists concentrated on the body's equator at the hypochondria, on the sides of the upper abdomen, where Mesmer located the common sensorium."[3] For the king's commission this bodily region is continuous with another organ accountable not only for magnetic predilection, but also for the spectacle of gender: the uterus. The capacities of the latter organ provoked the commissioners to add a supplement to their officially published experimental logic: a *Rapport secret,* or secret report, intended solely for the king, devoted to the effects of Mesmerism upon the physiognomic and moral constitution of women.[4]

As we will see, part of what the commission's reports indisputably do, as Neil Hertz states of a series of later French texts, is figure "a political threat as if it were a sexual threat."[5] Hertz's attention is devoted to the fetishizing or emblematizing work involved in the conversion of political to sexual threat; the endless experimental rehearsals that represent the commissioners' official protocol, however, resist condensation into a fetishistic plot. Rather, the threat of Mesmerism resides in the official report's apparently interminable experimental recreation of magnetic effect. This proliferation of Mesmeric effect is contained—and never fully contained—in the uterine function of receptivity, the function essential, as the commissioners see it, to Mesmerism's spectacular popularity. Yet receptivity, even as it summons a specific organ and sex, is not, like Edmund Burke's "abused shape of the vilest of women," an easily materialized cognate of male panic.[6]

The commission's two documents suggest that the organization of sex is both supplemental to a more general Mesmeric etiology and, of itself, able to anticipate the magnetic deformation of public space. Their focus upon the function and the organ of receptivity—the uterus—has less to do with the sex it would fix than with its ability to render tenuous the distinctions of visible and invisible, observation and imagination, rational publicity and public spectacle. My readings of the official and secret reports reference Jürgen Habermas's account of the eighteenth-century bourgeois public sphere, then, because Habermas predicates the eighteenth-century transformation of public subjectivity upon the stability of these very distinctions. Indeed, despite its lack of attention to the specifics of women's engagement in the eighteenth-century public sphere, Habermas's history is enmeshed in the orienting thematics of gender, if that category gains historical coherence, in part, as a function of its subject's claim upon the disembodying aptitude of reason. Reason, the medium of eighteenth-century politics' embourgeoisement as charted by Habermas, signals the dissolution of physical display into the abstractly inclusive medium of print discourse.[7] The commission's reports—both the publicly circulated one and its supplement—affirm the rich and volatile overlay of the history of the density of the public self and the history of the category of gender. Indeed, the ambiguity of the qualifier *public* as it surfaces in the commission's reports—its signification as "not exclusive" and its Habermasian affirmation of the cultivated and critical aptitude of the representative man of letters—will be redressed in the commissioners' recourse to the peculiarly elastic realm of anatomical tendency.

This essay takes the commission's two reports as remarkable documents in both the history of the bourgeois public sphere and the history of gender. At the same time, I will suggest that they show the confluence of the two categories, insofar as each might emerge from the difference between anatomical and discursive capacities of the self. In tracking the variously nested susceptibilities that account for Mesmerism's popular success, the commissioners render volatile the very coordinates that would fix this difference.

"La Séduction de l'esprit": The Official Report

The *commissaires de la faculté et de l'Academie chargés par le roi de l'examen du magnétisme animal* (commissioners of the Faculty of Medicine and the Royal Academy of Sciences, appointed by the king to investigate animal magnetism) were named on March 12, 1784. They included the doctors Michel-Joseph Majault, Charles-Louis Ballin, Jean d'Arcet, and Joseph-Ignace Guillotin, as well as the academicians Benjamin Franklin, Jean-Baptiste Le Roy, Jean-Sylvain Bailly, Gabriel de Bory, and Antoine-Laurent Lavoisier. Twenty thousand copies of the official report were published after it was sent to the king in August 1784; it was widely read and provoked a flood of printed responses.[8]

The rationale for the king's commission is cogently supplied by contemporary caricatures of Mesmer and his followers, which depict with lavish detail licentious charlatans and abandoned women, set in a confusion of pseudoscientific signifiers.[9] These images aim to expose the indecent pretensions of the Mesmerist and the erotic susceptibility of his patient. The more alarmist among them attempt to show how Mesmeric excitement deforms the relation of public bodies, stressing the incoherence of the scene around the baquet or, in one image, depicting a mob of Mesmerist dogs, working people, republicans, and one woman lying on her back with her legs in the air. Such caricatures would seem to take for granted the coextensivity of feminized gullibility and civic disorder.

The commission's official report, however, avoids this presumption, apparently bypassing the connection that the engravings reflexively affirm. It attempts, instead, to disprove the existence of "magnétisme animal," throwing its blindfolded experimental subjects into crisis by means of some dumbly ordinary prop. The success of this very protocol underlines the paradox occasioning the report: how to treat Mesmeric illogic, the nullity of animal magnetism as the commissioners themselves perceive it, as a force that nonetheless operates upon the crowd of patients gathered for "traitement public." While they publicly avoid an obviously prurient etiology, the commissioners will still place pressure upon the feminine, even more decisively than the caricatures locating the paradox of Mesmeric predilection inside the body of the crowd.

Early in the report, the commissioners declare that their own private reconstitutions of the Mesmeric seance, conducted by Mesmer's follower M. Deslon, yield no proof of the invisible fluid's existence: "none of them felt anything" (R 89).[10] The definitiveness of this experimental verdict, however, is rendered curiously anticlimactic by the section of the report immediately following these results, "Difference of the Effects at Public Treatment and at Their [the commissioners'] Private Treatment." Here the report states:

> The commissioners were forcibly struck by the difference between public treatment and their private treatment at the baquet. The calm and silence in one, the movement and agitation in the other: there, multiplied effects, violent crises, the stasis of body and spirit interrupted and troubled, nature exalted; here, the body without pain, the spirit untroubled, nature maintaining its equilibrium and its ordinary course, in a word the absence of all effects. One can no longer recover the enormous power which is so amazing at public treatment; magnetism, without energy, appears divested of all perceptible action. (R 20)

Insofar as it affirms the difference between not only an exclusive and a popular, but also a neutral and a susceptible body, this passage marks a structuring juncture. In it, the commissioners' own indifference to Mesmeric fluid—"none of them felt anything"—becomes sharply discontinuous from the response manifest at public treatment. Instead of acting as controls, who register universal experimental proof, the commissioners' nonresponse divides a "violent," "exalted" popular body from their own "calm." Mesmerism can never be tested in the commissioners' model—indeed "absent"—bodies; feeling nothing, instead of serving as proof, dramatizes the commission's failure to reenact public agitation. The domain of privatized experimental recreation, of an inevitably *failed* recreation, would thus seem to render the commissioners' resistance to Mesmerism continuous with the conditions of their authorship. Constitutionally exempt from the circulation of magnetic energy, the commissioners project in their report the remedial conditions of rational scientific discourse, sustained only in experimental failure.

At the same time that the report limns an atomized and rational readership, immune to the energy uniting the crowd around the baquet, it severs the commissioners' sympathetic connection to that crowd. This marks something of a break with the discourse of sympathy, whose central place in the emerging Enlightenment "science of man" inhered in its capacity to project, out of the indistinction of physiology and psychology, a bridge between individual feeling and general sociability. The commissioners, in effect, exchange sympathetic aptitude (the discourse of political economy) for specular distance (the discourse of "hard" science): their lack of sympathy for the crowd replaces affective proximity with, as they put it, "scrupulous fidelity" to the task of description (*R* 90). By annexing the powers of observation to those of reason, the commissioners oppose the sense of sight to its remainder, the domain of feeling: here we might read, in the words of one historian, the "unloosening of the eye from the network of referentiality incarnated in tactility. . . . [The] autonomization of sight."[11] In their lack of connection to the patients gathered for treatment, the commissioners' unsympathizing bodies barely surface in the Mesmeric scene as bodies at all, most strongly marked as such when the report notes their experimental displacements to Passy because of Franklin's gout. The difference between commissioners and crowd is not—as it might have figured in the prior century—one of self-discipline; as we will see, their difference is marshaled through the displacement of embodied organization into the register of publicity.[12]

After briefly defending its objects of experiment—all of them women, children, and members of *la classe du peuple*—as individuals whose disagregrated tendencies best represent Mesmeric predilection, the report turns to "a new object": "to determine to what degree the imagination can influence our sensations" (*R* 100). Thus begins a series of sixteen experiments that gain access to the Mesmeric imagination by obstructing its subjects' vision. The commissioners' anticipation of the course that such protocol will take dictates the multiple experimental dramas staged in the report: "We recognized that their responses were obviously determined by the questions we asked. The questions indicated where sensation should be felt; in place of directing magnetism in them, we merely activated and directed their imagination" (R 105). Trials eight and nine amply demonstrate the commissioners' success in "activating and directing" two women's magnetic response. I cite these trials at length to give a sense of both their intensely specular focus and their obvious iterability:

> One day the commissioners were all assembled in Passy, at M. Franklin's house, with M. Deslon, having asked the latter to bring with him some patients, and to choose, among the poor ones, those who would be most sensitive to magnetism. He brought two women; and while he was occupied in magnetizing M. Franklin . . . we separated them, and placed them in two different rooms.
>
> . . . One, Mrs. P**, had cataracts on her eyes; but as she could still see a little, we covered them. . . . We persuaded her that we had brought M. Deslon in to magnetize her: silence was recommended; three commissioners were present, one to ask questions, one to write, and the third to represent M. Deslon. We gave the impression of speaking to M. Deslon, asking him to begin; but nobody ever magnetized the woman: the three commissioners stayed aloof, occupied in observing only. After three minutes, the patient began to feel a nervous shiver; then successively she felt pain behind her head, in her arms, a prickling in her hands (her expression); she stiffened, struck her hands, rose from her seat, stamped her feet: the whole crisis was very pronounced . . .
>
> Two commissioners were with the other patient, Miss B**, who was prey to nervous ailments. We left her eyes uncovered: we sat her in front of a closed door, and persuaded her that M. Deslon was on the other side, busy magnetizing her. She was hardly a minute in front of the door before she began to feel chills; after another minute, her teeth chattered, despite an overall flush; finally, after a third minute, she fell completely in crisis. Her respiration sped up; she stretched her arms behind her back, violently twisting them and leaning her body forward; her entire body trembled; her chattering teeth became so loud, that they could be heard outside; she bit her own hand, strongly enough that the marks remained . . .
>
> The commissioners, who had wanted to understand the work of the imagination, and to appreciate the role that it could play in magnetic crisis, obtained all that they desired. It is impossible to see imagination's work more clearly exposed than in these two experiments. (R 115–17)

Certainly, these dramatically staged—and, extended into sixteen vignettes, almost shaggy dog–like—demonstrations of the superfluity of animal magnetism to Mesmeric effect can only represent "all that [the commissioners] desired." What is most striking in this experimental series, however, is the scrupulously indexed bodily residue for which they must claim equivocal credit. In repeatedly dissociating magnetic crisis from the abilities of M. Deslon, the commissioners themselves assume the force of his gaze or voice: rather than defusing Mesmeric crisis, the commission demonstrates its peculiar fungibility.[13] "All that they desired," then, entails proof of their own ability to produce crisis in P** and B** even while "occupied in observing only": demonstrating animal magnetism's nullity, paradoxically, entails the potentially limitless (sustained, at least, over sixteen variations) iteration of its crises. Ironically, these unsympathetic witnesses to popular predilection ("none of them felt anything"; "[they] were occupied in observing only") can only prove their overdetermined ability to affirm its predilections.

In showing the interchangeability of Mesmerist and commissioner, the report would seem to have radically abstracted both positions. In other words, recalling the caricatures described here, the disembodied agents of unfeeling observation prove themselves able surrogates for even the spectacularly manifest Mesmer, who wore flowing lilac-colored robes, carried a wand, and accompanied his performances with the glass armonica.[14] In showing that they can elicit Mesmeric crisis, the commissioners drain the magnetizer's spectacular presence of its force, registering the imbrication of supervisory rationality and feminized loss of self-possession. At this juncture the commissioners remove themselves from the magnetic scene, turning to the interior of the Mesmeric patient. The faculty of imagination must, the report concludes, induce Mesmerism's "effets physiques" (R 127). Disembodying both Mesmerist and animal magnetism entails embodying the imagination: the inside of the Mesmeric body is as spectacular as (her) outside.

As it turns out, Mesmeric imagination is both embodied and dislocated. The report situates the Mesmeric patient's "centre nerveux" as follows: "One knows the influence and the empire of the uterus over the animal economy" (R 130). Paris's deepest predilection is located in the lower abdomen, which the Mesmerist treated as the body's equator and, to the dismay of the commission, rubbed:

> The intimate relation of the colon, the stomach, and the uterus with the diaphragm is one of the causes of the effects attributed to magnetism. The regions of the lower stomach, exposed to different pressures, respond to different nervous networks [*plexus*] which there constitute a veritable nervous center, by means of which, abstraction made of the whole system, there certainly exists a sympathy, a communication, a correspondence between all of the parts of the body, an action and a reaction, such that the sensations

excited in this center agitate the other parts of the body, and such that, reciprocally, a sensation felt in one part agitates and imparts motion to the nervous center, which often transmits this impression to all of the other parts. (*R* 131)

This somewhat impacted description participates in the eighteenth-century discourse of nervous sensibility, relying upon an internal fund of sympathetic energy that places the body in intimate and iterable relation to itself. It marks an intriguing divergence from the account of sensibility traced by the historian George Rousseau, however, in its placement of this uterine "nervous center." For Rousseau, the "paradigmatic leap" enabling the eighteenth-century fascination with nerves—consolidated in Locke's "integration of ethics and physiology"—occurred in the late-seventeenth-century's "regionalization of the soul to the brain."[15] Rousseau states: "Once the soul was limited to the brain, scientists could debate precisely how the nerves carry out its voluntary and involuntary intentions. . . . [A] radically new assumption arose about man's essentially nervous nature. . . . [A] theory of knowledge . . . directly followed from . . . the physiology of perception."[16] If the brain, for Rousseau, anticipates an epistemology based in the nervous transmission of perception and intention, the official report appends to it a strangely supplemental cul-de-sac. While nerves "carry out" the brain's intentions and, alternatively, transmit impressions back to the brain, the Mesmeric nervous center is excluded from this two-way traffic. It exists in direct and brainless relation to the body, a site of sensory amplification that of itself has no directive other than to "transmit this impression to all of the other parts."

The autonomy of this uterine nervous center suggests the persistence of the classical conviction that "the womb is like an animal within an animal," whose (mis)function inheres in its ability to exert pressure or impart motion to its neighboring organs.[17] Certainly, the commissioners' "centre nerveux" is not supervised by the brain. Nor, "abstraction made of the whole system," do the functions of "sympathy, communication, [and] correspondence" represent modes of perception. The uterine region's function might be best evoked as that of receptivity—of the brainlike but brainless capacity to trap and reiterate Mesmeric impression. Of course, the "sensations excited" here are, recalling the commissioners' insensibility, already suspect: the nervous center, itself a brainless double of the brain, can only reproduce a phantasmatic original.

This process, if it corresponds to "imagination," provides the etiology for another, larger, nervous and brainless body: the crowd. The crowd is uterine-like in its ability to generate crisis out of almost nothing:

Many women are magnetized at once, and feel at first only effects like those of the commissioners during many of their own experiments. . . . Little by little the impressions communicate and reinforce each other, like one sees at theatrical spectacles, where the impressions are stronger when there are a lot of spectators, and above all in places where they have the liberty to applaud. . . . The same cause foments [*fait naître*] revolts. . . .

This great mobility [of sensibility], part natural and part acquired, in men as well as women, becomes habitual. These sensations once or several times felt, one has only to recall the memory, to raise the imagination to the same degree, to cause the same effects. . . . Thus public treatment now involves no more than touching the hypochondria, waving the finger or iron wand in front of the face; the signs are known. It is not even necessary that these means be employed; it suffices that the patients, eyes covered, think that these signs are repeated, are persuaded that a magnetizer acts: the ideas awaken, the sensations reproduce themselves. . . .

Touch, imagination, imitation, these are thus the real source of the effects attributed to this new agent known by the name animal magnetism. (*R* 134–39)

It is telling not simply that the endpoint of Mesmeric communicability is "revolt" but that the terms of such communicability—articulated as the "liberty" to unleash the mechanical contagion of applause—retain their connection to the uterine zone. The vocabulary of the original French, *fait naître*, fortuitously references the organ that is implicated in the transformation of commissioners into women into revolutionaries. Yet the metaphor of birth, to pursue this serendipitous organization of grammar, becomes most resonant in its failure to keep pace with the reproductive powers of habit. If the brainless amplification of sensations originally "like those of the commissioners" occurs in the womb of the nervous center and in the womb of the crowd, the commissioners' turn to habit would bypass even that scene of gestation: memory's resources enable "the sensations [to] reproduce themselves." Habit renders props such as the Mesmeric finger or iron wand superfluous to magnetic sensation; indeed, in contrast to a therapeutic drama analogous to "theatrical spectacle," the patient is now best "persuaded" when blindfolded. The opposition of a theatrical to an almost entirely interiorized Mesmeric scene threatens to install the forces of magnetism *inside* the patient:[18] if the commissioners' invocation of memory here would seem to signal their recourse to the organ that has had little play so far, the brain, this is an already uterine brain, whose ability to reproduce "the same phenomena" figures the dislocation of sensation itself.[19] Mesmeric interiority figures, intriguingly, a bizarre double of the internalizing field of sociability charted by the man of letters in the bourgeois public sphere: the paradox of interiority would be, then, that, for (at least) these eighteenth-century women and men, the body already *has* depth.

The commission's account of uterine publicity engages and disturbs the indices of sociability that make up the eighteenth-century subject. Insofar as this disturbance proceeds from the incongruity of virtual cues and hyperembodied susceptibility, it solicits Luce Irigaray's assessment of the philosophical stakes of the mind/body split. Indeed, Irigaray exploits the failure of this split, as inaugurated in Plato's cosmogony *Timaeus,* to realize itself in the world without the mediation of the figure that Plato designates the "mother," "nurse," or "receptacle"—a third term that, subsisting between matter and idea, would be the template in Plato's vision of the printing press–like replication of intelligible ideas as sensible things.[20] In reading Plato's myth, Irigaray recasts a masculine fantasy of autochthonous rationality, of reason that can (almost) realize itself in things, by imagining the unqualifiable ground of mediation between matter and idea as the feminine.[21] The importance, to the present reading, of Irigaray's appropriation of Plato's receptacle inheres in that organ's incoherence. Terminally inchoate materiality, what Judith Butler evokes in her amplification of Irigaray's text as "a matter that exceeds matter" or "unthematizable materiality,"[22] both funds and disrupts the operations of a rationality that would constitute itself from the difference of thing and idea. The commission's nervous center, the site of both an anatomical and a virtual proliferation of Mesmeric effect, recalls Irigaray's feminine; it confuses the medium of interiority itself.

Irigaray's feminization of a matter that exceeds matter engages not only the imbrication of Mesmeric anatomy and "revolt" but the structuring coordinates of the Habermasian account of the rise of rational publicity, urging a reading of the Mesmeric uterus as a supplement that, as Butler states, "cannot be contained within the form/matter distinction."[23] If the bourgeois public sphere is the briefly utopian endpoint of a history that affirms the progressive abstraction of the body, the commission's magnetic nervous center offers itself as that history's third term: constituted not, to be sure, in "feminine" embodiment but in a hysterical confluence of immaterial and somatic that would, apparently, gender Paris's Mesmeric body.

"Touch, imagination, and imitation," listed in the official report as the final cause of Mesmeric sensation, gesture towards the cues of the magnetizer and the presence of the crowd. Imagination is organized as a site of passage between magnetizer and crowd, serving the uterine function of amplification and intensification. Uterine interiority not only registers the confused proximity of material cues and virtual contagion as Mesmeric effect but threatens to perpetuate itself both in space and time:

> This [Mesmeric] art is even more dangerous, not only because it aggra-
> vates nervous maladies . . . in making them degenerate into habit; but if it is
> contagious, as one might suspect, the ability to provoke nervous convulsions,
> and to excite them in public treatment, is a means of spreading them
> throughout large cities, and even of afflicting the coming generations, since
> the ailments and the habits of parents are transmitted to their posterity. (*R*
> 146)

This is the warning with which the commissioners close their report: the threat of Mesmerism's transmission to posterity would conclusively embody uterine function. Their signatures, dated August 11, 1784, appear on the next page. They distill their results in the formula: "Imagination without magnetism produces convulsions, and magnetism without imagination produces nothing"(*R* 146). Such a calculation recalls the irony of their own insensibility to Mesmerism, which severs privatized experiment from the physiology of the crowd: here, in asserting magnetism's superfluity to the crowd's susceptible interior, the commissioners demonstrate that they have effectively denounced nothing, leaving as a remainder the "active and terri-ble power" (*R* 140) of sensations that can reproduce themselves. Indeed, uterine receptivity, with its potentially interminable iterative capacity, impels the commissioners themselves to produce one more report.

"L'Influence et l'empire de l'uterus": The Secret Report

The occasion of the commission's secret report on women can be anticipated in a contemporary engraving, *Le Magnétisme dévoilé* (fig. 2). In it the com-missioners stride past the tattered curtains framing a Mesmeric stage; hold-ing the *Rapport des Commissaires* aloft is the triumphant figure of Benjamin Franklin, whose service on the commission coincided with his last full year in Paris. Toward the opposite side of the stage fly a group of broom-riding char-latans (among them, Deslon and Mesmer) and several *citoyens,* one conspic-uously waving a *tricorne* hat as he departs through a door at the rear of the scene. In Paris, in 1784, Franklin had the almost iconic capacity to represent the demystifying forces of scientific rationality, yet he is visually subordinate to the figure sitting in the engraving's center, a blindfolded, bare-breasted, flailing-limbed woman whose Mesmeric tub collapses around her. The work's title, *Mesmerism Unveiled,* suggests that of the Mesmeric ephemera fluttering away in the face of science, *she* is the remainder waiting to be exposed; amplifying this suggestion is the ambiguity of her heavily muscled legs.

The engraving's composition hints at the acute split within the event of publicity occasioned by the secret report. This report, ratified by the commission's belief that "it was prudent to suppress an observation that should not be divulged," was "intended to be placed under the eyes of the King and reserved for his Majesty only" (*SR* 42–43). While a contemporary caricaturist could not know of the secret report's existence, this composition nonetheless dramatizes the difficult coincidence of two forms of publicity, representing, in the open secret of the naked woman, the imminent but not-quite-realized promise of the official report. At issue here is spectacular or theatrical display, constituted in the engraving itself, the stage upon which its action is set, and the visual intricacy of the fleeing Mesmeric "performers." Opposed to this is rational or discursive publicity, most obviously realized in the legibly printed title of the report, the rays of light shooting from it, and the stern, compacted mass of commissioners who hold the document aloft.

Yet within this parodic clash of rococo and its rationalizing antidote, the caricature reveals an impediment to the commission's discursive powers: the figure at center stage. While the rest of Mesmeric theater dissolves before the approaching commission, she remains in her tub, her relation to the competing forms of publicity around her unclear. Can her conspicuous and equivocal embodiment be reformed by the commissioners? Or does she fall outside the scope of their corrective claims? The print's commissioners do not even look at her: at the same time that she is visibly at the crux of this drama of demystification, she is as yet unrecognized and unrevised by the forces of rational science. Herself figuring the point of contact of Mesmeric spectacle and scientific discourse, she anticipates the paradoxical constitution of the secret report. Even though, as a text devoted to Mesmerism's erotic effect upon women, the secret report's topic was popularly elaborated and spoofed in print pamphlets, in caricature, and on the Parisian stage, its authors felt licensed to "divulge" it to an audience of only one.[24] The open secret of Mesmeric crisis is off the scale of rational publicity, beyond the bounds of official science, at the same time that, as the print portends, its centrality to Mesmeric etiology demands that it be represented.

The secret report is about five pages long; opposed to the seventy-odd pages of the official report, it is terse in stating what it is that makes women not only vulnerable but addicted to the effects of Mesmerism. We read again that the (male) magnetizer touches his (female) patient on the abdomen and

Fig. 2. *Le Magnétisme dévoilé.* (Reproduced by permission of the Bibliothèque nationale de France.)

even on the ovaries, or, again, "upon an infinity of parts in the most sensitive region of the body" (*SR* 43). Much more rapidly than in the official report, the imminence of that "most sensitive region of the body" to the sensation of a single patient is conflated with its imminence to an entire crowd of women:

> The Commissioners have recognized that the principle causes of magnetic effects are touch, imagination, and imitation; and they have observed that there are always many more women than men in crisis. This difference has its primary cause in the different organization of the sexes. Women in general have more mobile nerves, their imagination is more lively, more rarefied. . . . This nervous mobility, in giving them more delicate and more refined sensation, makes them more susceptible to the impressions of touch. In touching them in any place whatsoever, one could say that one touches them everywhere at once. The same mobility of nerves disposes them to imitation. As we

have already stated, women are like finely tuned strings wound to the same pitch. When one is put into movement, all the others resonate instantly. Many times the Commissioners observed that as soon as one women fell into crisis, the others would follow immediately. (*SR* 43)

In comparing women to "finely tuned strings," the commissioners draw upon an analogy whose importance to the discourse of nervous sensibility dates at least to the beginning of the eighteenth century, when the Earl of Shaftesbury states in his *Characteristics* (1711) that, "upon the whole, it may be said properly to be the same with the affections or passions in an animal constitution as with the cords or strings of a musical instrument";[25] Denis Diderot, translator of the *Characteristics,* wrote in 1769 of perception that "it has sometimes led me to compare the fibres of our organs with sensitive vibrating strings. A sensitive vibrating string goes on vibrating and sounding a note long after it has been plucked. . . . But vibrating strings have yet another property, that of making others vibrate."[26] By the date of the commission's reports, the notion of nervous fibers as musical cords, capable of vibrating and harmonizing with others, was in wide cultural circulation.[27] So, too, was the feminization of nervous "mobility."[28] An already formulated theory of "the different organization of the sexes," invoking the classical mobility of uterine complaints along musical-mechanical lines, might thus appear to account for the commissioners' relative brevity in ascribing to women heightened Mesmeric susceptibility.

Yet, as imagined by Shaftesbury, Diderot, and La Mettrie, an assembly of nervous fibers or musical strings together constitutes *one* individual or instrument; in the commission's report, it is "women [who] are like finely tuned strings wound to the same pitch."[29] A group of strings adds up not to one woman but to a crowd of them. The commissioners' conception of crowd behavior as a gendered tendency stresses a musical string's capacity, as Diderot puts it, to "make others vibrate"—not to account for complex internal functions like memory, as is the case for Diderot and the others cited here, but to evoke the reflexive communicability that operates between women in crisis. The definitive feature of a woman's response to Mesmerism, as the commissioners evoke it, is thus its simultaneity with every other woman's response. The specter of a sexual crisis that no longer inheres in discrete bodies or events funds a spectacle in which the discontinuity of feminine bodies serves only to augment the single sensation that each projects simultaneously. Nervous organization, in prescribing the simultaneity of gendered ecstasy with itself, is its own inverse, the single undifferentiated organ of the crowd.

Yet the secret report does carefully anatomize feminine crisis, which is manifest to the commissioners as follows:

The medical commissioners, present and attentive to the treatment, carefully observed what happened. When this kind of crisis approaches, the face flushes by degrees, the eye blazes, and these are the signs by which nature announces desire. We saw the woman lower her head, covering her eyes and forehead with her hand; unbeknownst to her, instinctive modesty guards her and prompts her to hide herself. However, the crisis continues and the eye becomes unfocused [*se trouble*]: this is an unequivocal sign of the total disorder of the senses. Such disorder can never be perceived by she who experiences it, but it never escaped the observing gaze of the doctors. As soon as this sign became manifest, the eyelids became humid, the respiration short and choppy, the breast rose and fell rapidly; convulsions began, as well as precipitous and brusque movements of the limbs or the whole body. For lively and sensitive women, the last degree of these sweetest emotions is often a convulsion. (*SR* 44)

As spectators, the commissioners see what "can never be perceived by she who experiences it": magnetized women's inability to both have and observe their crises recalls the blindfolded objects of official experiment, the intensity of whose reactions is severed from its real conditions of possibility. Like the dupes of the commission's official report, the secret report represents women whose sensation renders them the unseeing objects of a supervisory, if not voyeuristic, gaze.

The body in crisis that cannot see past itself is, in the official report, a public body, whose tendencies cannot be reproduced in the commission's private attempts at magnetism. The commissioners would be unfeeling observers, magnetized women their blindly feeling objects; the commission—whether in the face of a blindfolded object of experiment or as agents of science—invisible, the indecent exterior of these women—despite the dissimulating efforts of "instinctive modesty"—fully visible. Indeed, the commissioners' stress upon their unique capacity as observers would in the secret report seem to "decorporealize vision"[30] exactly insofar as it exempts that faculty from the feminized and feminizing fallout of Mesmeric susceptibility. The commission, in representing the functions of reason and observation, its members blending together into a single body of print, claim the powers of the implicitly masculine, disembodied ideal of rational public discourse elaborated by Habermas in his history of the bourgeois public sphere.

Yet the analogy of women-as-strings, which combine to form the single uterine organ that is the crowd, troubles the obvious difference between the discursive claims of the commission and the conditions of Mesmeric ecstasy. The strings evoked by the commissioners are not, after all, simply objects. As nervous fibers, agents of reiteration, amplification, and communication, these strings are situated between subject and object; indeed, as George Rousseau indicates, historical contention over the mediatory role of the nerves was reflected in the equivocal physical status of the nervous fibers themselves.[31] The debate over whether these fibers were solid or hollow—a debate over *what* they might transmit to the brain—encapsulates persistent historical confusion around the medium connecting the somatic and the passional. The Scottish physician and physiologist Robert Whytt (1714–66) frankly expresses this confusion:

> Such is the constitution of the animal frame, that certain ideas or affec-
> tions excited in the mind are always accompanied with corresponding
> motions or feelings in the body; and these are owing to some change made in
> the brain and nerves, by the mind or sentient principle . . . but what that
> change is, or how it produces those effects, we know not: as little can we tell,
> why shame should raise a heat and redness in the face, while fear is attended
> with a paleness.
> . . . [I]n these matters, we must confess our ignorance.[32]

The interest of this historical "ignorance" to the secret report inheres, very simply, in the nerves' function as place-holders: they hold open an unqualified gap between "mind" and "body." This is the space in which Irigaray would stress the constitutive instability of the mind/body split; in this realm of both medical ignorance and Mesmeric pleasure, the incommensurability of mind and body that would affirm the consistency of reason finds its unexpected, ecstatic supplement in the excitable interior of the crowd.

The secret report warns that what makes Mesmeric crisis morally dangerous is not its physiognomic content but its addictiveness:

> Magnetic treatment can only be dangerous to morality [*les moeurs*]. In
> proposing to cure patients who require a long treatment, one excites pleasant
> and cherished emotions . . . they are that much more dangerous, because it is
> easier to acquire the pleasant habit [*la douce habitude*]. (SR 44)

The report closes with final threat: "Nothing can prevent . . . these convulsions from becoming habitual, and spreading like epidemics in big cities; and from extending themselves to future generations" (*SR* 46). What the spread of "these convulsions" would seem to portend, now that it is articulated here, is the spread of gender itself: if women's instantaneously transmissible crises figure the absolute transparency of nervous contagion, then everybody in future cities and generations might acquire the sweet habit. Thus, the complement of the body in crisis, a body that can observe nothing beyond itself, is its access to a medium even subtler than print. At once the material object of the commission's gaze and the medium of a contagion that would make every body come together, the woman in crisis throws into excited proximity the coordinates of the commission's two publics, publics composed of unsympathetic print on the one hand and anatomical predilection on the other.

If Mesmeric women supplement a binary imagining of publicity, the secret report itself subverts the earnest experimental logic of the commission's official version. Another variation of the report's secret is, perhaps, that its science is Paris's ecstasy. Indeed, it is an irony of history that Guillotin, promoter of the eponymous instrument, should be among those letting Louis XVI in on the secret of magnetism's powers. For even if the magnetic fluid, as the commissioners insisted, was nothing, the king himself would come to feel the force of Mesmeric ecstasy.

Supplement: The Figure of Benjamin Franklin

Here I return again to *Le Magnétisme dévoilé*, to expose a deliberate omission in my prior reading concerned with the figure of Benjamin Franklin. I will briefly pursue it to suggest that we need not locate the excess of an abstracting narrative of publicity in an ecstatically magnetized woman: that Franklin himself symptomatizes the unqualifiable mediation of discourse and spectacle, observation and feeling, brain and its objects.

In this image, Franklin holds up the official report: he is continuous with it and with the transparent beams of reason shooting from it. Thus, the caricature positions Franklin, very literally, as constituent of discursive rationality, coextensive with or subordinate to the text that the commission has produced. Yet at the same time—and this is the omission from my prior reading—the engraving necessarily draws upon Franklin's appeal to the sensorium of some *other* public, one recognizing his face through the massive circulation of his image, through the spectacular popularity of his electrical experiments, and through his quaint republican charm, incarnated, for example, in his celebrated glasses and fur cap. Franklin, the representative of rational (print) publicity, is also visibly a mass-popular personality, whose almost cartoonlike physiognomy buttresses the report's claim to abstract truth.

Franklin's status in Paris as a public celebrity is documented by David

Schoenbrun, who states: "With or without his famous fur hat, his was the best-known face in France. His friend Chaumont, at his factory in the Loire, had manufactured a medallion, with a portrait of Franklin, that had been sold by the thousands throughout France. . . . This medallion was sold and worn even at the court of Versailles, to the annoyance of the king."[33] In contrast, Franklin's discursive position as representative of print publicity is evoked by Michael Warner, who states that Franklin, fashioning himself as a republican man of letters in England and America, repudiated "*personal* authority in favor of a general authority based in a negative relation to one's own person"—person signifying both self ("personality") and body.[34] For Warner, the literary Franklin "cashes in like no one else on the resource of negativity."[35] Thus, we have an intriguingly doubled Franklin, appearing at Versailles and disappearing in America's republican pretensions; aging, racked with gout and kidney stones during his final stay in Paris, and ageless, represented in the abstract virtue that is republican print; continually (re)embodied in popular renderings of his person, and disembodied by the mechanical reproducibility of the self he offered as a model of civic virtue. Schoenbrun's and Warner's accounts of Franklin's public persona, one assuming a specular and the other a print audience, are prefigured in *Le Magnétisme dévoilé:* Franklin is *both* "the best-known face in France" and the author who "cashes in like no one else" on his negative relation to his person.

The incompatibility of these accounts is striking: as with the form/matter distinction more generally, the print Franklin can be constituted only as the negation of his other, irrepressibly recognizable, self. In the display that would eclipse the king and the print persona that would provide a template of republican selfhood, these two Franklins condense the Habermasian narrative of publicity into two sides of one man. They are referenced in one image of that man, whose status as an agent of demystifying science is inextricable from the very conditions of publicity condemned in the commission's report. Indeed, if the caricature maps the hyperbolic sublimation of a body that nonetheless remains indefinitely recognizable, we might again locate rational publicity's third term in the indeterminate density of Franklin's persona. I close with Franklin, then, to suggest that his is a figure as much in crisis as the ecstatic woman at center stage: that if she supplements a binary drama of publicity, then so does Franklin himself. She troubles the mediation of official print and popular body; so, in this parodic enjambment of mutually exclusive selves, does he. Together, indivisibly, they constitute the tableau of Mesmeric publicity. If Mesmerism draws its powers from the unqualifiable interior of the crowd, then Franklin himself partakes of that ecstatic incoherence.

NOTES

1. In a sentence that spans the broadest trajectory of his study, Darnton states, "In its final stages, mesmerism expressed the Enlightenment's faith in reason taken to an extreme, an Enlightenment run wild, which later was to provoke a movement toward the opposite extreme in the form of romanticism." Robert Darnton, *Mesmerism and the End of the Enlightenment in France* (Cambridge: Harvard University Press, 1968), 39.

2. The text of the official report is reprinted in Alexandre Bertrand, *Du Magnétisme animal en France et des jugements qu'en ont portés les sociétés savantes, avec le texte des divers rapports faits en 1784 par les commissaires de l'Académie des sciences, de la Faculté et de la Société royale de médecine, et une analyse des dernières séances de l'Académie royale de médecine et du rapport de M. Husson; suivi de considérations sur l'apparition de l'Extase dans les traitements magnétiques* (Paris: J. B. Baillière, Libraire-Éditeur, rue de l'École de Médecine, n. 14. Février 1826). Passage cited, 72. Translations mine. Hereafter all references to the official report will appear parenthetically in the text with an *R*. I am grateful to Philip Stewart for his very helpful assistance with these translations.

3. Darnton, *Mesmerism*, 4.

4. The text of the secret report is reprinted, in French, in D. I. Duveen and H. S. Klickstein, "Benjamin Franklin (1706–1790) and Antoine Laurent Lavoisier (1743–1794): Part III. Documentation," *Annals of Science* 13.1 (Mar. 1957): 42–46. The authors state: "It is well known that Franklin and Lavoisier were among the commissioners from the Académie Royale des Sciences appointed in 1784 for the investigation of animal magnetism. . . . It is not generally known, however, that the same committee also drew up on this subject a secret report which dealt with delicate matters of 'morals' involved in it and which was intended for the King's exclusive use. It was published some fifteen years later in François Comte Neufchâteau's *Le conservateur, ou receuil de morceaux inédits d'histoire, de politique, de litterature, et de philosophie* (Paris, an XII [1799], 146–55)." All translations mine. Hereafter all references will appear parenthetically in the text with an *SR*.

5. Neil Hertz, *The End of the Line: Essays on Psychoanalysis and the Sublime* (New York: Columbia University Press, 1985), 161. See in particular chap. 9, "Medusa's Head: Male Hysteria under Political Pressure."

6. Edmund Burke, *Reflections on the Revolution in France,* ed. Conor Cruise O'Brien (London: Penguin, 1968), 165. In a famous passage of gendered panic Burke imagines the scene of the royal family's forced displacement from Versailles to Paris. The full citation is: "The royal captives who followed in the train [of the mob] were slowly moved along, amidst the horrid yells, and shrilling screams, and frantic

dances, and infamous contumelies, and all the unutterable abominations of the furies of hell, in the abused shape of the vilest of women."

7. This process was slowest in France, Habermas states, because for much of the century "the king largely monopolized public authority." Jürgen Habermas, *The Structural Transformation of the Public Sphere: An Inquiry into a Category of Bourgeois Society,* trans. Thomas Burger (Cambridge: MIT Press, 1991), 68. See esp. chaps. 1–4. Habermas stresses the slowness of the consolidation of a print public sphere in France, due to the absence of "developed political journalism," the nullity of the Estates General, the depth of class division, and, again, the fact that "the king largely monopolized public authority" (67–68). During the insular reign of Louis XVI, however, "the great ceremonial gave way to an almost bourgeois intimacy" (31). Habermas cites at length from Arnold Hauser, *The Social History of Art* (New York: Knopf, 1951), to substantiate this point: "At the court of Louis XVI the dominant tone is one of decided intimacy, and on six days of the week, the social gatherings achieve the character of a private party" (32). He locates the development of a properly "political" sphere of public debate in the journals of the physiocrats, particularly Turgot and Malesherbes, who "were called into government—the first exponents, as it were, of public opinion." Most central, however, is Necker, who "made public the balance of the state budget. . . . [T]he public's critical debate of political issues had proved its mettle as a check on the government, significantly at the nerve center of bourgeois interests. . . . From the time of Necker's *compte rendu,* this public sphere in the political realm . . . could no longer be effectively put out of commission" (69). Habermas evokes the French salon as a "peculiar enclave" (33) in which, to some degree, the rigid distinction of aristocracy and bourgeoisie was relaxed. His more general discussion of the inclusive power of print—particularly as it enables a fiction of cultivated literary "parity"—has recently been enlarged upon. See especially Michael Warner, *The Letters of the Republic: Publication and the Public Sphere in Eighteenth-Century America* (Cambridge: Harvard University Press, 1990).

8. The publication of the official report is discussed by Darnton, *Mesmerism,* 62–66; Claude-Anne Lopez, *Mon Cher Papa: Franklin and the Ladies of Paris* (New Haven: Yale University Press, 1990), 170–75; and Frank A. Pattie, *Mesmer and Animal Magnetism: A Chapter in the History of Medicine* (Hamilton, N.Y.: Edmonston Publishing, 1994), 142–58.

9. All of the prints referenced here are assembled in Darton, *Mesmerism.*

10. See Pattie, for an assessment of the commission's choice of Deslon as their object of investigation: "The reasons for going to d'Eslon's [the Mesmerist whom the commission investigated] were not officially disclosed. D'Eslon, being under the jurisdiction of French authorities, would have been more amenable to restrictions that might have resulted from the investigation. He was less touchy and hard to get along with Mesmer, and he spoke better French by far" (143).

11. Jonathan Crary, *Techniques of the Observer: On Vision and Modernity in the Nineteenth Century* (Cambridge: MIT Press, 1992). See chaps. 1 and 2, in which Crary discusses the late-seventeenth- and eighteenth-century positioning of vision relative to the other senses through the figure of the camera obscura. The dialectic of

the camera obscura—foreclosed by the nineteenth-century "industrialization of the senses" (19)—sustains a notion of sight, and the senses more generally, "as adjuncts of a rational mind and less as physiological organs" (60) alongside the notion of "a vision . . . in which tactility was fully embedded" (66).

12. From John Milton to Edmund Burke, at least, it is possible to trace the gendering of the faculty of perception as a crowd- and nation-building enterprise. See, for example, Milton's "The Reason of Church-Government Urg'd against Prelaty" (1642), which anticipates in the "sensual mistress," "wily arbitresses," and "pathetic handmaids" of an essentially venal sensorium his own aesthetic and corrective office as national poet. If Milton (and Burke) would, however, locate the material basis of the social in an essentially feminine asociality, they do not exempt themselves from it: discipline would establish a gradient, and not a break, between bodily appetite and the activity of writing.

13. The commissioners' attention to the impact of the magnetizer's gaze upon the imagination of his patient ("The gaze has the eminent power to magnetize" [R 121]) can be read alongside the rise of medical "management by spectacle," whose equivocalness, at an extreme, resided in the spectacular therapy of "fixing the patient with the eye." See Roy Porter, "Barely Touching: A Social Perspective on Mind and Body," in The Languages of Psyche: Mind and Body in Enlightenment Thought, ed. George S. Rousseau (Berkeley: University of California Press, 1990), 68–69. Porter recounts an anecdote according to which the Rev. Dr. Francis Willis, George III's mad doctor, gazes at Edmund Burke during a session of Parliamentary questioning—and forces Burke to turn away (68).

14. Pattie defends Mesmer's sartorial preferences, evoking "the statement, found in monotonous regularity in twentieth-century writing in English, that Mesmer appeared 'in a lilac gown.' There was nothing extraordinary, in the years before the French Revolution, about a lilac coat (habit) worn by a wealthy man" (190). Pattie adds in a footnote that "even the dessicated Voltaire appeared in magnificent clothing" (191).

15. George S. Rousseau, "Nerves, Spirits, and Fibres: Towards Defining the Origins of Sensibility," Blue Guitar (Messina) 2 (1976): 128, 139. Rousseau contends that the Kuhnian paradigm shift inaugurating Locke's "science of man" occurred in the works of Thomas Willis, particularly An Essay of the Pathology of the Brain (1681); Willis was Locke's tutor at Oxford. Rousseau suggests that the mid-eighteenth-century literature of sentiment represents the cultural absorption of this development: "no novel of sensibility could appear until a revolution in knowledge concerning the brain, and consequently its slaves, the nerves, occurred" (145).

16. Rousseau, "Nerves, Spirits, and Fibres," 135–40.

17. Ilza Veith, Hysteria: The History of a Disease (Chicago: University of Chicago Press, 1965), 23.

18. The opposition of theatrical to internally inspired sensation recalls Michael Fried's Absorption and Theatricality: Painting and Beholder in the Age of Diderot (Chicago: University of Chicago Press, 1980). Fried deploys these terms to designate strictly painterly resolutions of the relation between a work and its beholder; in charting the tension between "theatrical" and "absorptive" modes of pictoriality

and spectatorship, Fried opens ways of thinking about the equivocal status of theatricality and the absorptive individualization of spectatorship prized by Diderot. That absorptive spectatorship would represent a threat to the commissioners inheres in the most obvious difference between painterly and Mesmeric objects of perception: animal magnetism, despite its spectacular trappings, was invisible.

19. Porter states in *"Barely Touching*: A Social Perspective on Mind and Body" that "Franz Anton Mesmer himself was adamant that he performed his cures through the agency of a natural superfine medium, the animal magnetic fluid. . . . By contrast, it was his critics, especially the devastating French Commission of 1784, who insisted that Mesmer's cures were mere suggestion, were all due to transference from mind to mind" (76). Even more strongly, the commission here suggests that Mesmerism's effects are due to traffic within a *single* "mind": "transference" thus becomes reiteration or remembering.

20. See Luce Irigaray, "Plato's *Hystera,*" in *Speculum of the Other Woman,* trans. Gillian C. Gill (Ithaca: Cornell University Press, 1985), 243–365.

21. Plato, *Timaeus,* trans. Benjamin Jowett (New York: Macmillan, 1985), 31. Plato's fuller description of the receptacle follows: "The mother and receptacle of all created and visible and in any way sensible things . . . is an invisible and formless being which receives all things and in some mysterious way partakes of the intelligible, and is most incomprehensible" (33).

22. Judith Butler, *Bodies That Matter: On the Discursive Limits of "Sex"* (New York: Routledge, 1993), 47, 38. Butler gives a crucial reading of Irigaray's text, which extends and topicalizes its intervention in the "history of matter" (54).

23. See Irigaray, "Plato's *Hystera,*" 285: "Forms are moving in a (perhaps female) indefinite beyond and constantly risk being overwhelmed by a surplus, a remainder, which (theoretically) has not been taken into account and which would go beyond all calculation." Butler states: "This excessive matter that cannot be contained within the form/matter distinction operates like the supplement in Derrida's analysis of philosophical oppositions" (38).

24. Aside from the printed caricatures that I have referenced, there was a vast amount of written material produced upon the topic of Mesmerism's erotic impact upon women throughout the period of Mesmer's stay in Paris. See chaps. 9 and 10 of Pattie, *Mesmer and Animal Magnetism,* esp. chap. 10, "The Literature of 1784: Satires and Plays," which briefly discusses plays such as *Les Docteurs modernes* and *Le Baquet de santé,* presented together by the Comédie Italienne on November 18, 1784, and running for twenty-one performances. Darnton states of the former play: "It provided material for endless gossip, essays by literary pundits like La Harpe, and a bitter counterattack by Mesmer's supporters" (65). Pattie cites a passage from the satirical pamphlet *Mesmer justifié,* probably written by J.-J. Paulet, that nicely illustrates the conflation of the spectacular and the licentious popularly attributed to Mesmer: "Here the physician in a coat of lilac or purple, on which the most brilliant flowers have been painted in needlework, speaks most consolingly to his patient: his arms softly enfolding her sustain her in her spasm, and his tender burning eye expresses his desire to comfort her" (190).

25. Anthony, Earl of Shaftesbury, *Characteristics of Men, Manners, Opinions, Times,* vols. 1–2, ed. John M. Robertson (Indianapolis: Bobbs-Merrill, 1964), 290. The essay in which Shaftesbury makes this analogy is "Concerning Virtue or Merit"; its original date of publication was 1699. John Locke, who was Shaftesbury's confidant and medical advisor, discusses nervous perception in *An Essay Concerning Human Understanding* (1689) (Oxford: Clarendon Press, 1975); however, although Locke raises the central problem of the mediation between object and subject (brain) in terms of physical distance, he does not formulate the "string" analogy: "'Tis evident, that some motion must be thence continued [after perception] by our Nerves, or animal Spirits, by some parts of our Bodies, to the Brains or seat of Sensation. . . . [S]ome singly imperceptible Bodies must come from them [the objects of perception] to the Eyes, and thereby convey to the Brain some *Motion,* which produces these *Ideas,* which we have of them in us" (136).

26. Denis Diderot, *D'Alembert's Dream,* trans. Leonard Tancock (London: Penguin, 1966), 156.

27. The quantity of primary and secondary literary on sensibility and nervous fibers in the eighteenth century is vast; primary texts in the French Enlightenment, and, more specifically, within French materialist thought that are directly relevant here would have to include Julien Offray de La Mettre, *L'Homme machine* (1748), Étienne Bonnot, Abbé de Condillac, *Traité des Sensations* (1754), and Diderot, *D'Alembert's Dream.* George Rousseau provides a useful survey of early British medical and scientific texts. *The Languages of Psyche* contains an extensive bibliography of primary and secondary texts, both French and English, concerned with sensibility and the body. Veith discusses several French doctors who contributed to the theorization of nervous disorders, François Boissier de Sauvages (1706–67) and Joseph Raulin (1708–84) (Veith, *Hysteria: The History of a Disease,* 166–70). Additional secondary texts mostly concerned with the medical and literary development of sensibility in England are: John Mullan, *Sentiment and Sociability: The Language of Feeling in the Eighteenth Century* (Oxford: Clarendon Press, 1988); and Ann Jessie Van Sant, *Eighteenth-Century Sensibility and the Novel: The Senses in Social Context* (Cambridge: Cambridge University Press, 1993).

28. Van Sant usefully cites from the physician Robert Whytt's *Observations on the Nature, Causes, and Cure of those Disorders which are commonly called Nervous, Hypochondriac, or Hysteric, To which are prefixed some Remarks on the Sympathy of the Nerves* (1768). Whytt's assessment of feminine sensibility coincides with that of the commission: "Women, in whom the nervous system is generally more moveable than in men, are more subject to nervous complaints, and have them in a higher degree" (105).

29. La Mettrie's discussion of fibers proceeds as follows: "Just as a violin string or harpsichord key vibrates and produces sounds, so also the strings of the brain echo or repeat the spoken words that produce the sound waves that strike them." *Man a Machine,* trans. Richard A. Watson and Maya Rybalka (Indianapolis: Hackett, 1994), 42. La Mettrie, unlike Diderot or the commissioners, limits the musical metaphor to the sense of hearing.

30. Crary, *Techniques of the Observer*, 39.

31. See Rousseau, "Nerves, Spirits, and Fibres," 134–38. Rousseau opposes late-seventeenth-century mechanists, who attempted to prove "that all nerves were in fact hollow tubes through which the quasi-magical fluid secreted by the brain flowed," to animists or monists. Although by the eighteenth century the hollow nerve theory had gained precedence, hollowness remained an unproved anatomical criterion, sustaining the nerves' ambivalent physicality.

32. From Robert Whytt, *Observations on the Nature, Causes, and Cure of those Disorders which have been commonly called Nervous, Hypochondriac, or Hysteric: to which are prefixed some Remarks on the Sympathy of the Nerves* (3d ed.; 1767); cited by Veith, *Hysteria: The History of a Disease*, 161.

33. David Schoenbrun, *Triumph in Paris: The Exploits of Benjamin Franklin* (New York: Harper and Row, 1976), 150. For another detailed account of Franklin's popularity in Paris, already cited, see Lopez, *Mon Cher Papa*.

34. Warner, *Letters of the Republic*, 81.

35. Warner, *Letters of the Republic*, 96. I would note here that many of Franklin's texts do not submit easily to being drained of "presence" (Warner's word): even the abstract grid of virtues offered in his autobiography as a model of disciplined selfhood would bear the marks of Franklin's failings, a trace of his "person" as ineluctable and inimitable as a fingerprint.

PART 2. Engendering Virtuality

The Inevitable Virtuality of Gender
Performing Femininity on an Electronic Bulletin Board for Soap Opera Fans

Robyn R. Warhol

A recent television advertisement for MCI heralds the new utopia of the Internet. "There is no age," the ad asserts, in a child's voice; "there is no race" (spoken by an adult with Asian features); "there are no genders" (spoken by a woman); "there are no infirmities" (signed in American Sign Language): "there are only minds." I could not disagree more. The problem with this ad is that it assumes "race" and "gender," "age" and "infirmities," are essential properties of the body. If there "is no race" in circumstances where the body is not physically present, then *race* would be identical to *skin color,* and its meanings would be legible in physical facts. Critical race theory has called that assumption into question, pointing out that the body is "racialized" when cultures superimpose significance upon skin color, so that race is not so much a property of bodies as of discourse. As, for instance, Elizabeth Abel's or Ruth Frankenberg's work on "whiteness" reveals, race is relational, contingent, and arbitrary: it consists of sets of assumptions, attitudes, and heritages that remain problematically present, even when the body is out of sight or—being visible—provides ambiguous racial clues.[1] If "there are only minds" on the Internet, they are minds that reproduce the cultural effects of race, just as they do of gender, and the utterances they produce in cyberspace will be racialized and gendered, if those terms mean anything at all in a nonessentialist analytical context. I maintain that gender, like race, is a function and a factor of "minds," not— as this ad implies—simply of corporeal bodies. Indeed, there *are* genders on the Internet, and, if they are "only virtual genders," that makes them so much the more visible, so much the more available for analysis. The Internet detaches individual subjects' gender performances from the perceived sex of their bodies and places those performances clearly on view within the text on the computer monitor.

Hasn't gender always been virtual, anyway? Or does the idea of "virtual gender" necessarily imply an opposite term in a binary pairing, something like "real gender" or "actual gender" or "bodily gender"? And what—in the context of contemporary gender studies—would that opposite term mean? I propose to work through a set of binarisms (including sex/uality vs. gender, nature vs. culture, and real vs. virtual) implied in the concept of virtual gender, in order to detach the concept from those implicit oppositions and to show its usefulness for current feminist theory. I will consider the implications of virtual gender for the theory of performativity and discuss a location in cyberspace—a soap opera discussion group—where traditional, middle-class femininity is being continually performed. I will argue that gender—by which I mean the gestures, the styles, the inflections, the looks, the diction, the feelings this culture marks as "feminine" or as "masculine"—is being constructed and reconstituted on the Internet every day. *What* the participants say, the content of their conversation, hardly conforms to cultural norms of femininity: they are critical, analytical, even vehement in their opinions. But *how* they say it, the discursive strategies they employ in framing their utterances, strikingly resembles the patterns that sociolinguists call "feminine talk." In the "As the World Turns" discussion, this is as true for the posters who present themselves as men as for those who sign their messages as women.

Maybe the first opposition *virtual gender* brings to mind would be *virtual sex*, a "generic term" for sexual relations in cyberspace, or for "erotic interaction between individuals whose bodies may never touch, who may never even see one another's faces or exchange real names."[2] If virtual sex is intercourse without bodies, then virtual gender must be disembodied masculinity and femininity. But the virtual sex / virtual gender pairing points to a now familiar conundrum of gender studies. *Sex* has two meanings. Depending on the context, *sex* refers to the genital classification of a body (as in "Sex: M or F"), and it also means erotic encounters (as in "having sex"). Although (or perhaps because) the original distinction in gender studies between *gender* and *sex* did not assign the erotic denotation to *sex* in that pairing, *sexuality* has come to be almost interchangeable with *gender* in its academic usage, as if the libidinal connotations of *sex* spilled over the boundaries of the sex/gender opposition and flooded both terms. Or, if that assertion goes too far, one could say that there is now a slippage between analyses of gender and analyses of sexuality, so that the two topics have collapsed into each other. This is especially evident in studies of virtual sex, in which partners often assume cross-gendered personas, entering into virtual relationships as men when their embodied identities are female, and vice versa. In this sense studies of virtual sex have involved analyses of virtual gender, especially since cyberspace allows individuals an unprecedented freedom to create newly gendered versions of their assumed identities. I am interested, however, in observing that gender is not always or exclusively expressed through sexual relations, whether "virtual" or "real"; I would argue that in contemporary American culture gender is an inescapable factor of every aspect of daily experience, both bodily and discursive. I want to pursue the question I have raised—whether gender is ever "real" as opposed to "virtual"—and to consider in light of that question what may be happening with gender in cyberspace locations that do not focus overtly on erotics or sexuality.

When gender studies began two decades ago, feminists distinguished between sex, which was understood as natural, determined by biology, and gender, which was seen as artificial, constructed by cultures. Through the late 1980s theorists, historians, anthropologists, and cultural critics began showing ways in which sex is constructed, too, so that the body could no longer be taken as an unambiguous product of biology or as a sign of real sexual difference. After Foucault, after deconstruction, after the myriad feminist applications of poststructuralist thought, the opposition between nature and culture just doesn't work anymore, no more than do the oppositions between reality and artifice or between sex and gender, for that matter. If we want to talk about virtual gender in the late 1990s, we need to understand it as something other than the opposite of "real gender."

Recent feminist theory enables us to see gender not so much as an entity in opposition to sex but, rather, as a process, a performance, an effect of cultural patterning. If it causes problems by raising questions about what its opposite might be, the concept of virtual gender also has certain advantages, in that it emphasizes this arbitrary, contingent, and imaginary nature of gender itself. Rather than setting up an eminently deconstructable opposition between virtual gender and real gender, this essay will refer to gender—understood as something that is always and inevitably virtual—in the ongoing textual conversation among members of a "feminine" online cyberspace community. The text in question is the America Online electronic bulletin board devoted to discussing the CBS / Proctor & Gamble soap opera "As the World Turns."

Soap opera discussion groups are an unusually feminine location in cyberspace, devoted as they are to detailed commentary on a genre historically associated with and addressed to women.[3] This essay will analyze the gendered self-presentation of participants in the "As the World Turns" group, about fifty persons whose nominal sex cannot be known but whose gender performance can be read in the style and content of their discourse. In seeing the bulletin board and the soap opera genre itself as examples of what Teresa de Lauretis has called "technologies of gender,"[4] I will follow Cathy Schwichtenberg's suggestion "to forge ahead by posing gender as a process of negotiation with culture rather than as the assumption of necessarily feminine qualities, attributes, or identifications."[5] Indeed, the gender performances on this bulletin board suggest that middle-class, white norms of femininity are alive and well in cyberspace, endlessly reiterating and reinforcing the process of feminization that soap opera viewers undergo by following their favorite serial stories over the long term.[6]

As queer theory has made eminently clear, one of the problems with feminist theory's traditional sex/gender distinction is that it tends to reproduce heterocentric culture's inclination to simply fold sexuality into that binary pairing. Under that system someone whose sex is female and gender is feminine is automatically assumed to be erotically attracted to masculine males; the idea that a lesbian might also be feminine or that a feminine man might appeal to a feminine woman disrupts the neat symmetry of the sex/gender system. As Judith Butler has so influentially argued, feminisms must resist the sway of compulsory heterosexuality (as Butler adapts Adrienne Rich's idea) in its construction of a continuum from sex to gender to sexuality and its implication that the one is obviously readable in the other two: to free women from gender oppression, feminist theory needs to be able to resist the assumption that the female body must be feminine and must be one half of a heterosexual dyad.[7] If we accept Butler's reasoning (not to mention the whole history of gender studies—from Simone de Beauvoir's idea that "one is not born, but rather becomes a woman," through Judith Fetterley's model of how female readers become "immasculated" in the process of reading male-centered canonical texts, to de Lauretis's concept of "technologies of gender") we have to conclude that gender is always virtual—and that this doesn't mean it isn't crucially important in the lived experience of every (potentially multiply) gendered subject.[8] Still, the advantage of analyzing gender as a construct has always been the opportunity it poses for detaching gender—that is, any given culture's idea of what is appropriate for men or for women—from the seemingly deterministic realm of the body. As I have mentioned, I want to go still further, to detach gender from sexuality, too. I am interested in performances of discursive femininity that are not specifically sexual, libidinal, or erotic in their content.

Recent work in feminist theory and gender history has effectively deconstructed the idea that the other side of the sex/gender opposition, the sex/body/nature side, is more real than gender, or, in other words, is not itself a construction. From Donna Haraway's and Emily Martin's critiques of scientific narratives of sex and gender; to Thomas Laqueur's histories of how sex has been "made"; to Marge Garber's work on cross-dressing and Julia Epstein and Kristina Straub's collection of essays on gender ambiguity;[9] to Butler's challenges to the idea that the body is "sexed" in any stable way—gender theory has dissolved the notion that sex is somehow real, that it transcends historical or cultural influence. Following this scholarly tradition, both sex and gender are virtual in the sense that neither can be understood as real or actual: "culture" has invaded both sides of the sex/nature–gender/culture syllogism.

To be sure, the original binary distinction between sex and gender was a triumph over the patriarchal view of traditional gender roles as natural to the two sexes. In similar ways the new intrusion of culture into the sex side of the binary triumphs over the natural notion of heterosexual difference. I think that's playing itself out in the gender performances of "As the World Turns" viewers on America Online, particularly for men who are full participants in the feminine discourse there: in cyberspace it's easier than in other forms of social intercourse to put the body aside, to "perform" femininity regardless of one's genital or libidinal sex/uality.

That means, of course, that a man may present himself online as a woman, and a woman may pose as a man. This is an observation that is strikingly absent in much of the work that has been done so far on gender and the Internet. The otherwise wonderful essays in *Wired Women* (a recent collection edited by Lynn Cherny and Elisabeth Reba Weise) tend to generalize about what "male posters" and "female posters" do when they write Internet messages.[10] While one might be able to test these propositions against specific cases when the electronic communications are being exchanged among people the researcher knows in other contexts (as in Ellen Ullman's amusing and insightful piece about falling in love with a coworker over e-mail [3–23] or Michele Evard's optimistic essay detailing the online encounters of her male and female elementary school students [188–206]), studies of Internet fan groups can only rely on posters' self-representations (and on self-perpetuating stereotypes of the masculine behavior of men and the feminine behavior of women) to draw conclusions about the sex of persons who write Internet messages.[11] Indeed, Martine Rothblatt's "manifesto on the freedom of gender," *The Apartheid of Sex,* hails cyberspace as the realm where the tyranny of sex and gender stereotypes must eventually begin to break down: "Technology will be used to try on genders and to pave the way for people being liberated from a single birth-determined sex," she declares; "cyberspace prepares us for the postapartheid twenty-first-century unisexual world."[12] At least one spectacular case has already demonstrated how effectively a person can transcend bodily sex to perform the "other" gender: Allucquère Rosanne Stone recounts what happened when a male psychiatrist created a female persona for an Internet discussion group and then—overwhelmed by his creation's success at gaining virtual friends and lovers and by mounting suspicions among "her" readers that the contradictions in her life story suggested "she" was, in some sense, lying—tried to kill her off; despite their expressed doubts, many of the receivers of her messages had been utterly convinced by the textual performance of feminine personality that constituted "Julie Graham" and expressed deep grief and anxiety when they believed she had a fatal illness.[13] When her creator came clean and tried to claim Julie's online friends as his own, hardly anyone was interested anymore (80).

That online gender is always or only what I have just called a textual performance raises a further terminological issue for gender studies. In what follows I will be emphasizing Butler's idea of gender (not to mention sexuality) as performative and using that term (as Butler herself does) in its specifically linguistic sense. As Eve Sedgwick pointed out in 1993, Butler's concept of performativity has had the effect of "placing theater and theatrical performance at front and center of questions of subjectivity and sexuality";[14] in the late 1990s studies focusing on the body, sexuality, and gender still tend mainly to construe *performance* and *performativity* in the theatrical sense.[15] As Sedgwick resurrected the distinction between the linguistic and theatrical usages of the word to theorize a "queer performativity" at work in Henry James, I want to revisit that distinction as a way to understand how online textual performance works to create and to reinforce mainstream, heterocentric notions of gender.

What precisely does Butler mean when she writes, "Gender is not a performance that a prior subject elects to do, but gender is *performative* in the sense that it constitutes as an effect the very subject it appears to express"?[16] In speech-act theory J. L. Austin originally distinguished between "statements, or *constative* utterances, which describe a state of affairs and are true or false, and another class of utterances which are not true or false and which actually perform the action to which they refer (for example, 'I promise to pay you tomorrow' accomplishes the act of promising). These he calls *performatives*."[17] A performative speech act is an utterance that does not affirm but constitutes its referent, such as "I bet," "I dare you," or "I now pronounce you man and wife." This is the sense of the performative to which J. F. Lyotard refers in *The Postmodern Condition,* and it is this sense—rather than the theatrical sense of *performance*—that principally informs Butler's influential essay "Imitation and Gender Insubordination."[18] In theatrical usage (or in common conversation among anyone other than speech-act theorists) a performance is an act that is put on, a fictive identity assumed by a real person for the benefit of an audience. That sense of the word assumes an opposition between *reality* and *performance,* an opposition that mirrors the pairings of *sex* and *gender, nature* and *culture,* or, for that matter, *real gender* and *virtual gender.* But the linguistic usage deconstructs that opposition, for the performative utterance constitutes its own reality: it is "neither true nor false"; it is not, like the theatrical performance, an artifice.[19] When Butler speaks of gender as performative, she is not saying that the individual subject is "putting on an act" of gender, for that would imply that the individual subject has an actual gender to place in opposition to that act. As Butler puts it, "There is no 'proper' gender, a gender proper to one sex rather than another" (312); furthermore, "there is no 'I' that precedes the gender that it is said to perform" (311). If gender is performative, that means online utterances conforming to "masculine" or "feminine" norms of discourse don't express or mime or even imitate gender; they constitute it.

In this sense gender can be understood "as contingent and multiple—as a process rather than an *a priori* category," as Schwichtenberg puts it in "Reconceptualizing Gender: New Sites for Feminist Audience Research" (169).[20] Schwichtenberg argues for abandoning the sexual difference model of gender (which, because of its reliance on Lacanian constructs of identity, divides subjects into just two genders, masculine and feminine, in correspondence with two sexes). She's interested in women who identify as female but are often mistaken as male and in lesbians who reject traditional femininity in their own self-presentation. Schwichtenberg suggests that more work should be done in feminist audience research (which makes local, demonstrable claims about gender, not the broad universalizing claims of Lacanian psychoanalysis and Screen theory) to represent the differences among women. She says we need to consider the women who don't like soap opera or romance, who prefer sports, or who identify with male heroes:

> To examine such disparities between gender and genre would enable us to respond to the need to more stringently problematize and pluralize the notion of gender. Indeed, the *a priori* of the "feminine" would by necessity

become less pristine and more nuanced in the process of exploring those dif-ferences between and among women, particularly women's variant forms of identification. (171)

While I acknowledge Schwichtenberg's point, I would argue that her approach can be as useful for studying the gender performance of women who *do* "like soap opera or romance" as of their less traditionally "femi-nine" counterparts. Thinking of femininity as a process rather than as an a priori category can give us a more vital and vivid picture of what feminine existence in the late 1990s is like, rather than making the tautological assumption that femininity is what feminine heterosexual women experi-ence, whatever that might be.

Schwichtenberg's specific prescription for feminist audience analysis is mainly to include lesbians (the "persistent blind spot of feminist cultural studies" [172]), but I want to adapt an offhand suggestion she makes: "an audience researcher could utilize discourse analysis as a means to code gen-der identifications as they emerge from respondents' commentary, rather than approach the audience group as gendered *a priori*" (178). Although Schwichtenberg doesn't mention electronic bulletin boards (EBBs) as a good potential source for such analysis, they would seem to lend themselves well to her approach, because the researcher can observe what gender a partici-pant is performing but can't know the biological sex behind the performa-tive utterances of gender. Participants' online names carry connotations of gender and/or of sex (some of the most strongly marked in the group I am studying are "HappyKitty," "CyndiH," and my current favorite, "Jon-GWM29," whose name changed from last year's "Jon GWM28" in true personals-ad style). But those connotations are obviously virtual constructs and are not testable against the observer's perception of "real" bodies, because the conventions of online communication mean that only the observer's own body is literally present at the discussion. As C. Lee Har-rington and Denise Bielby have mentioned, the EBB obviates many of the complications of ethnographic research in general, as it allows the observer to participate, as it were, unobserved. They remark of their own research on the creation of virtual community through EBBs: "Our approach contrasts with earlier work on audiences that relies upon viewers' reports to inter-viewers or upon ethnographers' observations of the viewing process. As a result, our approach minimizes the problems inherent in interviewer inter-vention, including concern over the politics of the analyst's interpreta-tion."[21] While I am less confident that my reading of the gender perfor-mances of the "As the World Turns" EBB discussion group would somehow transcend politics—indeed, I am sure that my own definitions of such politically charged terms as *femininity* will have to pervade my every assertion—I agree that the EBB presents a seemingly unique opportunity to study gender without considering the evidence of physical bodies or letting my own markedly female and feminine presence intrude into the discussion I am analyzing. For three years I have "lurked" on the "As the World Turns" bulletin board; while participants express fantasies about the assumed presence of the show's stars or of the writers and producers ("The Powers That Be," or "TPTB") among their readership, no one seems to suspect a feminist academic is out there, listening in, looking for signs of gender.

If gender is indeed performative in the linguistic sense, then the utterances on the electronic bulletin board are not, properly speaking, signs of gender. They *are* gender, or, rather, they constitute the process that creates and reinforces the participants' gender identity. Who are the participants? According to the 1994 version of the members' packet produced by the "As the World Turns" group on America Online, the thirty-six regular participants range in age from fifteen to the mid-forties, with the majority being in their thirties. The group includes six members who represent themselves as men; one of them signs his postings together with his wife, but the others are independent members of the group. The group consists mainly of dedicated fans of "As the World Turns," which has been on the air continuously since 1956: only three members have followed the soap for five years or less; four have watched from five to ten years; six have watched from ten to twenty years; six from twenty to thirty; and nine of the members have watched continually for thirty to forty years. Not everyone who posts messages to the list has a profile in the packet, but most of the members who are profiled make regular postings. Their subscriptions to America Online suggest that each of them has the educational and economic privilege to get access to computers with modems, to pay a monthly fee for the service, and to find the leisure time to use it. If their class status is legible in their presence on the Internet, their racial identities are usually not: very seldom, over the three years I have followed the list, has a poster referred directly to her own race, usually in connection with racial themes on the soap opera. For example, "Matt n Meg" writes:

> This subtle racism isn't so subtle. Even a white girl from Virginia like me can see it. We get our first look at Devere and he's a black guy who abused Shannon. Meanwhile Duncan has left his perfect BLACK wife for a ditzy WHITE woman and can't decide who he loves. Give me a break. This is so racist its pathetic.

Sometimes a poster will identify herself as "an African-American woman" in a message that is not otherwise overtly marked with signs of racial difference from the implicit white norm of the group. The group's social politics could be described as liberal-to-Left: they routinely criticize the script not only for its racism but for antifeminism (e.g., portraying professional women as ditzy and emotionally dependent) and for homophobic avoidance of same-sex love stories.

"Matt n Meg"'s tone of critical outrage is, oddly enough, very typical of the discussion on this list. To say that the group is feminine is not at all to say that their attitude toward the soap itself or toward its characters is passive, accepting, or nurturing. While all the participants are avid fans of the series, the discussion typically focuses on shortcomings and failures of characterization, plot, acting, and production techniques as well as of the moral and ideological valences of the storyline. Indeed, the discussion covers all the topics that Susan Clerc attributes to "fandom," "whether online or off." The fans

> discuss characterization; express their affection for, or dislike of, particular characters; alert each other to appearances by the actors on talk shows or in other roles; compile lists of useless information [e.g., on the ATWT list, "THINGS TO DO WHILE WAITING TO CONNECT TO AOL: 1. Your 1996 taxes; 2. Complete your BA degree; 3. Watch your hair grow; 4. Finally clean your keyboard; 5. Count the tiles on the ceiling 200 times; 6. Think about commercials you saw during the Super Bowl; 7. Scribble I HAVE NO LIFE on a notepad . . ."]; speculate about what would have happened if some feature of a story had been different . . . ; compare series, seriously and not so seriously . . . ; make up drinking games . . . ; and hash over any number of other issues arising from the aired episodes.[22]

The "As the World Turns" group also avidly discusses the long- and short-term plot strategies of the soap; the production values of individual episodes (e.g., camera angles, settings, background music, costumes and hairstyles); the comings and goings of head writers for the series; the latest gossip about actors' contract renewals; and what can only be called the poetics of soap opera (e.g., identifying textual cues that predict certain story outcomes, analyzing the use of flashbacks and repetition, debating the desirability of plots' coming to closure, and comparing and contrasting the current storyline with the back-story the group so laboriously reconstructs from time to time). Sometimes they also write alternative versions of the plot line, producing everything from humorous parodies of current scenes to elaborate scripts that fit the genre of "fan fiction" and would take hours to perform. Participants identifying themselves as men and as women take part in all these activities, as Clerc asserts they do in fan groups that are devoted to more masculine or more gender-neutral television series than soaps. As Nancy K. Baym found in her study of the virtual community generated in a set of Usenet soap opera discussion groups, however, the community is markedly feminine in its discourse (if not in the subjects or content of the discussion), especially its participants' emphasis on emotions and relationships and their avoidance of the practice of "flaming," or barraging rude or hapless posters with violently abusive messages.[23]

I wish I could say that detaching gender from sex and from sexuality, looking at performances of feminine "talk" that are separated from female bodies, reveals a new and unexpected form of femininity. That's not what I find. The discursive qualities of the conversation on the "As the World Turns" EBB conforms, for the most part, to what sociolinguists have been saying about "women's talk" for at least twenty years. The participants, like the women in the sociolinguistic studies summarized by Lynn Smith-Lovin and Dawn T. Robinson, are likely to express agreement or ask for others' opinions, to acknowledge points made by other speakers, and to encourage communication and disclosure; they are "supportive of others," generally unassertive, and "likely to use questions (especially tag questions), hedges, qualifiers, disclaimers, and other linguistic forms conveying uncertainty."[24] The posters say, "I totally agree," so often that they abbreviate it as "ITA." They are always ready to offer a compliment to one another but deprecate themselves when receiving one;[25] they express strong sentiments but backpedal with humor ("just kidding!") and "emoticons," or punctuation indicating friendly intentions [e.g., ;)—a sideways smiley-face with a wink; G for "grin," LOL for "laughing out loud," and ROTFL for "Rolling on the Floor Laughing"];[26] they refer to domestic and familial concerns in their own lives much more often than to overtly political or public matters;[27] they lecture "newbies" on conversational etiquette, especially when someone naively posts messages with the "all caps" button on (as "Donnafair" put it: "We don't yell on this board and we *try* not to flame. If you can't live like that, then please [sic] with the SOD [Soap Opera Digest] board. Thanks.");[28] they defer—sometimes ironically—to others' views on controversial matters (often introducing a remark with "IMHO," or "in my humble opinion," or even "JMHO," "just my humble opinion");[29] they use the EBB in the way that women are supposed to use conversation in general, as a location for community and an opportunity to foster (virtual) intimacies.[30]

Of course, anyone logging onto the America Online discussion of "As the World Turns" could find some examples of comments that conform to masculine styles of discourse: postings can be aggressive without backpedaling, unresponsive to other posters' messages, or downright rude. As a literary critic—not, alas, a sociolinguist—I cannot present a convincing statistical analysis of the incidence of feminine "moves" in the online conversation. Instead, I offer an almost random selection of characteristic comments from three consecutive and representative days of the discussion, to give a sense of the feminine gestures, inflections, and styles performed daily on this bulletin board:

"JnGriz" hedges on a strong feeling about a character, citing "just my humble opinion": "I really wish the writers would mature her and make her less selfish and self-absorbed. I think this would be believable (not to mentioned welcomed) since she is now a mother and motherhood usually makes people less selfish. JMHO, JnGriz"

"BSimons727" refers to family experience to disagree with another poster's point then qualifies her position by calling it "just" her experience: "Both of my parents had/have a living will and the DNR clause is in there. In their living will they state that no extraordinary measures should be taken to keep them alive (including a DNR clause), which is what I think Kim was getting at (though the use of the term "vegetable" may have been misleading). My mother had hers reviewed and updated just before having some major surgery as did my father—neither of which were (at least initially) terminal conditions. Just my experience with living wills."

"Snera" adds a smiley emoticon to soften what might look like sarcasm in reference to a participant's report of having spotted soap stars in New York City: "Wow Teri I am jealous!! You could write a weekly column on your brushes with soap stars! Happy Searching!! :-)"

"Tchrsings" uses the same emoticon to modify a strongly felt but unpopular opinion: "If someone had killed my husband, I would be distracted and obsessed, too. I think Lily is burnt out and on edge, plus the fact that there is no love lost between her and Emily. Give Lily a break—she will be back to normal soon, as soon as she is back in the arms of the man she belongs with!!! :-)."

"Rickstern2," embroiled in a rare eruption of "rudeness" on the list, acknowledges supportive messages with not one emoticon but two: "Thank you for the over two dozen responses I have received over one member's immature behavior. It was very nice of you :) Special thanks to Donnafair, Leapyear56 and Tchrsings :) ."

"UCSBsweat," who always signs postings as "Steve," adds another ameliorative voice to the many who hastened to remind angry posters of the list's prevailing etiquette: "I enjoy both JonGWM's and Rickstern's posts, and I think the tension between these two 'camps' is really the result of miscommunication. I think that sometimes we read and post messages too hastily and don't really digest the full meaning of someone's statements. I think that it might be most appropriate for those parties involved in this 'dispute' to agree (at least) to limit 'flames' to private email, rather than the boards."

"PatriciaGM" quite gratuitously adds a qualifier to an uncharacteristically violent sentiment about the recently deposed head writers: "Tchrsings: I love your phrase for the Valente/Black/Stern regime: The Reign of Terror—and now they have all been guillotined, thank goodness! (Figuratively speaking of course)."

"KLE007" appends a wink to an ironic comment on a particularly vehement posting from "Donnafair": "Donna, stop being so polite!!! Tell us what you really think ;) Donna fair, Donna Fair, let down your hair!!!!"

"Maryjorens" endorses another viewer's opinion and chooses a particularly feminine adjective (*fabulous*) to describe one actor's work: "I feel the same way! ATWT has been resurrected! Kelly is a fabulous actress—it must have been very difficult to do that scene for both of them."

"Jon GWM 29" chooses markedly feminine diction (*yummy, honey, quite, tidbits*) and adds a winking emoticon for good measure: "Tom was yummy as usual. Hal was quite loud as usual. LOL when Margo said she usually doesn't break the rules. Honey, that's her way of LIFE!! Gotta run! I'll be back on tonight to finish up all my tidbits! ;)"

My point in providing this sampling is to observe that the "maleness" or "femaleness" of most of these participants in the discussion is obscure. Surely "JonGWM29" is a twenty-nine-year-old gay white man, probably "Patricia GM" and "Maryjorens" are women; "UCSBsweat" (aka Steve) must be a man. But what if they are not? And what sex does "Tchsrings" or "JnGriz" denote? Even if the assiduous sociolinguist could find out, the participant in the discussion cannot. In this sense it simply does not matter whether these are men or women taking part in the discussion; if we cannot know their sex, we can observe their performances of feminine gender. Community building and intimacy may be feminine goals, but in cyberspace they are not exclusively available to women. The soap opera bulletin board is a place where men can join the virtual community as well as experiment with cross-gendered performance without perhaps intending to and without specific reference or recourse to their own or anyone else's sexuality.

This virtual community may not be self-conscious about the "feminine" connotations of the values that guide its discourse, but many of the members are clear in their expressions of those values. In the aftermath of the spat between two posters representing themselves as men, "Rickstern2" and "JonGWM29," "Snera" participated (as had "UCSBsweat") in the collaborative process of making peace. She remarked on the medium in which the dispute had arisen: "Sometimes the written word becomes misconstrued because we don't have the benefit of facial expression, intonation etc. to convey our true meanings. Is it possible that this was blown out of proportion? If so, lets all take a deep breath, make apologies where necessary and lets get back to the fun we always have on this board! Lois :-)" The emoticon ending "Snera's" (aka Lois)'s comment adds a valence of irony to her point. The feminine "intonations" of the discourse come through clearly, especially in response to such unusual incidents of discord. As "RDoe831" puts it in a pointedly metadiscursive observation, the participants in this group try to treat one another like (feminine) members of their own families: "I love this board and the warm feelings and many, many chuckles it gives me. I read it last after the other boards, because I want to sign off feeling at PEACE with myself. This is the only board that seems to hold itself together, actually talking to each other like we're face to face. What I said above to Irene is the way I would say it to my mother—whom I've disagreed with many times about ATWT."

The "As the World Turns" discussion group is a virtual extension, after all, of the embodied influences that first inspired each viewer's devotion to the soap. Most of the viewers who have followed the story for decades connect "As the World Turns" with specific members of their own families, mentioning it was her "Grandma's soap" (CyndiH); or that she "began watching ATWT with her mom during summer vacations" (HappyKitty); or that "his parents watched the show, and he has been a viewer as long as he can remember" (Joey5307); or that "she grew up watching ATWT with her grandmother"; or that "she began watching ATWT in the 60s, with her mother and grandmother" (NPeveler); or that "her college sorority sisters got her hooked" (OhUJest); or that "it was her grandparents' show" (Smoooch2). Scholars such as Mary Ellen Brown celebrate soap opera as an entry into a community of viewers, where flesh-and-blood persons express their feelings, critical and celebratory, about the text.[31] The existence of the VCR and the electronic bulletin board make possible an extension of the family group, the college dorm crowd, or the community of coworkers who might meet "as women" to discuss soap opera. One viewer, "Mariann924," remarks in her member's packet profile: "I'm the only person I know, off-line, who is glued to the soaps, knows all the actors' real names, and buys all the soap opera magazines—that is why I love this BB [bulletin board]. I've had nobody to talk to for many years!" The virtual community includes men, too, in an expanded version of the gendered audience, engaged in the unremitting daily process of feminization. Just another technology of gender, cyberspace has a long way to go before femininity disappears. For what it's worth, I believe the real world—not to mention the virtual one—would be greatly impoverished if that were to happen.

NOTES

1. Elizabeth Abel, "Black Writing, White Reading: Race and the Politics of Feminist Interpretation," *Critical Inquiry* 19.3 (1993): 470–98.

2. Shannon McRae, "Coming Apart at the Seams: Sex, Text and the Virtual Body," in *Wired Women: Gender and New Realities in Cyberspace*, ed. Lynn Cherney and Elizabeth Reba Weise (Seattle: Seal Press, 1996), 242–64.

3. Michele Evard reports that "less than ten percent of the public messages [on Usenet newsgroups] are written by women," despite the fact that "an estimated 36 percent of Internet-accessing accounts belong to women," in "'So Please Stop, Thank You': Girls Online," in Cherny and Weise, *Wired Women*, 188. Susan Clerc, "Estrogen Brigades and 'Big Tits' Threads: Media Fandom Online and Off," in Cherny and Weise *Wired Women*, 73–97, provides a discussion of women's participation in Internet "fandom" discussions devoted to primetime and syndicated TV shows. According to Clerc, women post fewer messages to those discussions than men do, and male participants remark on women's talkativeness, even when male viewers are in fact dominating the conversation (85). Clerc (whose examples come from Usenet groups and not from commercial services such as America Online) does not discuss soap opera fans.

4. Teresa de Lauretis, *Technologies of Gender: Essays on Theory, Film, and Fiction* (Bloomington: Indiana University Press, 1987).

5. Cathy Schwichtenberg, "Reconceptualizing Gender: New Sites for Feminist Audience Research," in *Viewing, Reading, Listening: Audiences and Cultural Reception*, ed. John Cruz and Justin Lewis (Boulder: Westview Press, 1994), 171.

6. See my essay "Feminine Intensities: Soap Opera Viewing as a Technology of Gender," *Genders* 28 (1998): <http://www.genders.org>, for an analysis of the gendering effects of long-term soap opera viewing.

7. Judith Butler, "Imitation and Gender Insubordination," in *Inside/Out: Lesbian Theories, Gay Theories*, ed. Diana Fuss (New York: Routledge, 1991) and *Bodies That Matter: On the Discursive Limits of "Sex"* (New York: Routledge, 1993); hereafter all references to the latter work will appear parenthetically in the text. Also Adrienne Rich, "Compulsory Heterosexuality and Lesbian Existence," in *Blood, Bread, and Poetry, Selected Prose, 1978–1985* (New York: Virago Press, 1986).

8. Simone de Beauvoir, *The Second Sex*, trans. H. M. Parshley (1952; rpt., New York: Vintage Books, 1989); and Judith Fetterley, *The Resisting Reader: A Feminist Approach to American Fiction* (Bloomington: Indiana University Press, 1978).

9. For example, see Donna J. Haraway, *Simians, Cyborgs, and Women: The Reinvention of Nature* (New York: Routledge, 1991); Emily Martin, *The Woman in the Body: A Cultural Analysis of Reproduction* (Boston: Beacon Press, 1990); Thomas Laqueur, *Making Sex: Body and Gender from the Greeks to Freud* (Cambridge: Harvard University Press, 1990); Marjorie Garber, *Vested Interests: Cross-Dressing and Cultural Anxiety* (New York: Routledge, 1992); and Julia Epstein and Kristina Straub, eds., *Body Guards: The Cultural Politics of Gender Ambiguity* (New York: Routledge, 1991).

10. Lynn Cherny and Elizabeth Reba Weise, eds., *Wired Women Gender and New Realities in Cyberspace* (Seattle: Seal Press, 1996).

11. Ellen Ullman, "Come In, CQ: The Body on the Wire," in Cherny and Weise, *Wired Women*, 3–23; and Evard, "'So Please Stop, Thank You,'" 188–206.

12. Martine Rothblatt, *The Apartheid of Sex: A Manifesto on the Freedom of Gender* (New York: Crown Books, 1995), 153.

13. Allucquère Rosanne Stone, *The War of Desire and Technology at the Close of the Mechanical Age* (Cambridge: MIT Press, 1995), 65–82.

14. Eve Sedgwick, "Queer Performativity: Henry James's *The Art of the Novel*," *GLQ: Journal of Lesbian and Gay Studies* 1.1 (1993): 1–16. Passage cited, 1.

15. See, for example, the essays collected in Sue-Ellen Case, Philip Brett, and Susan Leigh Foster, eds., *Cruising the Performative: Interventions into the Representation of Ethnicity, Nationality, and Sexuality* (Bloomington: Indiana University Press, 1995), as well as the other essays in the present collection that refer to "performativity."

16. Butler, "Imitation and Gender Insubordination," 314.

17. Jonathan Culler, *On Deconstruction: Theory and Criticism after Structuralism* (Ithaca: Cornell University Press, 1982), 112; see the original formulation of "The Performative" in J. L. Austin, *How to Do Things with Words* (Cambridge: Harvard University Press, 1962), 5–6, 26–38.

18. Jean François Lyotard, *The Postmodern Condition: A Report on Knowledge* (Minneapolis: University of Minnesota Press, 1984).

19. Sedgwick shows that deconstructionists and even Austin himself eventually collapsed the distinction between the performative and the constative, recognizing "performativity" as "a property common to all utterance" ("Queer Performativity," 2). Butler's work nevertheless maintains the distinction, if only allusively. To be sure, the most interesting work on performativity also deconstructs the commonly held notion that a theatrical performance is an artifice, as opposed to something "real"—for example, Joseph Litvak, *Caught in the Act: Theatricality in the Nineteenth-Century English Novel* (Berkeley: University of California Press, 1992); and Case, *Cruising the Performative*.

20. Schwichtenberg, "Reconceptualizing Gender: New Sites for Feminist Audience Research." Hereafter all references will appear parenthetically in the text.

21. Denise Bielby and C. Lee Harrington. "Reach Out and Touch Someone: Viewers, Agency, and Audiences in the Televisual Experience," in *Viewing, Reading, Listening: Audiences and Cultural Reception,* ed. Jon Cruz and Justin Lewis (Boulder: Westview Press, 1994), 81–100. Passage cited, 82.

22. Clerc, "Estrogen Brigades," 76.

23. Nancy K. Baym, "Interpreting Soap Operas and Creating Community: Inside a Computer-Mediated Fan Culture," *Journal of Folklore Research* 30.2–3 (1993): 143–76.

24. Lynn Smith-Lovin and Dawn T. Robinson, "Gender and Conversational Dynamics," *Gender, Interaction, and Inequality* (New York: Springer Verlag, 1992), 122–56.

25. N. Woolfson, "An Empirically Based Analysis of Complimenting in American English," in *Sociolinguistics and Language Acquisition,* ed. N. Woolfson and E. Judd (Rowley, Mass.: Newbury House, 1983), 82–95, calls this "downgrading"; Pamela S. Kipers, "Gender and Topic," *Language and Society* 16.4 (1987): 543–57, reports she found it invariably to happen in exchanges of compliments between women but not men.

26. See Mary Crawford, "Just Kidding: Gender and Conversational Humor," in *New Perspectives on Women and Comedy,* ed. Regina Barreca (Philadelphia: Gordon and Breach, 1992) for an account of gendered joking.

27. Kipers's study challenges the truism that women discuss "more trivial" topics than men; her work confirms that women discuss home and family more often than men, but it also shows that women rate the topics of their discussions as being more important than men rate their own less domestic topics as being.

28. Laurel A. Sutton, "Cocktails and Thumbtacks in the Old West: What Would Emily Post Say?" in Cherney and Weise, *Wired Women,* 169–87, distills a code of "netiquette" from the online behavior of her female subjects.

29. Smith-Lovin and Robinson, "Gender and Conversational Dynamics," 124.

30. Clerc, "Estrogen Brigades"; and Julia Wood, *Gendered Lives: Communication, Gender, and Culture* (Belmont, Calif.: Wadsworth Publications, 1994), both cite Deborah Tannen, *You Just Don't Understand: Women and Men in Conversation* (New York: William Morrow, 1990), to make this generalization. Baym, "Interpreting Soap Operas," bases a similar conclusion on her own data.

31. Mary Ellen Brown, "Motley Moments: Soap Operas, Carnival, Gossip, and the Power of the Utterance," in *Television and Women's Culture: The Politics of the Popular,* ed. Mary Ellen Brown (London: Sage, 1990), 183–98.

Remembering and Forgetting
Feminist Autobiography in Performance

Charlotte Canning

I remember / que soy de allá / que soy de aqui / un pie en
New York . . . / un pie en la Habana.
  —Carmelita Tropicana, *Milk of Amnesia /*
  Leche de Amnesia

We share the story that is known. Whether people know it or
not, it is as I call it, part of their collective memory. Personal
stories are the same. My listeners also know my personal
story because my personal story is all of our story.
  —Robbie McCauley, intro., *Sally's Rape*

Reflecting on her work, Robbie McCauley wrote, "I wanted to do a kind of
theater I felt I remembered from before I was born."[1] As if echoing
McCauley, Carmelita Tropicana / Alina Troyano stated that her piece was
about: "Losing memory and recuperating memory. Finding out what the
recuperation of memory has to do with things we construct, like identity."[2]
These memories are galvanizing and each performer recalls them in state of
great urgency and is compelled to express these memories in performance.
Robbie McCauley and Carmelita Tropicana are both solo performers based
in New York City who have toured their work nationally. Occasionally
working with others as well, both women write and perform their own
material. All their pieces engage with the difficult issues of gender, race, and
sexuality as well as family, political struggle, and community. The performances created out of this engagement with memory are McCauley's *Sally's
Rape* (1991) and Tropicana's *Milk of Amnesia / Leche de Amnesia* (1994).
The two pieces interrogate the use of memory and in doing so offer new
feminist ways to understand the gendered experience of identity, history,
and autobiography.

The assumption in both pieces is that memories of the past shape present actions and discourses. The two discourses, memory and history, which are elided in their lived experiences, construct who McCauley and Tropicana/Troyano understand themselves to be. Their memories provide "a potential for creative collaboration between present consciousness and the experience or expression of the past."[3] Both performers thus struggle over a past with which they can live productively and which will serve as part of an empowering basis for social and political action. They find the construction of history and identity offered through the narratives of the dominant discourse debilitating because those narratives do not support or elucidate their memories and specific lived experiences of gender, sexuality, and race. Official history comes from the memories of those who are both in power (who license the version of history) and empowered by it (who ensure its existence by testifying to its accuracy and positioning those experiences that challenge it as inaccurate, unimportant, or fabricated). This is particularly potent for these two women as their resistant memories and identities insist on the specificity of experience—as women, as African American, as Cuban American, as rape survivor, as lesbian, as artists, and as politically aware subjects. These memories continue to construct present and future action and events precisely because these performers understand and represent them in their specificity.

That these two performers choose autobiography as the vehicle to articulate their relationships with history and memory is not surprising as autobiography is a narrativization of memory. Autobiography can operate both as a way to mark and own memories and as a way to communicate the memories as experienced in context. It is an attempt, as Sidonie Smith argues, to intersect those communicated memories with a narrative form that offers resistant understandings of women's lives:

> An effort of recovery and creation, an exploration into recapturing and restating a past, autobiography simultaneously involves a realization that the adventure is informed continually by shifting considerations of the present moment. For example, the autobiographer has to rely on a trace of something from the past, a memory; yet memory is ultimately a story about, and thus a discourse on, original experience, so that recovering the past is not a hypostatizing of fixed grounds and absolute origins but, rather, an interpretation of earlier experience that can never be divorced from the filterings of subsequent experience or articulated outside the structures of language and storytelling.[4]

This long quotation indicates the complex interdependence of past and present, memory and experience, and, by implication, history and revision.

Smith argues for a feminist conception of autobiography that necessarily positions it as both "recovery" (attempting to preserve and record past action, events, or people) and "creation" (the invention and representation of such narrativizations of past, present, experience, and history that reject traditional forms based in "androcentric fictions," that is, forms created for and by men [174]). This doubled task foregrounds that memory is not a stable record of previous moments dictated by male norms but already a "story about" those moments derived from a challenge to "gender ideologies and the boundaries they place around women's proper life script" (44). Employing memory in the construction of history does not offer an authoritative foundation for that construction but a way to use those memories within the structures of representation.

That the autobiographical process is extremely labile, that it "approximate[s] but never recapture[s] the past," is what makes it such a productive forum for women like McCauley and Tropicana, who represent their memories as significant challenges to the ways in which those memories have been constructed (46). Through their feminist structuring of memory they are able to intervene in and seize ownership of the ways in which such structures are conventionally constructed in and utilized by oppressive discourses. McCauley and Tropicana join other women who have used the narrativization of memory "as a means of 'talking back.' "[5] By "talking back," women, who experience themselves as separate from the roles and identities assigned them by patriarchal dominant discourses, revise autobiography, allowing them to

> find narrative and rhetorical strategies through which to negotiate the laws of genre and the calls to provided subjectivities. Not merely passive subjects of official autobiographical discourse, they become agents of resisting memory and creative misprision. (Smith, *Subjectivity*, 22)

Smith's interest is primarily in the feminist ways in which women engage with the histories and practices of subjectivity through their written autobiographies. But her observations work well for an investigation into the feminist ways women actively resist and reinvent history through the live performance of their autobiographical memories. bell hooks's deployment of the term is also productive. *Talking Back* is also the title of a bell hooks's anthology. In that volume *talking back* comes from hooks's experience as a child in the black communities of the South. In this context *talking back* meant "speaking as an equal to an authority figure. It meant daring to disagree and sometimes it just meant having an opinion."[6] Talking back is not simply a metaphor either for challenging authority or for resistant agency when considered in the context of live performance but a race- and gender-marked feminist strategy that aggressively resituates women's memories as authoritative sites for constructing a resistant and revisionary identity and history.

Gender, specifically the experience of being a woman, is crucial to the feminist conceptions of history, memory, and autobiography elucidated here. While the assumptions made about women's experience do not make essentialist claims to universality and homogeneity, they do claim that these experiences define what it is to be a woman in their cultures. It is from these experiences that the possibilities of talking back emerge. What McCauley and Tropicana explore is a world they have experienced through gender but also a world and a past that has experienced them through gender. Their histories are interventionist in their explorations, assessing and evaluating what gender has meant and what they are going to make of those meanings through the active agency of their memories. Cultures have marked them as women, and what they explore they explore through that identification. The history they construct is deeply connected to identity and personal history. But it is not history as reduced to the single individual or identity politics. Instead, it is a complex intertwining of community—both acknowledged and implied—lived experience, and politics. Caren Kaplan observes that autobiographies that break with the universal subject redefine the possibilities of autobiography and reveal the power dynamics encoded within. These resistant autobiographies "require more collaborative procedures that are more closely attuned to the power differences among participants in producing the text."[7] These autobiographies are situated within communities because it is within the links between the personal and the political, memory and history, and individual and community that the challenges to traditional narratives emerge. Live performance, the most "collaborative" and communal form of representation women can employ, allows these women more possibilities for creating resistant autobiographies.

Autobiography in performance resonates communally as it has the potential to present simultaneously to a community of spectators the self-representation of autobiography and the more collective representation of history. The spectators assume an important role as their presence allows the performance to explore quite literally the assumption that history is more than the story of or investigation into a single individual (but certainly including single individuals) and to investigate how the, if not discrete then distinct, discourses of history, autobiography, and performance intersect with one another. Performance also points to the ways in which memory is itself a performance. Always a repetition, highly suggestible, and open to influences of subsequent production and reception, memory exists as a contingent representation constructed and authenticated by lived experience made powerful through retelling.

The autobiographical performance of memory, gender, race, sexuality, and history occurs strategically in comparable but distinct sites of intersection in each piece. In *Sally's Rape* and *Milk of Amnesia* memory occurs within and through the female body and is experienced physically through pain and pleasure. Similarly, memory's opposite, forgetting, is also articulated through autobiographical performance in all its contradictions as potentially either a privilege or disempowerment and how that potential is directed by gender, race, and sexuality. What is not remembered affects and effects what is remembered, thus tying memory and forgetting together, less as opposites than as different aspects of the same strategy. Finally, memory is also a specific resistance to oppression. It challenges the historical models of memory and experience offered by dominant discourses and in that challenge opens possibilities for change. McCauley and Tropicana use performance to confront traditionally gendered and racialized constructions of memory, identity, and history and in doing so offer significant models for licencing change that spring from and authorize memories and experiences usually discredited by oppressive discourse.

One of the primary constructions of memory in both pieces is a rejection of the traditional split between mind and body. Memory is not simply a mental process, both women argue through their performances; instead, it is concomitantly mental and physical, intellectual and sensual. As Sidonie Smith notes, "the autobiographical subject carries a history of the body with her as she negotiates the autobiographical 'I'" (22–23). In performance the female autobiographical body is not elsewhere or textually inscribed through writing; it is physically present sweating, moving, and "with [its] entry there is mess and clutter all around" (20). Autobiographical performance is a way to *embody* history—actually to take it on one's body and repeat it for physically present spectators. As they play out explorations of memory, McCauley and Tropicana each demonstrate the physical and material "mess and clutter" of "carr[ying]" history in her body.

In *Sally's Rape* the physicality of memory is particularly foregrounded from the beginning of the performance and works to frame the piece as, among other things, a visceral remembering. In the prologue McCauley and her performance partner, Jeannie Hutchins, discuss the nature of the piece they are about to perform. Seated on chairs on an otherwise bare stage, they agree, after some false starts, on Hutchins's words that "it's about getting culture."[8] McCauley quickly focuses that "getting" of culture on the body.

She gestures toward the gendered markings of class that her family valued: "Cups and saucers. Charm school. White gloves" (220). Hutchins, agreeing with McCauley, describes a friend who was "being groomed to be a southern belle" and had to walk with a book on her head in order to attain the correct posture, but McCauley vehemently rejects Hutchins's memory:

> We didn't worry about books on our heads. We already had this *up* thing. I guess that was the African in us before I even knew it. But we (*walking, Jeannie following*) had to contain our hips. To keep tucked up. Slightly seductive but not too much . . . (*at the bench*) and when . . . you know this part. (220)

Hutchins does know and demonstrates the proper, ladylike way to sit— "you touch the front of the seat with the back of the calf, and then you descend without bending at the waist" (220). The procedure ends with a crossing of the legs at the ankles. *Sally's Rape* begins with the ways in which class, race, and gender are physically encoded. Those discourses are carried in the body, and their effects are visible to others.

The exchange about learning how to contain one's body provides a crucial frame to the piece. The exchange between McCauley and Hutchins emphasizes the ways in which the physicality of memories is always experienced through gender and race. McCauley and Hutchins mark the learned class behavior of being a woman that is demonstrated through properties (e.g., teacups) and restraint (i.e., "we had to contain our hips"). While the stories of learning to hold one's body in "appropriate" positions come from the experiences of both performers, it is McCauley's memories that propel *Sally's Rape* forward. She rejects Hutchins's analogy of the southern belle because it opens a space for racist revision and appropriation. She challenges the co-opting familiarity of the analogy with a memory of Africa filtered through the historical, cultural, and political ways it must be contained and changed to meet the expectations of the African American, middle- and working-class, female body. The performance foregrounds from the first the importance of memory but of a complex notion of memory—one that is simultaneously physical, gendered, racial, historical, and political.

Carmelita Tropicana, too, foregrounds a complex construction of memory. Like McCauley, that memory's construction is framed from the outset by its physical properties and experience. One constituent of physical memory is the very character of Carmelita Tropicana herself. Since the early 1980s Alina Troyano has been a part of New York's alternative performance scene as Carmelita Tropicana. More than a simple stage character, Tropicana is the only way Troyano was able to begin performing. As theorist David Román remarked, "Alina Troyano didn't give herself permission to be on stage as Alina, she had to create Carmelita."[9] In *Amnesia* the invention of Carmelita is tied into both Troyano's reluctance to perform and her fears about homophobic backlash on her job. It is also a significant departure for Tropicana/Troyano as it marks the first time she has allowed "Alina Troyano" to appear on stage. As the disembodied voice-over identified as the "Writer" and never seen on stage, Troyano explores her emigration to the United States, the construction of Tropicana, and her 1993 visit to Cuba in monologues that provide transitions between scenes. Woven around this is Tropicana's narrative begun after she hits her head during a chocolate pudding wrestling match and develops amnesia.

Connecting both narratives is Cuba. Tropicana/Troyano is emphatic that the physical experience of memory is the crux of *Amnesia*. "I wanted to give people Cuba. Whether or not Cuba is familiar to you, I wanted to give you a taste of it. . . . I wanted people to experience Cuba in the way that I do."[10] She realizes this by beginning with a contrast of the tastes of Cuba with the very different tastes of the United States. She implies that her awareness of the specifics of the "taste" of Cuba began when she entered the United States. "I didn't like it here at first. Everything was so different. I had to change. I had to acquire a taste for peanut butter and jelly. It was hard. I liked tuna fish and jelly."[11] The differences between her previous and current cultures is illustrated by the different tastes and textures in each. At first the seven-year-old resists the new tastes of the United States and defiantly throws her milk away. She is caught by a nun whose "beady eyes screamed: You didn't drink your milk, Grade A, pasteurized, homogenized, you Cuban refugee." This moment proves to be a catalyst.

> I knew from my science class that all senses acted together. If I took off my glasses I couldn't hear as well. Same thing happened with my tastebuds. If I closed my eyes and held my breath I could suppress a lot of the flavor I didn't like. This is how I learned to drink milk. It was my resolve to embrace America as I chewed on my peanut butter and jelly sandwich and gulped down my milk. This new milk that replaced the sweet condensed milk of Cuba. My amnesia had begun. (95)

Assimilation, she suggests, is a matter of altering one's senses to reconcile the unfamiliar, the disconcerting, with that which is familiar and reassuring. The Writer dislocates her senses in order to grapple with the larger dislocations she has experienced. She reorients her physical experiences to distance her memories of the familiar and desirable and embrace a new set of experiences. This physical process has serious effects. As she assimilates physically, she also begins to forget physically. Thus, the process of adjustment is also one of obliteration and loss, and that process is recorded in her body. As her body digests the new culture, it begins to expel the former.

In memory's narrativization within representation "recollection is about the confrontation with absence and forgetting."[12] Both McCauley and Tropicana face this "confrontation" and the dangers it poses. In doing so, they do not narrativize merely the embattled memory but also the process and stakes of forgetting. The performers confront different sides of forgetting. For McCauley the struggle is not with her own forgetting but against those who are privileged to forget, while she cannot. Tropicana, whose "amnesia had begun" and is trying now to remember, struggles to claim her agency.

Much of what motivates *Sally's Rape* is the fact that the memories McCauley carries with her are different from the dominant historical narratives told by white people. Telling her Great-Great Grandmother Sally's story (and blurring that story with that of Sally Hemings) is one way to confront the absences in what McCauley has been taught as history.[13] With Jeannie Hutchins speaking the white girl's lines, McCauley recalls an encounter that forcefully confronted her with the dominant historical narrative that works to erase the past that she inherited.

> *McCauley:* In 1964 . . . a U.S. history major from Smith College said:
> *Hutchins:* I didn't know white men did anything to colored women on plantations.
> *McCauley:* I said, "It was rape." Her eyes turned red, she choked on her sandwich, and quit the job.
> *Hutchins:* Was the Smith College graduate (*she points at a different section of the audience with each new term*) lying, denying, or dumb?
> *McCauley:* Well, how could she be dumb? She actually graduated from Smith College—that's an ivy school. Well, I think it the way she was taught history for the last four hundred years.[14]

This is only one link McCauley makes between how what is possible in the present has everything to do with the operations of history. Sally's story has been erased in part so that white women do not have to confront their complicity in the rape of African American women and white men can escape responsibility for their perpetuation of such crimes. The "Smith College graduate" can graduate from a prestigious school, major in U.S. history, and be completely ignorant of the gendered material exigencies of plantation life in which she herself is implicated. The race and gender of forgetting are positioned here as reaffirmations of white male supremacy. While McCauley acknowledges a line of descent from rape, the absence of that acknowledgment outside African American communities erases her from memory. McCauley comments on this erasure to Hutchins: "It angers me that even though your ancestors may have been slaves . . . history has given you the ability to forget your shame about being oppressed by being ignorant, mean, or idealistic . . . which makes it dangerous for me" (228). What McCauley points to is not so much the actual experience of slavery or oppression but the memories of those experiences and the importance of memory in influencing actions. Those who have forgotten their own past can thus deny the existence of oppression or privilege by offering a view of history that does not account for past actions.

Carmelita Tropicana / Alina Troyano, too, wishes to challenge the erasure of herself as both a Cuban and an American woman, but for her it is an internal struggle around the forgetting demanded by assimilation. The lack of memories makes her particularly vulnerable to oppressive forces that shape and mold her. She remarks about her condition, "I want to remember so much I get these false attacks. In desperation, I appropriate other people's memories" (100). Without memories Tropicana/Troyano is at the mercy of discourses that would shape her without regard to her own experiences or identities, and she has no tools with which to resist the dangers of having amnesia.

The earliest strategy was Troyano's invention of Carmelita Tropicana.

> I couldn't stand in front of an audience, wear sequined gowns, tell jokes. But she could. She who penciled in her beauty mark, she who was baptized in the fountain of America's most popular orange juice, in the name of Havana's most popular nightclub, she could. She was a fruit and wasn't afraid to admit it. She was the part I'd left behind. She was Cuba. (98–99)

In Tropicana, Troyano's conflicting identifications found a performative voice. Latina stereotypes, lesbian culture, her Cuban birth, and her "naturalized" American citizenship found humorous and parodic expression. Tropicana was more than a stage character for Troyano; she was a named part of her fragmented sense of herself. "[Lesbianism] works to unsettle rather than to consolidate the boundaries around identity, not to dissolve them altogether but to open them to the fluidities and heterogeneities that make their renegotiation possible."[15] Carmelita Tropicana / Alina Troyano as lesbian raises the stakes of her amnesia because she refuses the homophobic heterosexism of both cultures and resituates what might otherwise be a polarized nationalist struggle. Neither solely Cuban nor solely American, Tropicana/Troyano rejects the usual "boundaries" of such conversations in order to animate the "fluidities and heterogeneities" that are powerful constituents of her memories. Tropicana/

Troyano's sexuality further throws the oppressiveness of forgetting into relief. As she finds ways to embrace her sexuality publically through performance, she finds ways around the loss of Cuba. Later in the piece she will reinforce the links between her lesbian identity and her Cuban one with a memory of her emerging sexuality. She remembers as a child kissing her Nanny. "She had long hair tied into a ponytail, red lips, and dreamy eyes like a cow. I ran to her and jumped on her and kissed her creamy cheeks. . . . My heart was beating fast, I was sweating. I knew then that was no ordinary kiss" (105). Troyano/Tropicana "renegotiates," in Biddy Martin's terms, the boundaries around identity by connecting the lost Cuba with the found transgressive sexuality. Carmelita is a confrontation to her own amnesia.

In *Amnesia* Tropicana/Troyano returns to Cuba, to the beginning, to what might be configured as the origin. But what she finds there is just as complicated as what she left in the United States, "origins" exist only as memories. Finally in Cuba "I tell my driver Francisco I want to see, touch, feel, hear, taste Cuba. All my orifices open" (102). Implicit here is the sexuality that Tropicana/Troyano has intertwined with Cuba. Her "orifices" are "open," suggesting that all her senses, as well as her sexuality, are necessary to re-member Cuba. Cuba is not generic but sexualized, gendered, and specific. Despite this openness, nothing happens. Tropicana desires Cuba, but Cuba resists her.

Similarly, the Writer finds familiarity and recognition similarly elusive. She comments on the contradiction between her "return" to Cuba and her inability to "recognize" anything. "I am like a tourist in my own country. Everything is new. I walk everywhere hoping I will recall something. Anything. I have this urge to recognize and be recognized. . . . But it doesn't happen" (105). Without memory, without history, the identity she experiences is profoundly lost and disempowered. She is almost unable to act and, instead, is often acted upon. The process embedded in Tropicana/Troyano's narrative is one that moves from paralysis to action. "The amnesia that Carmelita Tropicana calls attention to is the elision of a profound sense of displacement that marks the exile subject's ontology."[16] As she cannot remember, she has no history, no autobiography. Her story must be reconstructed through a sedimentation of new experiences and reconstructed memories.

Despite the difference in struggle—McCauley with others, Tropicana with herself—the focus is the same. Both performers understand that the urgency of forgetting is a way to obliterate resistance. If the source of contention disappears, then presumably the contention will disappear as well. Memory is resistance, whether forgetting is evidence of privilege or disempowerment. The most striking and horrifying moment of resistant memory comes from the moment that is at the heart of *Sally's Rape*. Taking off her dress, McCauley stands naked on an auction block (a bare cube) as Hutchins leads the audience in chanting, "Bid 'em in" (230). McCauley speaks in agony of the experience of being ruthlessly examined and sold. "On the auction block. They put their hands all down our / bodies / to sell you, for folks to measure you" (230). The scene quickly breaks and resumes. Clothed, McCauley returns to the auction block, this time to curl up on it. She describes her knowledge of Sally: "I am I am Sally being done it to I am down on the ground being done it to" (231). As Deborah Thompson points out, for McCauley "presenting her body naked on an auction block is her history. It's a necessity, a memory written on her body."[17] This is obviously a place where the physicality and resistance of gendered memory intersect. McCauley's intention in representing these events, particularly representing them as first-person, present-tense autobiographical memory, is to tell the story of slavery repeatedly in order to prevent denial and fight the racism that rooted in slavery. "It has to do with speaking my memories . . . the memories in my bones—those kind of tensions we were born with because those experiences are passed down and if we bear witness we're able to continue."[18] Speaking, "bearing witness," and remembering are here positioned as radically resistant acts that point to the sources of racism and refuse to allow those sources to be erased as well as the gendered specifics of being a woman slave.

This kind of action is part of a larger African American strategy of memory.

> In this nation infamous for its . . . historical forgetfulness, African Americans have been the ones who could not forget. . . . The legacy of slavery and the serried workings of racism and prejudice have meant that even the most optimistic black Americans are, as the expression goes, "born knowing" that there is a wide gulf between America's promises and practices.[19]

One is born with memory, that memory is larger than one's lived experiences, and it is that larger quality, along with memory of lived experience, that provides strategies for resistance. Knowing that forgetting slavery would have dire consequences not simply for herself or African American communities but for the entire United States, McCauley vulnerably risks herself to revisit Sally's/McCauley's memories of horror and oppression specific to women and demonstrate those memories' currency for the present—"a stance toward history that is braced by the awareness that the past . . . has never really *passed*."[20] Memory is a crucial component for change because it urgently demonstrates both the consequences of racism and the possibilities for eradicating it.

The complex difficulties of bringing change about are marked when Hutchins follows the auction block scene with an account of the supportive attention she received in a rape crisis center. McCauley sharply contrasts this with Sally's experience of repeated violation, "ain't no rape crisis center on the plantation" (233). McCauley offers Hutchins a chance to perform the auction block scene herself, but ultimately Hutchins finds that, as a white woman, she cannot (and historically did not have to). McCauley asks Hutchins, who stands fully clothed where McCauley was naked a few moments before, "Do you have anything to say?" When Hutchins shakes her head, McCauley responds, "That's something right there" (234). Hutchins's refusal marks, in McCauley's estimation, a step forward, a public declaration of the specifics of historical experience where white and black women cannot simply compare one another's pasts, where race creates historical privilege, and where a reassuring version of the past in which those differences are ameliorated through analogy can be prevented.

Woven throughout *Sally's Rape* are examples of the illusions those in power endeavor to construct and what McCauley and Hutchins eventually reject—a more palliative version of the past.

> I'm going against the myth of romance of the slave master and the overseers with the slave women, even Thomas Jefferson. I'm going against the myth because it was a power thing, so we call it rape. Sometimes it was actual, brutal rape; sometimes it might have been romantic. It doesn't matter. It was rape in the sense that we know what rape is now. (215)

McCauley's refusal of the romanticization of sex between white men and African American women on the plantation is a refusal of a powerfully reoccurring trope in U.S. history. Her specific mention of Thomas Jefferson references a host of romantic narratives about plantation life and demonstrates their power seemingly to ameliorate the effects of slavery.

> Any student of slavery knows it is a waste of effort to play the numbers game. It is even hard to convince some historians that the thousands of slave mulattoes were not all products of mutual consent. Documents, records, and statistics have become tangled issues within our combative field. Memory can provide alternative substantiation.[21]

For African American women the experience of rape on the plantations was a forceful reminder about how the discourses of racial and sexual oppression were intertwined. McCauley works to "provide alternative substantiation" because without it the official narrative disempowers and erases her. Using memories—both hers and those she inherited—creates powerful opposition.

In resistance to forgetting, Tropicana/Troyano works to name and write a history that accurately reflects the complexities of Cuban-American experience. Writing about precisely these kinds of struggles, Gustavo Pérez Firmat stresses that "Cuban-American culture is a balancing act."[22] The discourses she must "balance" through resistance intersect in profoundly challenging ways. The homophobia and sexism of both the United States and Cuba pose a risk to Tropicana/Troyano as a lesbian, the virulent anticommunism of United States / Cuban-American politics threatens her ability to offer a critique of the Cuban Revolution from the Left that aligns her neither with the Revolution nor the Right groups of the United States nor a romantic depiction of prerevolutionary Cuba. *Amnesia* is the site where Troyano/Tropicana performs the "balancing act" and explores the conflicting constituents of her history.

Twice Tropicana has what she calls a "CUMAA," or "Collective Unconscious Memory Appropriation Attack."[23] The first time she experiences the life of Hernando Cortez's horse when he and the Catholic Church arrived in Cuba to subjugate the indigenous peoples. The horse witnesses the death and horror with a growing sense of agony. The history of colonization is recounted through an unwilling and naive participant who arrives with the conquerors but is himself conquered and tamed. The complexity of "New World" hybrid identities complicates Tropicana/Troyano's search, and as she noted earlier, much of it depends on location. The history of conquest and colonization marks the conscious construction and performance of subjectivity as well as evokes the experiences of women and lesbians whose own less empowered positions can prevent them from acting.

Similarly, the effects of the U.S. economic embargo of Cuba are played out through another CUMAA, this time a piglet who is taken from his mother to live in a city apartment. Eventually, he is slaughtered, and it is his death that coalesces Tropicana/Troyano's memory. These appropriative experiences that Tropicana predicted she would need in order to reconstruct herself permit her to act from what had become a disabling location. The contradiction in her memories and histories were so strong that she no longer had agency. Constructing a new set of memories, however, allowed for the construction of an empowered identity and demonstrates that knowledge of the past and embracing lived experiences can be an empowering feminist place from which to act. Part of the feminist solution that is played out in the performance is one that Troyano identified previously—

the construction of Carmelita Tropicana. Carmelita, who "went on . . . one night and . . . never came off," allows Troyano to embody contradictions that constitute identity without resolving them into a coherent assimilated, homogeneous identity.[24] Carmelita's exuberant feminist parody simultaneously embraces and interrogates culture, history, and resistence. Another part of the solution to the profound challenges facing Tropicana/Troyano's desire for agency is the performance of *Milk of Amnesia* itself. Through these strategies she can "def[y] the exilic plot of giving up a 'lost' self. Rather, through a practice of exilic remembering, the past is brought firmly into the present."[25] By refusing to abandon the past and recognizing the formative role it plays in the present, Tropicana/Troyano offers a sense of history that is resistant: she will not stop being Cuban, nor will she forgo being American. She embraces her differences, no matter how contradictory they may be. At the end of *Amnesia* Tropicana/Troyano re-members herself and embraces her "culturally fragmented, sexually intersected" identity, but, as she goes on to say, "I don't esplit" (109). She concludes: "My journey is complete. My amnesia is gone. After so many years in America I can drink two kinds of milk. The sweet condensed milk of Cuba and the pasteurized homo kind from America" (109–10). As exile, Tropicana/Troyano can now acknowledge both identities, construct the hybridity that will allow her to be Cuban and American, and establish herself in a subsequent nationality without erasing the previous one.

This sort of feminist truth-telling— a self-representation of a woman's lived experience connected to larger discourses of history, politics, and culture—is a crucial contribution to the ongoing project of feminist critique and change. Close to the end of *Sally's Rape* Robbie McCauley tells Jeannie Hutchins: "They say Sally had them children by the master to save us. How come they thought she had a choice? Survival is luck. Or unlucky" (236). McCauley marks here both how African-American women have been written into and out of history. Implying choice denies rape, and McCauley refuses to simplify or distort Sally's story by attributing it to empowered options and good fortune. Tropicana/Troyano begins to find her way out of amnesia by listing several things she does remember. Among them is that the "slang word for dyke is *bombera,* firefighter. So maybe if I yell, 'Fire,' '*fuego,*' would all the dykes come out now?" This memory is a feminist marking of the places that produce her memory. Even though she has claimed earlier that her lesbian persona Carmelita Tropicana is inextricably linked to Cuba ("She was a fruit. . . . She was Cuba"), Tropicana/Troyano recognizes the homophobia of Cuba as a place where she cannot "see" any lesbians and that would not necessarily welcome her identification of lesbian with Cuba (107). As a feminist, however, she resists this by fore-grounding the absence. Both these moments are examples of feminist strate-gies of performed autobiography that identify oppressive discourses (tradi-tional narrativizations of slave women or homophobia's erasure of lesbians) and radically confront those discourses by refusing their sexist, misogynist modes of operation.

The interpretive strategies of feminist self-representation empower both performer and spectator. For the performer this doubled feminist move—the contradicted "I" of autobiography and performance that is simultane-ously first- and third person—talk back and challenge oppression as articu-lated through stable histories of the dominant discourse. These stable histories would rewrite Sally's rape as romance or Carmelita's amnesia as a benefit of assimilation and deny McCauley and Tropicana/Troyano's mem-ories. For the spectators the feminist tellings of women's lives are con-structed by live bodies physically present in the same space. This dynamic is feminist because the autobiographies are presented not simply to claim authority for the performers but also to reach out to the spectators, identify them as collaborative and communal partners in the telling of women's lives, and encourage them to seize the means to tell their own lives. By doing so, feminists can offer significant challenges to power structures that would oppress and deny their experiences and memories.

I imagine that McCauley and Tropicana/Troyano would respond to the question "Is it possible for us to think otherwise, as cultural actors evidently do, and conceive of 'past' events being truly effective in the present—con-ceived of them, that is, as not really past?" that it is not simply possible but absolutely imperative.[26] A feminist past would open greater possibilities for a feminist present, and a feminist present would, in turn, make a feminist future imaginable.

NOTES

1. Robbie McCauley, "Thoughts on My Career," in *Performance and Cultural Politics*, ed. Elin Diamond (New York: Routledge, 1996), 265.

2. David Román, "Tropicana Unplugged: An Interview with Carmelita Tropi-cana," *TDR* 39.3 (1995): 81.

3. Jonathan Boyarin, "Space, Time, and the Politics of Memory," in *Remap-ping Memory: The Politics of TimeSpace*, ed. Jonathan Boyarin (Minneapolis: Uni-versity of Minnesota Press, 1994), 22.

4. Sidonie Smith, *A Poetics of Women's Autobiography: Marginality and the*

Fictions of Self-Representation (Bloomington: Indiana University Press, 1987), 45. Hereafter all references will appear parenthetically in the text.

5. Sidonie Smith, *Subjectivity, Identity, and the Body: Women's Autobiographical Practices in the Twentieth Century* (Bloomington: Indiana University Press, 1993), 20. Hereafter all references will appear parenthetically in the text.

6. bell hooks, *Talking Back: Thinking Feminist, Thinking Black* (Boston: South End Press, 1989), 5.

7. Caren Kaplan, "Resisting Autobiography: Out-law Genres and Transnational Feminist Subjects," in *De/Colonizing the Subject: The Politics of Gender in Women's Autobiography,* ed. Sidonie Smith and Julia Watson (Minneapolis: University of Minnesota Press, 1992), 119.

8. Robbie McCauley, *Sally's Rape, Moon Marked and Touched by the Sun,* ed. Sydné Mahone (New York: Theater Communications Group, 1994), 219. *Sally's Rape* was first performed in 1989. Since that time McCauley and Hutchins have toured the piece nationally, performing in a diverse range of venues. Citing lines from *Sally's Rape* is complicated, as much of the text is improvised on set themes; thus what is actually spoken varies from performance to performance. The lines performed in the video documentaries *Sphinxes without Secrets* and *Conjure Women,* quoted in Raewyn White's article in *Acting Out* and published in *Moon Marked and Touched by the Sun* (itself a transcription of a performance in November 1991), differ widely. I have not limited myself to the published version in exploring the piece. Hereafter all references will appear parenthetically in the text.

9. Identifying who is being discussed is complicated in reference to *Milk of Amnesia.* Saying that Alina Troyano has performed for over fifteen years as Carmelita Tropicana is somewhat misleading, as Tropicana has never been indicated as "character" in programs, interviews, or reviews. In most materials she is simply referred to as Carmelita Tropicana. In the Román interview she is identified as Tropicana, and the authorial credit for *Amnesia* is also Tropicana. I will refer to her as Tropicana/Troyano in this article because I think it is crucial to acknowledge Troyano in this context, as she indicates that this is the first performed material in which Troyano appears, although *appears* is inaccurate given that she is a taped voice-over.

10. Román, "Tropicana Unplugged," 93.

11. Carmelita Tropicana, *Milk of Amnesia / Leche de Amnesia,* TDR 39.3 (1995): 94. Similarly to McCauley, Tropicana/Troyano is flexible in her approach to her piece. She is willing to change it depending on venue and resources. Hereafter all references will appear parenthetically in the text.

12. Michael Roth, *The Ironist's Cage: Memory, Trauma, and the Construction of History* (New York: Columbia University Press, 1995), 204.

13. For an excellent examination of the complexities around the Jefferson/Hemings controversy, see Annette Gordon-Reed, *Thomas Jefferson and Sally Hemings: An American Controversy* (Charlottesville: University of Virginia Press, 1997).

14. Robbie McCauley, *Sally's Rape, Sphinxes without Secrets,* dir. Maria Beatty (1992). Interestingly, in the published version of *Sally's Rape* the assessment of the Smith College graduate is somewhat different.

> *Jeannie:* . . . Yeah she was dumb. I keep telling you that.
>
> *Robbie:* Why do I feel like crying . . . because she went to Smith College . . . I think of the dumb educated bourgeois thing in me. . . .

The epistemological responsibility shifts somewhat in this version, although McCauley goes on to say, "The point is Smith College, all those colleges are places that people should go to learn things that help the world." The emphasis is still on the institutional suppression of knowledge, but there is an interesting vacillation around the issue of individual responsibility. McCauley, *Sally's Rape, Moon Marked,* 225.

15. Biddy Martin, "Lesbian Identity and Autobiographical Difference(s)," in *Life/Lines: Theorizing Women's Autobiography,* ed. Bella Brodzki and Celeste Schenck (Ithaca: Cornell University Press, 1988), 103.

16. José Esteban Muñoz, "No Es Fácil: Notes on the Negotiation of Cubanidad and Exilic Memory in Carmelita Tropicana's *Milk of Amnesia/Leche de Amnesia,*" *TDR* 39.3 (1995): 76.

17. Deborah Thompson, "Blackface, Race, and Beyond: Rehearsing Interracial Dialogue in *Sally's Rape,*" *Theatre Journal* 48.2 (1996): 137.

18. Robbie McCauley, interview, *Conjure Women,* dir. Demetria Royal (1995).

19. Geneviève Fabre and Robert O'Meally, intro., in *History and Memory in African-American Culture,* ed. Fabre and O'Meally (New York: Oxford University Press, 1994), 3.

20. Fabre and O'Meally, intro., 3.

21. Catherine Clinton, "'With a Whip in His Hand': Rape, Memory, and African-American Women," in Fabre and O'Meally, *History and Memory,* 209.

22. Gustavo Pérez Firmat, *Life on the Hyphen: The Cuban-American Way* (Austin: University of Texas Press, 1994), 6.

23. Firmat, *Life on the Hyphen,* 6.

24. Alisa Solomon, "The WOW Café," in *The Drama Review: Thirty Years of Commentary on the Avant-Garde,* ed. Brooks McNamara and Jill Dolan (Ann Arbor: UMI Research Press, 1986), 310.

25. Muñoz, "No Es Fácil," 79.

26. Boyarin, "Space, Time," 2.

Theorizing Early Modern Lesbianisms
Invisible Borders, Ambiguous Demarcations

Harriette Andreadis

Little is generally known with certainty about the history of female same-sex erotics and the ways in which such an erotics might have been constructed throughout early modern Europe. A textual history reaching back to classical times identifies and describes tribadism and tribades as a class of sexually transgressive and socially ostracized females; yet, apart from these demonized transgressors, the construction of female erotic relations has remained underexamined and undertheorized. It is my contention in this essay that early modern English women from the ostensibly respectable classes who might have transgressed into territories of physical intimacy would almost certainly not have defined themselves and their behaviors in the terms offered by then-available publicly circulated vocabularies, nor in fact would they have been likely to name themselves or their behaviors in ways that they and their culture would have understood as transgressive. I believe that women of the "middling sort"[1] who wished to retain social status, which more often than not would have included heterosexual marriage and children, used strategies of silence about sexual practice that allowed them both to acknowledge their erotic desires and to evade opprobrium. Literature by women in England during the early modern period, before about 1700, often suggests the manner of these evasions and suggests the ways in which a female same-sex erotics, what I call "an erotics of unnaming," might have been constructed quite apart from the public, male-generated discourse of transgression.

The project of recovering early modern understandings of female same-sex erotics is complicated by our working description of early modern constructions of identity and by our struggles to refrain from imposing upon them our own notions of selfhood. Recent scholarship has made it apparent that the modern subject or "self" understood as individual identity and characterized by, among other qualities, unity, interiority, self-consciousness, autonomy, and coherence, was not fully formulated before the eighteenth century, though it was certainly in the process of developing during the late sixteenth and early seventeenth centuries. As Catherine Belsey's work in the drama demonstrates, the notion of a subject that included interiority was emerging only in a halting fashion during this earlier historical moment in England:

> The unified subject of liberal humanism is a product of the second half of the seventeenth century, an effect of the revolution. Broadly this seems to me to be so. Liberal humanism, locating agency and meaning in the unified human subject, becomes an orthodoxy at the moment when the bourgeoisie is installed as the ruling class. Signifying practice, however, is not so well ordered as to wait for the execution of Charles I in 1649 before proclaiming the existence of interiority, the inalienable and unalterable property of the individual, which precedes and determines speech and action.[2]

In contrast to our own, early modern constructions of identity seem generally to have been determined by external or social attributes—the sum of a constellation of such characteristics as class, sex, occupation, familial, regional (e.g., urban/rural, north/south) and national origins, as well as religious and political affiliations. An even relatively subjective personal identity was not, then, analogous to what we now experience as gendered selves constructed by an individualist psychology. With this difference in mind, readings of early modern texts in search of "lesbian community" seem manifestly absurd, though understandable in light of the contested social positions of sexual minorities in the twentieth century and their attempts to move from marginality into a social mainstream, so-called.

In discussing the social genesis of the self, Charles Taylor notes that "conversation partners [are] essential to . . . achieving self-definition" and remarks that "a self exists only within . . . 'webs of interlocution,'" a point also made by Regenia Gagnier: "'the self' is not an autonomous introspectible state—a Cogito or a unique point of view—but is instead dependent upon intersubjectivity, or the intersubjective nature of language and culture."[3] This philosophical perspective on the nature of the constructed self—that the self exists only intersubjectively—is perhaps most useful in our efforts to comprehend early modern understandings of the nature of identity. With respect to female same-sex erotic transgression during the early modern period in England, what we will find is that an identity defined by specific behaviors indeed had been distinguished by the language community; however, as we shall see, it was an identity characterized primarily by its alterity, by its "otherness" and consequently by its foreignness and its un-Englishness.

The problem for us is not, then, that there was no distinguishable category for female same-sex erotics. The problem is, rather, how women who might have chosen or been drawn into intense emotional and erotic connections with other women would have thought about those relations if (1) these women were not included in the mostly male language community that was aware of same-sex transgressive sexuality, or if (2) these women were aware of transgressive identities yet did not associate their own feelings or behaviors with those identities, or even if (3) these women were aware of transgressive identities yet rejected the possibilities of their own connection with those identified as "other."

The then-available signifiers for female same-sex transgressivity were, as is now generally known, the nouns *tribade* and *tribadism,* which were used in conformity with classical precedent throughout the early modern period to describe the activities of women who engaged in sexual activity, as it was then understood, with other women.[4] More colloquially, tribades were also called "rubsters" in English or "fricatrices" or "confricatrices" after the French and Latin.[5] Like other terms we have become aware of, such as *lollepot* in seventeenth-century Dutch and *tommy* in eigtheenth-century English, and like our modern American uses of *dyke* and its variants (*bull dyke, diesel dyke, bulldagger,* etc.), or the early twentieth-century use by the Bloomsbury Group of the more genteel *sapphist,* these terms operate in precise contexts, often determined by class, and engaging, at various times and in different places, nuances of disapprobation and reappropriation, or even of affirmation, that are marked temporally and geographically. The realities represented by any given locution are not usually amenable to direct comparison with constructions of erotic behavior from another time or place, so that we have to allow for the possibility that certain forms of erotic expression (e.g., oral/genital or manual/genital contact) between women might not have been considered sexual before the twentieth century within a masculinist paradigm that reads and defines all erotic behaviors in terms of a heterosexual model.

Literally defined, then, a tribade was one who achieved sexual gratification by rubbing; in conjunction with this definition, some early texts also mention that these women had preternaturally enlarged clitorises, which they used "in the manner of a man." The enlarged clitoris and female appropriation of male sexual behaviors seem to have been an obsessive concern of anatomists and other male writers and are mentioned with nearly compulsive regularity whenever tribadism is the subject of discussion. These persons were most often said to belong to the classical world or to be denizens of foreign lands, so their existence was consigned to exotic locales by travel narratives as well as by medical and midwifery texts.[6] Jane Sharp's observations, in *The Midwife's Book* (1671), reiterate ideas readily available in earlier anatomy texts:

> Commonly it [the clitoris] is but a small sprout, lying close hid under the wings, and not easily felt, yet sometimes it grows so long that it hangs forth at the slit like a yard [penis], and will swell and stand stiff if it be provoked, and some lewd women have endeavored to use it as men do theirs. In the Indies and Egypt they are frequent, but I never heard but of one in this country: if there be any, they will do what they can for shame to keep it close.[7]

These "lewd women" and their transgressions are placed at a safe remove from everyday English life. It is noteworthy here that toward the latter end of the seventeenth century, in a text intended for women and women midwives, Sharp avoids naming the transgressive women in question though names were readily available. Sharp's reluctance to name may have been occasioned by the female readership of her book and an unwillingness to circulate a name perhaps otherwise unavailable to them. Or it may be part of the phenomenon, which I have described elsewhere, in which women who could be identified as engaging in the particularly "lewd" acts of tribadism were regarded with increasing condemnation as we move from the sixteenth into the seventeenth century, so that dissemination of knowledge about their activities became more widespread at the same time that it began to be suppressed.[8] An example of the continuity of ideas about transgressing women, particularly their association with Sappho and their exoticizing, or othering, is to be found in the anonymous mid-eighteenth-century *Satan's Harvest Home* (1749):

> Sappho, as she was one of the wittiest Women that ever the World bred, so she thought with Reason, it would be expected she should make some Additions to a Science in which Womankind had been so successful: What does she do then? Not content with our Sex, begins Amours with her own, and teaches the Female World a new Sort of Sin, call'd the Flats, that was follow'd not only in Lucian's Time, but is practis'd frequently in Turkey, as well as at Twickenham at this Day.[9]

As this passage demonstrates, an acknowledgment of the existence of transgressive women closer to home takes place as we enter the eighteenth century and a more elaborate discourse of identification is being used, the slangy game of "Flats" that presumably refers to a rubbing without benefit of male protuberance or supplementation. By 1781 *tommy* may have been the colloquial analogue for *molly,* at least in London.[10]

In contrast to our limited information about female same-sex erotic relations, a great deal more is generally known about male sexuality and the traditions of male-male sexual relations since ancient times, no doubt because the lives of men are lived more publicly and documented more extensively. Thus, we have available narrative accounts—though they are as yet partial and speculative—of the emergence of a sodomitical subculture that included "molly houses," or early gay bars, in late-seventeenth- and eighteenth-century England and Europe.[11] Whether there might have been a similarly emergent culture of female same-sex erotic activity is now being addressed with more careful historical analysis and from a more adequately theorized perspective than has previously been the case. Recently, Bernadette Brooten's *Love between Women: Early Christian Responses to Female Homoeroticism* furnishes a much-needed historical and theoretical bridge between our knowledge of female same-sex relations during classical times and the early modern period. Brooten's study provides the early cultural contexts of female homoeroticism in the transmission of Sappho, Greek erotic spells, astrological texts, medical treatments, and dream analyses, through Egypt from the Greeks into early Christian Roman times.[12] Although Brooten's extensive analysis in part 2 of Paul's Letter to the Romans, 1:18–32, patristic writings of the second and third centuries, and church sanctions of the fourth and fifth centuries, is also highly informative, it is her account of the transmission of the classics into early Christian times that helps illuminate the complex sources of early modern female same-sex eroticism. As we have seen, it was classical sources and their translations that provided names and identities for transgressing women in early modern England.

The literary and other textual evidence of these and other sources now available to us demonstrates unambiguously that same-sex physical behaviors between women were known and feared by men. In some ways and at some times this knowledge and fear were presumably communicated to women, though it may not always have been explicitly articulated or fully conscious, depending on class and other environmental or social factors. There is reason to believe, for instance, that, as more women became literate and gained access to texts previously accessible only to men, they also gained access to a broader range of sexual information and understanding, despite efforts by men and by other women like Sharp to bowdlerize texts for women.[13] It is also apparent that these behaviors were considered transgressive and not desirable for women who might wish to maintain a respectable social standing, who might in other words wish to remain among "the better sort." What, then, of those women of the middling sort, or of even higher status, whose connections with other women must have transgressed into the territories of physical intimacy, whether genital or not? I use *must have* deliberately here to indicate that, like Terry Castle, I assume that individuals are inclined to use, and in fact do use, their bodies—both alone and with each other—in the great variety of ways available to them physiologically, however they might define, or avoid defining, or even avoid acknowledging, these uses.[14] In light of this assumption it is not improbable that women of all classes and social strata, those who were willing to be ostracized as well as those who were not, performed acts that, were they to be named, would be considered transgressive—that is, not normative because not heterosexual—by others or by themselves.

How might those respectable women who transgressed into territories of physical intimacy have defined for themselves the nature of their erotic feelings and activities? What literary and social forms might their definitions have taken? Or, from another perspective, in the case of women to whose literary voices we do have access, "what did these women who wrote in impassioned ways about/to/for other women actually do with each other?" These are questions to which we have no empirical answers and to which we may have to be satisfied with speculative yet educated answers for the period before about 1700. Although in the future there may be found diaries or other similar artifacts describing actual instances of same-sex female sexuality and the relationships in which they thrived or there may emerge cases of prosecution that describe in detail sexual acts between women, for the time being we must theorize without such corroborative evidence concerning the verifiable *facts* of women's relations.

The case of Anne Lister (1791–1840) is an apparent, though rather late, exception to this dilemma. Lister's diaries demonstrate a clear definition of the nature of sexual acts between women. Lister's use of code to name her sexual behaviors (i.e., *kiss* = *orgasm*) is certain evidence of her consciousness of transgression and her conscious struggle to find sexual companionship is a clear indication of erotic communication between women of the better sort by the end of the eighteenth century.[15] Anna Clark describes Anne Lister as one of those "individuals [who] deliberately construct their own identities with three elements: their own temperaments and inherent desires; their material circumstances; and the cultural representations available to them."[16] This understanding of the construction of an identity outside the bounds established by a formally sanctioned social community might perhaps be useful in thinking about the ways in which some early modern women during the sixteenth, seventeenth, and earlier eighteenth centuries, before Anne Lister, might have negotiated socially as well as personally unacceptable erotic feelings and desires. As we have seen, individual temperaments and desires, or what we now think of as personal identities, were subordinated without question to material and social circumstances for most persons during the early modern period. These circumstances were also particularly limiting to women in the early modern period: the necessity to marry in order to maintain respectability was for most women simply a fact of life, as it often still is. Cultural representations of tribades and of tribadism would have made identifying with them unlikely, if not impossible, for any woman who did not court social ostracism, which would have meant the loss not only of social status but almost surely of the means of material survival as well.

Yet without being named, *without being spoken,* certain otherwise transgressive acts might simply be understood by the individuals involved as physiological gestures embodying mutual feelings of friendship, love, and/or affection. Without naming, there is no point at which to establish a series of boundaries between affection, eroticism, and sexuality.[17] That such boundaries were not clearly established—or even thought necessary—for (certainly sheltered) women of certain classes and circumstances is what I want to suggest here through my exploration of the vocabulary that might or might not have been available to them. And yet, as Caroline Woodward has already noted of eighteenth-century women, their "silence . . . about their sexual lives may have been an effective strategic practice,"[18] allowing them to acknowledge desire as they simultaneously evaded opprobrium. The behaviors underlying such a strategic evasion could not be called, or even said to be "like," lesbianism; but they could be called transgressive when or if they were identified as tribadism. But unnamed, particularly before about 1700, the behaviors that were identified with the transgressions of tribades would not have stigmatized the women who engaged in them, nor would they have caused them to self-identify as transgressive. An "erotics of unnaming" could thus serve as a socially strategic evasion of what would certainly have been a devastating social opprobrium. Because we cannot know for certain how such transgressing women might have described for themselves their same-sex erotic behavior, we can take note of the social constructs that developed to accommodate and perhaps to contain a constellation of passionate emotions and behaviors. It has become increasingly clear that the primary social framework that provided both erotic opportunities and discursive camouflage for women in the sixteenth and seventeenth centuries is that of "female friendship" and that it was followed in the eighteenth century by the rhetorical constructs of female "romantic," or "passionate," friendship.[19]

In the absence of visible subcultures identified as transgressive, such as the eighteenth-century molly houses known to serve men interested in same-sex connections, social structure flexes to include within itself unacknowledged transgressions and unnamed nonnormative behaviors.[20] Secure social status may be maintained by individuals through their refusal to make an association, in either language or consciousness, between their behavior and socially identified transgression. Everyone thus colludes in accepting as normative the dominant social structures and ideology. This collusion, exemplified here by the silencing (or unnaming) of female sexualities, is simply part of the process whereby culture constructs and demarcates the acceptability of sexual and erotic relations within particular boundaries and individuals respond in complex ways that both court and avoid transgression of those boundaries.

Michael McKeon has recently described the process by which the assumptions of patriarchalism were of necessity brought to consciousness and separated out in "the emergence of modern patriarchy [which] is coextensive with the emergence of gender difference."[21] In seeing Robert Filmer's *Patriarcha* as marking "not the triumphant ascendancy of patriarchal thought, but its demise as tacit knowledge, the fact that it is in crisis," McKeon argues that "the long-term and uneven shift from patriarchalism to modern patriarchy entailed a separation out of elements which had formerly been tacitly understood and experienced as parts of an integral whole—the cosmos, the social order, the family, economic production."[22] His account includes a description of how this shift facilitated the emergence of the modern system of gender difference and the coalescence of the discourse of sexuality as formerly only tacit understandings and experiencings separated themselves out from an unconscious social matrix.

McKeon's notion of tacit understanding is useful in suggesting how the sexual naming of female same-sex eroticism during this period participates in the social dismantling of tacit knowledge. Along, then, with the emergence of the discourse of sexuality, the older system of the tacit knowledge of erotic practice gives way to naming as subcultures become known and as certain erotic activities are recognized as sexual rather than as part of a larger complex of behaviors earlier embedded in a social context of "friendship." This process has already been described in detail for male behaviors and subcultures. It is a process that also took place with respect to women's behaviors within female social structures: absent a male organ—or "supplementation" by an ancillary appendage, be it a dildo, an enlarged clitoris, or other prosthetic device—sexuality was (and in some quarters still is) hard to define with respect to women with each other; with the eventual naming of what had been only tacitly acknowledged, certain erotic behaviors would of necessity have been included in the range of activities now defined as sexual. No doubt this process occurred later for women than for men, whose more public display of same-sex sexual activities in parks and molly houses evidenced the behavior of a clearly established subculture by the later seventeenth century. As long as women acceded to male precedence and did not transgress by assuming male prerogatives (i.e., cross-dressing), there seems not to have been much reason to explore or to name what women might do with each other's bodies. Following the Restoration in England, however, and the more general social license openly indulged by various individuals, especially by members of the aristocracy, the demise of the tacit ironically may very well have become a means of repressing unwelcome female transgressivity. The effect of naming—and the more public the naming the more profound the effect—was to bring to the consciousness of individuals the connections between their behaviors and named transgressions. In this way to name may be to inhibit and to constrain.

The history of the textual availability of a language for female sexuality bears out this speculation. Earlier, tribades and tribadism were described by men, and knowledge of their existence was available only to men in the Latin texts published throughout early modern Europe. The language for identifying this behavior and the persons who engaged in it did not become available in English until the classics began to be translated from Latin into the European vernaculars, at which time this vocabulary also became available to educated women. As we have seen in the passage from Jane Sharp's midwifery manual, the acquisition of knowledge and the displacement of tribades to exotic locales through a familiar trope were enabled simultaneously. This new availability of vocabulary and information probably occurred earlier and/or slightly differently in the Continental vernacular languages, though the process of accessibility is likely to have been similar in England and in English. As Sharp's language suggests, an inhibition in the accounts of tribadism appears to have been taking place as an understanding of the possibilities for exotic transgressions led to the eventual identification and naming of those same behaviors closer to home. A developing consciousness of the demarcations separating transgressive from conforming behaviors may have provided the impetus for inhibition. Profound changes in the cultural understandings of same-sex sexual behaviors among women occur clearly in conjunction with the increasing availability of vernacular print cultures. Not coincidentally, or surprisingly, these changes are associated with class and literacy.

The aftermath of the dissemination of knowledge during the Renaissance and the increasingly open availability of sexual discussion following the

Restoration permitted the intensification of public discourse about sexuality in general and female same-sex sexuality in particular. We find male concern with women's same-sex erotic relations to be a pervasive theme in English literature before the Restoration. The influence of Ovidian myth effected the transformations that we note so frequently in the drama of Shakespeare and Lyly, to mention only two of the most obvious instances, in which the resolution to the dilemma of two women in love is a sex change miraculously achieved in advance of the possibility of any real sexual discomfort between two women. Following the Restoration, we note the emergence of the explicit idea of female same-sex relations in the writings of women willing to appear publicly transgressive and not loathe to name or to play at transgression, as in Delarivière Manley's Cabal in *The New Atalantis* (1709) and in several of Aphra Behn's poems. This phenomenon seems to mark a major break with the past and a movement into new forms of erotic and sexual understanding.

The consequence of an accelerated dissemination of sexual knowledge about female same-sex relations in a variety of texts, then, created a coherent verbal construct and began to make possible a codification of certain behaviors as transgressive and as violations of social norms in a way both more concrete and far-reaching than could have been accomplished simply by an oral tradition.

We can recognize in the latter half of the seventeenth century a splitting off of discourses from each other, a divergence of the discourses that name transgressiveness from those that do not. For instance, in the sixteenth century the language and understanding of educated men who read Latin before the translation of reference works and the like into the European vernaculars clearly named female same-sex transgressive sexuality. Later, at the end of the seventeenth century, the language of women willing to be transgressive continued to name transgressiveness, albeit at times more coyly and covertly, as in the case of Manley. Throughout the seventeenth century, however, a middling sort of "respectable" women—who were becoming educated and for whom texts were being made available in the vernacular (though often bowdlerized)—would have wanted to retain their status and to gain patronage as poets; to do so, they used the eroticized and romantic discourses of a heterosexual pastoralism to describe relations and behaviors that might have been identified as transgressive.

Since I have been most concerned with the poetic expressions of same-sex erotics between women during the early modern period, I have argued that, insofar as poetry is a vehicle for the expression of impassioned feeling between literate Englishwomen, we can describe that poetry as an erotically charged communication of same-sex intimacy, yet an intimacy that often seems to reach beyond conventional notions of acceptability within, say, the context of friendship. In a number of instances, most notably that of Katherine Philips, there seems to exist sufficient biographical evidence to suggest that these poetic intimacies were genuinely felt representations of actual experience. The availability and the use of secondary, biographical materials in any attempt to speculate about what these women did or felt is critical. Nevertheless, such materials still do not tell us unambiguously how these women—intelligent, literate, educated, materially comfortable— might have regarded, or even named, themselves. It seems doubtful that they would have wanted to categorize themselves as the infamous tribades they might have been made aware of in translations of the classics or in other contemporary texts. Since their experience of a same-sex erotics would not have been congruent with then available definitions of tribadism as defined by transgressive behaviors, their experience would have remained unnamed and certainly unacknowledged in its possible transgression.

In order to account for the indications of same-sex erotics we encounter in women's literary productions, especially in their use of the conventions of heterosexual poetry and in their assertions of chaste love, we should first note that, within a context of patriarchal definitions of sexuality, female same-sex eroticism *is* chaste insofar as it does not emulate male penetrative behavior—that is, insofar as it does not involve the use of phallic prostheses or preternaturally enlarged clitorises. This is an idea very much at variance with modern understandings, both secular and religious, of "chastity"; nevertheless, there is reason to believe that this indeed was the case during the early modern period and before in Europe, as it continues today to be a prevailing notion about female sexuality in many non-Western cultures.[23] "Respectable" women, as the writers we deal with generally regarded themselves, were likely to have looked on tribades (if they had heard of such women) as exotic, transgressive, and very much removed from themselves and their own understandings of their behaviors. If, as a function of their impassioned feelings for each other, they happened also to explore each other's bodies, they were not likely to have *named* their behaviors using a language then understood as sexual. For example, manual stimulation, oral contact (cunnilingus), and other erotic expressions need not be, and often are not, considered sexual in contexts defined by a masculinist sexual paradigm. Women may have been able to retain their respectability by living in conformity with prevailing social constructs that demanded marriage and children while giving expression to their feelings for other women through the conventions of "chaste" romantic friendships, especially by the eighteenth century. The literary shape taken by a same-sex erotics between women was most frequently a poetic one, though it is being increasingly recognized that the prose literature of female community produced by women during the late seventeenth and eighteenth centuries is rich with erotic subtexts. Recent studies of Jane Barker's *A Patch-Work Screen for the Ladies* (1723) and Sarah Scott's *Millenium Hall* (1762) draw attention to the ways in which a female same-sex erotics was coming to be constructed and expressed through literary representations of accepted structures of celibacy, contemplation, and female community, even before the later-eighteenth-century formulation of romantic friendship.[24] The real tensions seem to me to have occurred when the romantic attachments of friends came into conflict with the demands of social conformity, as they did in the famous case of the 1778 elopement of Eleanor Butler and Sarah Ponsonby, the Ladies of Llangollen, before they settled down into a chastely coupled kind of respectability.[25]

Reconstructing an accurate and adequately nuanced history of female same-sex erotics in early modern England requires the dismantling of our binary understanding of sexuality and the disruption of our genitally inflected notions of eroticism.[26] Until now, attempts to create "cultural narratives" of lesbianism—attempts, that is, to establish a historical "tradition" of lesbian identity by lesbian literary critics—have tended to reinscribe contemporary paradigms by reading earlier literature, for the most part that of the eighteenth and nineteenth centuries, through the lens of the identity politics of the last quarter of the twentieth century. My own vantage point with respect to this critical tendency is aptly summarized by Sally O'Driscoll, who, in a recent essay, writes that it is impossible to posit "a transhistorical or transcultural Lesbian Self" and that, despite an awareness of lesbian erotic practice, "evidence [before 1900] of what would now be termed lesbian sexual acts did not produce the equivalent of a twentieth-century lesbian identity."[27] My project extends backward into the earlier periods in England the assumptions of O'Driscoll's "outlaw reading" of Eliza Haywood's mid-eighteenth-century novel *La Belle Assemblée*.

Critics trying to establish a historical "tradition" of lesbian identity often reveal through their vocabularies the difficulties implicit in their efforts. For example, rather than problematize the notion of "lesbian" itself, at least one literary critic not wanting actually to attribute lesbianism to literary work in an earlier period has used the phrase *lesbian-like*[28] to describe behavior and identity that seem to be recognizable or familiar to a twentieth-century reader. Another critic, taking her cue from the use of "protofeminist," describes as "protolesbian" identities we believe we recognize.[29] This precarious precipice of neologisms is generated by the powerful desire to discover the antecedents of current paradigms. Anna Clark's conclusions about the early-nineteenth-century erotic life of Anne Lister with other women exemplifies the conflation of scholarly analysis with modern identity politics and with the continuing vigor of 1970s ideas of "woman-identified women":

> Anne Lister was not able to create a lesbian network, let alone a subculture, because of her chronic concealment, and duplicity tangled her love relationships into webs of deceit and competition. Romanticism justified her lesbianism as part of her nature, but its focus on the unique individual also hampered her ability to support other lesbians. Meeting the masculine and learned Miss Pickford helped Anne realize that there were other women such as herself in the world, but her scornful treatment of her friend prevented them from developing more solidarity.[30]

Notions of network, support, and solidarity operate here to evoke modern lesbian-feminist paradigms of "community" and thus to create normative expectations for the past. Elaine Hobby, like Clark and others, uses an unproblematized *lesbian* in her description of Katherine Philips and remarks that "the lesbian community then, as now, had its divisions,"[31] revealing that an unexamined and certainly misleading assumption is the foundation of her otherwise more nuanced historical understanding. In effect, a terminology that is not problematized back-projects the relatively recent notion of lesbian identity.[32]

Gesturing toward an unambiguous history with which modern individuals can identify, lesbian academics have too often replicated what Jennifer Terry has described as "the 'hidden from history' model which launched the field of women's history in its early days."[33] In *The Apparitional Lesbian* Terry Castle marshals an explicit rationale for the essentialism that drives efforts to recover lesbian cultural narratives. Her arguments for a pre-1900 "libidinal self-awareness" and her efforts to "'recarnalize' matters" outside the fashionable parameters of queer theory and the new postmodern paradigms bring a certain panache, not to mention seductiveness, to essentialist readings:

> And indeed, I still maintain, if in ordinary speech I say, "I am a lesbian," the meaning is instantly (even dangerously) clear: I am a woman whose primary emotional and erotic allegiance is to my own sex. Usage both confers and delimits meaning: the word is part of a "language game," as Wittgenstein might say, in which we all know the rules.[34]

But it hardly resolves the problems of historical, social, or geographical particularity either in the present or before 1850.

This approach, usually less eloquently articulated, appears to serve the interests of lesbigay rights agendas but eventually undermines them by not providing a more nuanced view of the past. Lesbians especially have been vulnerable to the intellectual simplifications of identity politics since Adrienne Rich's "lesbian continuum" posited a de-eroticized lesbian identity that supplied cultural feminism with an intellectual framework.[35] "Queer theory,"[36] on the other hand, has tended to elide the particularities of identity politics under an umbrella term that purports to include practices that transgress heteronormativity, but, while queer theory may seem to argue for the social constructedness of the broad spectrum of variant sexualities and genders, it does not usually take into account the complex historical situatedness and evolution of ideas about the body and sexuality before about 1850.[37] If, then, we are to arrive at a nuanced reconstruction of our antecedents, the dual projects of *theorizing* the historical nature and understandings of female same-sex relations and of *recovering* historical materials that address the existence of female same-sex erotics must proceed in tandem, and they must do so with a clear sense of the problems inherent in current theories that cannot accommodate the particulars of a historicized understanding.

Until recently, Lillian Faderman's pathbreaking 1981 study, *Surpassing the Love of Men,* set the evasive tone for the critical work that followed. Her discussions of Montaigne's idealized views of friendship in the *Apology to Raymond Sebond* and of the poetry of Katherine Philips are good examples of readings that strain to ignore or to redefine the erotics of particular texts and to expunge from them any hints of corporeality.[38] Although lesbian scholars, grateful to Faderman for having introduced the subject of female same-sex erotics before 1800, now have been correcting and complicating her perspective, a number of heterosexual critics (both female and feminist) have perpetuated Faderman's reluctance to affirm the presence of a nonnormative female same-sex erotics. The remarks of the editors of one anthology of early women poets that Katherine Philips "is chiefly important for her exaltation of Platonic friendship between women" and that "some of her champions choose to ignore her own stipulation that such friendship be free from carnal interest"[39] gloss over both the traditionally multivalent implications of the Renaissance rhetoric of friendship and the complexities of defining carnality during the early modern period.

Much of the textual material about female same-sex behaviors that was eventually available in England was Continental because these behaviors were more generally known, prosecuted, and openly named earlier on the Continent than they were in England.[40] Because many instances of same-sex sexual transgression mentioned and repeated in these early modern textual sources (including prosecutorial records) concern women who cross-dressed or lived what we might understand as transgendered lives, recent scholars sometimes have conflated the issue of same-sex eroticism with issues of transvestism. But, despite the perceived identity between sexuality and gender roles raised by cross-dressed persons during the early modern period, the actual occurrence of a connection between transgressive sexuality and gender role seems not to have been usual and is misleading as an index of sexual behavior. Instances of transvestism, because they do not necessarily involve motives for erotic transgression, prove to be a blind alley for the recovery of early modern constructions of female sexuality in England.[41] Further, an emphasis on cross-dressing women tends to focus on the liminal and the grotesque, on the socially marginal, thereby valorizing the exception insofar as it places the marginal at the center and refocuses concern away from the majority or the general run of women. The continuities and complexly signifying practices of other more generally sanctioned social forms, particularly those of female friendship, are thus obscured, and the perhaps more common indications of female same-sex erotics are overlooked.

Additional possibilities of how same-sex eroticism might have been enacted in the larger context of social conformity and class distinction need to be considered. The complex interplay between individual behavior and social demand that takes place as women negotiate their relations with each other in the environments of patriarchy demands more scholarly attention. How women poets of the sixteenth, seventeenth, and even eighteenth centuries gave their feelings for each other verbal form is an expression of their cultural embeddedness in historically variable understandings and definitions of erotic behavior and in the almost certain probability that those understandings and definitions were not uniform throughout English society but varied according to social class (e.g., aristocratic vs. gentry vs. middling vs. laboring classes) and geographic location (e.g., urban vs. rural). Certain behaviors, both physical and verbal, that may seem to us similar to what we are accustomed to defining as lesbian may have been a tacitly accepted cultural element in certain segments of society, especially before the introduction of a Latinate sexual terminology by anatomy and medical texts, as well as by translations of the classics, in the late sixteenth century, and may not necessarily have been recognized as transgressive.[42]

I have already explored some of the implications of this theoretical perspective in my work on Katherine Philips and other women writers of this period. I believe that, while it may be impossible to know for certain what these women actually "did" physically, it is important to recognize their erotic uses of conventional heterosexual rhetoric in their addresses to each other and to acknowledge the possibilities for erotic behaviors that they may not have recognized or named as sexual and which may have motivated their poetic expressions of passion for each other. It is in the context of these understandings that we can discuss the nature of the erotic friendship poetry by women in the sixteenth, seventeenth, and eighteenth centuries and recognize the ways in which it develops a kind of shadowed language of erotic ellipsis to express a possibly transgressive content. This process of an erotics of unnaming has already been noted many times in twentieth-century lesbian writing, both in poetry and prose, a primary example being the coded erotic writing of Gertrude Stein. We might want to acknowledge that the elliptical expression of erotic feeling in women's writing may, as a tradition, begin in English in the early modern period just before the Restoration—and long before any construction of a lesbian identity as we know it—with the friendship poems of Katherine Philips.

The dissonance between the fixed categories according to which Western cultures increasingly seem to have defined sexual relations and the fluidity of the erotic desires and understandings experienced by individuals must be continually kept in mind in our attempts to recover the constructions of earlier historical moments. Once individuals become conscious of sexual possibilities in arenas not previously named, avenues become available for the demarcation of cognitive and sexual boundaries, and a policing, and silencing, of sexual borderlands becomes possible. In early modern England a silencing of the relations between women had not yet taken place because the sexual borderlands demarcating transgression had yet to be defined.

NOTES

1. Though class status is invoked here to focus on women of a particular social position, I have purposely avoided problematizing ideas of class in themselves. Instead, I have chosen to reinscribe the language and understanding of social position likely to have been operative for the subjects of my study. The intent of this rhetorical strategy is to sustain the focus of this essay on early modern understandings of status and behavior. In using the "language of 'sorts' of people," I follow the work of Keith Wrightson in questioning the classical hierarchy of social order customarily accepted by students of the early modern period: "in the later sixteenth century the English elaborated an alternative vocabulary of social description which reveals a world of social meanings untapped by the formal social classifications of literary convention, and . . . this language of 'sorts' of people was ubiquitous in late

Elizabethan and early Stuart England" (36). See Wrightson, "'Sorts of People' in Tudor and Stuart England," in *The Middling Sort of People: Culture, Society and Politics in England, 1550–1800,* ed. Jonathan Barry and Christopher Brooks (New York: St. Martin's Press, 1994), 28–51.

2. Catherine Belsey, *The Subject of Tragedy: Identity and Difference in Renaissance Drama* (London and New York: Metheun, 1985), 33–34. See also John Lyons on the possible connections between the popularity of Venetian mirrors and the great number of self-portraits during the sixteenth century; though there is not "a comparable growth of self-portraiture in prose literature" (69), there is, as Belsey demonstrates, a perhaps commensurate display of interiority in the dramatic soliloquies of Shakespeare and his contemporaries. See Lyons, *The Invention of the Self: The Hinge of Consciousness in the Eighteenth Century* (Carbondale: Southern Illinois University Press, 1978).

3. Charles Taylor, *Sources of the Self: The Making of the Modern Identity* (Cambridge: Harvard University Press, 1989), 36; see also 528n. 12; and Regenia Gagnier, *Subjectivities: A History of Self-Representation in Britain, 1832–1920* (New York and Oxford: Oxford University Press, 1991), 11.

4. Katharine Park provides a detailed analysis of the interdependency of ideas about hermaphrodites and tribadism in early modern France in "The Rediscovery of the Clitoris: French Medicine and the Tribade, 1570–1620," in *The Body in Parts: Fantasies of Corporeality in Early Modern Europe,* ed. Carla Mazzio and David Hillman (New York: Routledge, 1997), 171–93. Patricia Simons furnishes evidence of the presence of *donna con donna* in the paintings of Renaissance Italy in her essay, "Lesbian (In)visibility in Italian Renaissance Culture: Diana and Other Cases of *Donna con Donna,*" *Journal of Homosexuality* 27.1–2 (1994): 81–122. Valerie Traub pursues the dissemination of the Ovidian myth of Callisto as a transgeographical phenomenon in Europe but does not focus on problems of historicity in the case of England in "The Perversion of 'Lesbian' Desire," *History Workshop Journal* 41 (1996): 23–49. For a synopsis of this scholarship about female same-sex relations in early modern Europe, see also Harriette Andreadis, "Workshop Summary of Early Modern 'Lesbianisms': History, Theory, Representation," in *Attending to Early Modern Women,* ed. Susan Dwyer Amussen (Newark: University of Delaware Press, 1998), 96–98.

5. Terry Castle lists "a whole slangy mob" of words that have "always" been available "for pointing to (or taking aim at) the lover of women." See Castle, *The Apparitional Lesbian: Female Homosexuality and Modern Culture* (New York: Columbia University Press, 1993), esp. 9. Rictor Norton and Randolph Trumbach give accounts of the various names used to describe same-sex female transgressors in eighteenth-century England. See Norton, *Mother Clap's Molly House: The Gay Subculture in England, 1700–1830* (London: GMP Publishers, 1992), esp. 232–47; and Trumbach, "London's Sapphists: From Three Sexes to Four Genders in the Making of Modern Culture," in *Third Sex, Third Gender: Beyond Sexual Dimorphism in Culture and History,* ed. Gilbert Herdt (New York: Zone Books, 1994), esp. 111–21. Theo Van der Meer provides this information for the Netherlands in

"Tribades on Trial: Female Same-Sex Offenders in Late Eighteenth-Century Amsterdam," in *Forbidden History: The State, Society, and the Regulation of Sexuality in Modern Europe,* ed. John C. Fout (Chicago: University of Chicago Press, 1992), esp. 203.

6. The "projection of sexual irregularity onto the exoticized bodies of women of another race and continent was a familiar trope in early modern European topographical literature" (Park, "Rediscovery," 172–73). Valerie Traub makes a similar point about exoticism and travel narratives, especially Nicholas de Nicholay's *Navigations into Turkie* (1585) and Ogier Ghiselin de Busbecq's (or Busbequius's) "Turkish Letters" (85–89). Busbequius's *Travels into Turkey,* initially published in Latin in 1589 and reprinted many times in various languages into the nineteenth century, was first "Englished" in a London edition in 1694 and was commonly cited in conjunction with female same-sex relations. See Traub, "The Psychomorphology of the Clitoris," *GLQ: A Journal of Lesbian and Gay Studies* 2.1–2 (1995): 81–113.

7. Quoted in Kate Aughterson, ed., *Renaissance Woman: A Sourcebook* (New York: Routledge, 1995), 129.

8. See Harriette Andreadis, "Sappho in Early Modern England: A Study in Sexual Reputation," in *Re-Reading Sappho: Reception and Transmission,* ed. Ellen Greene (Berkeley: University of California Press, 1997), 105–21.

9. *Satan's Harvest Home* (London, 1749) 18 [sig. D1ᵛ]. Norton, *Mother Clap's,* 233, also cites this passage. See Andreadis, "Sappho," for descriptions of Sappho in early modern editions of her poetry and in medical, anatomical, and other contemporary texts that mention her.

10. Norton, *Mother Clap's,* 232–47, reviews the evidence for these locutions in chapter 15, "Tommies and the Game of Flats." That this vocabulary was common has yet to be confirmed by textual examples in addition to the unique instances now known. It is of course always also possible that these vernacular usages rarely made their way into surviving texts and that the absence of additional instances might not negate their existence as common discursive currency, at least within certain social circles probably not of the better sort.

11. Alan Bray and Randolph Trumbach have provided the now-standard analyses of an emergent male subculture. See Bray, *Homosexuality in Renaissance England* (London: Gay Men's Press, 1982); and "Homosexuality and the Signs of Male Friendship in Elizabethan England," in *Queering the Renaissance,* ed. Jonathan Goldberg (Durham: Duke University Press, 1994), 40–61; and Trumbach, "London's Sapphists" and "Sex, Gender, and Sexual Identity in Modern Culture: Male Sodomy and Female Prostitution in Enlightenment London," in *Forbidden History: The State, Society, and the Regulation of Sexuality in Modern Europe,* ed. John C. Fout (Chicago: University of Chicago Press, 1994), 89–106.

12. See Bernadette Brooten, *Love between Women: Early Christian Responses to Female Homoeroticism* (Chicago: University of Chicago Press, 1996), esp. intro. (1–28) and "Part One: Female Homoeroticism in the Roman World: The Cultural Context of Early Christianity" (29–188). Brooten's analysis is a powerful and careful corrective to the work of the late John Boswell, which virtually ignored women

in its emphasis on male homosexuality, and to Judith Brown's work, whose under-theorized assumptions about the nature of "lesbian" behaviors was for a long time the only available study of female homoeroticism in this period. See Boswell, *Christianity, Social Tolerance, and Homosexuality: Gay People in Western Europe from the Beginning of the Christian Era to the Fourteenth Century* (Chicago: University of Chicago Press, 1980); and Brown, *Immodest Acts: The Life of a Lesbian Nun in Renaissance Italy* (Oxford: Oxford University Press, 1986).

13. Andreadis, "Sappho," illustrates this process by analyzing representations of the contemporary reputation of Sappho.

14. For a sustained and rigorously elaborated essentialist perspective, see Castle, *Apparitional Lesbian*, 1–20.

15. See Helena Whitbread, ed., *I Know My Own Heart* (New York: New York University Press, 1992); and Jill Liddington, "Anne Lister of Shibden Hall, Halifax (1791–1840): Her Diaries and the Historians," *History Workshop: A Journal of Socialist and Feminist Historians* 35 (1993): 45–77.

16. Anna Clark, "Anne Lister's Construction of Lesbian Identity," *Journal of the History of Sexuality* 7.1 (1996): 23–50, esp. 27.

17. Bray comments on the "cleavage . . . between an individual's behaviour and his awareness of its significance" (*Homosexuality,* 68); see also Bray, "Homosexuality and the Signs of Male Friendship," for a later refinement of his views.

18. Carolyn Woodward, "'My Heart So Wrapt': Lesbian Disruptions in Eighteenth-Century Fiction," *Signs* 18.4 (1993): 845.

19. Martha Vicinus describes the "raves" of Victorian schoolgirls. These appear to have been a way of defining and isolating female same-sex relations to adolescence and to boarding schools. See Vicinus, "Distance and Desire: English Boarding School Friendships," *Signs* 9.4 (1984): 600–622.

20. I include in "visible subcultures" groups tacitly acknowledged by a dominant culture as part of its purpose in containing and marginalizing nonnormative relations. So, for instance, molly houses served to locate and to contain "sodomites."

21. Michael McKeon, "Historicizing Patriarchy: The Emergence of Gender Difference in England, 1660–1760," *Eighteenth-Century Studies* 28.3 (1995): 300.

22. McKeon, "Historicizing Patriarchy," 296 and 300. He provides in this essay a useful survey of the recent literature on the molly subculture and its distinction from "precedent sodomitical activity" (307); see especially his review of the work of Bray and Trumbach (307–12; 319n. 47–50; 320n. 55).

23. [K. Limakatso] Kendall, for instance, has found that this is the case in modern Lesotho. See "Looking for Lesbians in Lesotho: Homophobia Is a White Devil's Disease" (MS, 1995).

24. On the erotically charged language of women's poetry, see Harriette Andreadis, "The Erotics of Female Friendship in Early Modern England," in *Women's Alliances in Early Modern England,* ed. Karen Robertson and Susan Frye (Oxford: Oxford University Press, 1999), 241–58. See also Kathryn R. King on Barker in her essay "The Unaccountable Wife and Other Tales of Female Desire in Jane Barker's *A Patchwork Screen for the Ladies,*" *Eighteenth Century* 35.2 (1994):

155–72; and on Scott, George E. Haggerty, " 'Romantic Friendship' and Patriarchal Narrative in Sarah Scott's *Millenium Hall,*" *Genders* 13 (1992): 108–22.

25. Elizabeth Mavor's account of their life together continues to be standard. See Mavor, *The Ladies of Llangollen: A Study in Romantic Friendship* (London: Penguin, 1973).

26. The work of Thomas Laqueur, though contested, has brought considerable attention to the fact that early modern constructions of the body and of sexuality do not conform to the binary system of male/female prevalent since the rise of modern science in the West. See Laqueur, " 'Amor Veneris, vel Dulcedo Appeletur,' " in *Fragments for a History of the Human Body,* ed. Michael Feher et al. (New York: Zone Books, 1989); and *Making Sex: Body and Gender from the Greeks to Freud* (Cambridge: Harvard University Press, 1990). For corrective commentary on Laqueur, see Katharine Park and Robert Nye, "Destiny Is Anatomy: Review of *Making Sex* by Thomas Laqueur," *New Republic,* Feb. 10, 1991, 53–57.

27. Sally O'Driscoll provides a neat summary of the theoretical stances on both sides of the identity categories debate and outlines the far-reaching implications of using modern categories to read earlier literatures. See O'Driscoll, "Outlaw Readings: Beyond Queer Theory," *Signs* 22.1 (1996): 37 and 43.

28. For the origination of this coinage, see Martha Vicinus, "Lesbian History: All Theory and No Facts or All Facts and No Theory," *Radical History Review* 60 (1994): 57–75.

29. See Deborah Meem, "Eliza Lynn Linton and the Rise of Lesbian Consciousness," *Journal of the History of Sexuality* 7.4 (1997): 537–60. At the same time that Meem says, "I use the term 'protolesbians' to refer to women of the late nineteenth century who would today be called lesbians" (537n. 4), she remarks that the novelist Eliza Lynn Linton "cannot name—no one could in 1880" (551) the identity of a female character whose erotic desire clearly is directed toward other women, despite the availability of the phrase "L'amour sapphique" in England as early as the 1870s (547). "Cannot name" might more productively be understood as "will not name," a mark of middle-class reluctance to name what is proscribed and hidden rather than an indication of the lack of names for female same-sex erotics before 1900.

30. Clark, "Anne Lister's Construction," 50. Despite her familiarity with current literature about language available to describe female same-sex relations during Lister's lifetime, Clark does not problematize *lesbian.*

31. Elaine Hobby, "Katherine Philips: Seventeenth-Century Lesbian Poet," in *What Lesbians Do in Books,* ed. Elaine Hobby and Chris White (London: Women's Press, 1991), 202. Emma Donoghue makes available a broad range of early modern literary materials that suggest the nature of same-sex erotics, yet she does not provide an adequately theorized context in which to place those materials or a problematized language through which to discuss them. See Donoghue, *Passions between Women: British Lesbian Culture, 1668–1801* (London: Scarlet Press, 1993). See also the review by Jonathan Brody Kramnick, "LGSN Review: The Lesbian Century," *LGSN: Lesbian and Gay Studies Newsletter* 22.2 (1995): 29–30.

32. The work of the late-nineteenth-century German sexologists Heinrich

Ulrichs and von Krafft-Ebing in systematizing a "scientific" understanding of a "third sex" is now well-known, along with the four part classification of the female "invert" by Krafft-Ebing that influenced Havelock Ellis. See Esther Newton's classic study of Radclyffe Hall's *The Well of Loneliness* for a description of the genesis of what was to become the modern lesbian identity ("The Mythic Mannish Lesbian: Radclyffe Hall and the New Woman" *Signs* 9 [1984]: 557–75).

33. Jennifer Terry, "Theorizing Deviant Historiography," in *Feminists Revision History,* ed. Ann-Louise Shapiro (New Brunswick: Rutgers University Press, 1994), 277.

34. Castle, "Apparitional Lesbian," 10, 11, and 15.

35. See Adrienne Rich, "Compulsory Heterosexuality and Lesbian Existence," *Signs* 5.4 (1980): 631–60.

36. I use quotes to draw attention to the fact that I wish to problematize the intellectual constructs described by "queer theory."

37. O'Driscoll, "Outlaw Readings," esp. 30–37, furnishes a useful analysis of queer theory.

38. See Lillian Faderman, *Surpassing the Love of Men: Romantic Friendship and Love between Women from the Renaissance to the Present* (New York: William Morrow, 1981), 65–73. I have summarized the debates about defining lesbian identity in another context (Andreadis, "The Sapphic-Platonics of Katherine Philips, 1632–1664," *Signs* 15.1 [1989]: 34–60, esp. 57ff., 57n. 50; 58nn. 51–52).

39. Germaine Greer et al., eds., *Kissing the Rod: An Anthology of Seventeenth-Century Women's Verse* (New York: Farrar, Straus and Giroux, 1989), 188. See also Merry Weisner's cautions against reading lesbianism in *Women and Gender in Early Modern Europe* (Cambridge: Cambridge University Press, 1993).

40. For example, see Theo Van der Meer, "Sodomy and the Pursuit of a Third Sex in the Early Modern Period," in *Third Sex, Third Gender: Beyond Sexual Dimorphism in Culture and History,* ed. Gilbert Herdt (New York: Zone Books, 1994), 137–88, particularly his accounts of sodomy, including female same-sex relations, in the Netherlands during the early modern period. Van der Meer, in "Tribades on Trial," also takes up the question of the prosecution of female same-sex offenders in late-eighteenth-century Amsterdam. See Katharine Park and Lorraine Daston's analysis of the complexities in sexual definition raised by the early modern French preoccupation with hermaphrodites, in "The Hermaphrodite and the Orders of Nature: Sexual Ambiguity in Early Modern France," *GLQ: A Journal of Lesbian and Gay Studies* 1.4 (1994): 419–38. See also Clark, "Anne Lister's Construction," esp. 26n. 14, which laments the lack of evidence for the existence of "lesbian networks or subcultures" in England, even as late as the late eighteenth and early nineteenth centuries; the situations in Paris or Amsterdam were of course quite different and subcultures were identifiable among otherwise marginalized women, that is, those who were not respectably attached to a male-dominated household (e.g., actresses, dancers, prostitutes).

41. Recent studies of transvestism during the early modern period can be found in Rudolf M. Dekker and Lotte C. Van de Pol, *The Tradition of Female Trans-*

vestism in Early Modern Europe (New York: St. Martin's Press, 1989); and in essays collected in Julia Epstein and Kristina Straub, eds., *Body Guards: The Cultural Politics of Gender Ambiguity* (New York: Routledge, 1991).

42. The anatomy texts of Ambroise Paré (1575) and Thomas Vicary (1548 and 1577), among others, were widely translated and disseminated throughout Europe. See Laqueur, "'Amor Veneris, vel Dulcedo Appeletur'"; Andreadis, "Sappho in Early Modern England"; and Park, "The Rediscovery of the Clitoris," for detailed analyses of the dissemination of Latinate sexual terminology and early modern understandings of female sexual pleasure.

The Game Girls of VNS Matrix
Challenging Gendered Identities in Cyberspace

Kay Schaffer

> We are the virus of a new world disorder
> Disrupting the symbolic from within
> VNS Matrix

Early in 1992 VNS Matrix released its "Cyberfeminist Manifesto for the 21st Century" to the world. The venue: Adelaide, South Australia—hardly a prominent city in worldwide, cyberculture terms. The format: a visually and textually arresting 6 × 18 foot billboard on a major, arterial road. The message: "the clitoris is a direct line to the matrix . . . VNS Matrix . . . mercenaries of slime . . . corrupting the symbolic from within . . . we make art with our kunst . . . we are the future" (fig. 3). In her book *Zeroes and Ones* Sadie Plant refers to the event as a nodal point for cyberfeminist activity, an extension of Donna Haraway's essay "A Cyborg Manifesto" of the 1980s (the essay, interestingly, also was first published in Adelaide).[1] The manifesto presaged the opening of VNS Matrix computer art installation All New Gen at the Experimental Art Foundation Gallery in Adelaide in 1993. The installation received national interest, critical acclaim, and wildly enthusiastic reviews.[2] Since the time of that modest, low-budget installation augmented versions of All New Gen have traveled around the world. The installation has been displayed at cybernetic art exhibitions, multimedia conferences, and international electronic media art shows, gathering devotees in its wake. Soon the prototype for an All New Gen CD-Rom interactive disc, entitled "Bad Code," will be released, affording new audiences further subversive pleasures, complements of All New Gen and her emergent matricicial creatix, in the VNS Matrix team.

This essay examines cyberfeminism's contributions to postmodern understandings of gendered bodies and gendered selves through an investi-

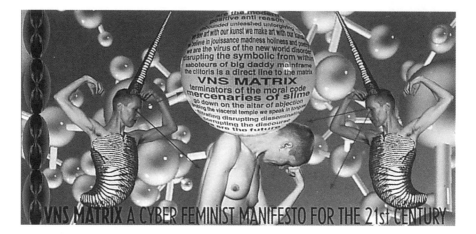

Fig. 3. VNS Matrix, "Cyberfeminist Manifesto for the 21st Century." (Courtesy of the artists.)

gation of the cyberfeminist artwork of VNS Matrix. The work of VNS Matrix conjoins an oppositional feminist politics with explorations of alternate sexual modalities and postmodern subjectivities. A growing number of postmodern feminist theorists couple these new forms of nongendered (or post-phallic) explorations with radical transformations within the social and cultural order. A number of feminist and queer theory contributors to the anthology *Sexy Bodies: The Strange Carnalities of Feminism,* for example, critically attend to transformations in culture effected through alternative modes of pleasure and desire. These alternate modes depend not on Freudian hierarchical models of sexuality but on feminine collaborative ones; on horizontal rather than vertical zones of desire; on a sexuality that assumes no a priori body. Contributors to *Sexy Bodies* explore the "perverse" undertones of carnality that might lead to new alliances and connections about and between bodies, desires, pleasures, and power.[3] The cyberart experiments of VNS Matrix are one such example. Are they, and others like them that proliferate in an ever-expanding cyber-community, capable of producing personal, social, and political transformations as these contemporary feminist and queer theorists suggest? What are their subversive elements? Are they capable of dismantling present forms of subjectivity and desire? To what extent might alternative modes of identity, subjectivity, sexuality, and politics offered within the realm of interactive technology lead to a transformation of social and cultural practices?

All New Gen: The Game

Welcome to the world of ALL NEW GEN: the radically transgressive, interactive computer game for non-specific genders.

Thank you for playing.

You are invited to join All New Gen and her DNA Sluts—the super powerful Patina de Panties, Dentata, and the Princess of Slime—in their battle against Big Daddy Mainframe and his technobimbo sidekicks—Circuit Boy, Streetfighter and other total dicks—whom you will encounter in the Contested Zone. This is a zone where gender is a shuffable six-letter word and power is no longer centered in a specific organization.

Rules of the Game:
All battles take place within the Contested Zone, a terrain of propaganda, subversion, and transgression. Your guides through the Contested Zone are the renegade DNA Sluts, abdicators from the oppressive superhero regime, who have joined All New Gen in her fight for data liberation.

The path of infiltration is treacherous and you will encounter many obstacles. The most wicked—Circuit Boy—a dangerous technobimbo, whose direct mindnet to Big Daddy renders him almost invincible.

You may not encounter All New Gen, as she has many disguises. But do not fear; she is always in the matrix, an omnipresent intelligence, anarcho cyber terrorist acting as a virus of the new world disorder.

You will be fuelled by G-slime. Please monitor your levels. Bonding with DNA Sluts will replenish your supplies.

Be prepared to question your biological construction.

There will be opportunities throughout the game for pleasurable distraction.

Be aware that there is no moral code in the Zone.

Enjoy[4]

Thus begins one's journey into All New Gen, an interactive computer artwork and multimedia installation piece produced by the Sydney-based VNS Matrix collective in 1993. Although the call to arms echoes the pitch of Gameboy computer games like Nintendo's popular Donkey Kong and Super Mario Brothers or Sega's Sonic the Hedgehog, this is no game for children. All New Gen mirrors the world of high-tech games but in an ironic and transgressive way. It has been designed for big (bad) girls who understand that the enemies, hazards, and obstacles they face mirror those of the high-tech, top-down world of contemporary, masculine technoculture.

Players of the game immerse themselves within a politics of resistance to that culture while at the same time exploring new forms of postmodern sexuality and subjectivity.

After logging on to All New Gen, the first question asked of game players is: "What is your gender? Male, Female, Neither." "Neither" is the correct answer, since clicking the Male or Female icon sends players spinning on a loop that takes them out of the game. Having taken up one's nonspecific gendered identity, players align themselves with ANG (All New Gen) and the DNA Sluts in the Contested Zone. Their aim is to "screw up" Big Daddy Mainframe, would-be Master of the World. ANG's mission, like that of her creatrix, the VNS Matrix collective, is to "hijack the toys from techno-cowboys and remap cyberculture with a feminist bent."[5] In this their approach is similar to other cyberfeminist projects, such as those of Sadie Plant, Linda Dement, Netchicks, and Geekgirls. But, unlike their techno-abled sisters, these girls blend technological skill with a keen sense of politics and a sophisticated grasp of feminist theory. The combination produces a unique inducement to ludic play that not only extends Donna Haraway's call for new cyber-forms of postmodern subjectivity but also retains her call for an oppositional politics.

In the cyber-art installation, in which the computer plays a central role, players are confronted with a complex interactive environment. The display space of the All New Gen includes light boxes, quick-time animations, wall-sized poster art, rows of telephones with lines connected to the All New Gen characters, and a Bonding Box. The Bonding Box affords players the physical pleasures of comfortable foam flooring, cushions, a serving tray, and a bottle of ("real" not virtual) sake, and computer access to the Matrix, where an erotic video plays, featuring female bonding in nonspecific gendered scenarios.

Players interact with the computer by clicking on icons that introduce them to a number of narratives, characters, settings, and scenarios. They can access multiple All New Gen technoworld narratives, which shift from the tight, hard, clipped feel of a Raymond Chandler thriller (*Beg, Bitch and Snatch were in a dark place, superbonding with some exotic tribal constructs. The feathers were flying*); to identity games infused with techno-babble (*She weeps tears of code. Her thoughts are classified. She has forgotten her password. She is corrupt*); to the feminine, erotic, free verse imaginings of Luce Irigaray (*Some Codekids had distributed a message over the Net: You must find your own bliss . . . jouissance is in the cunt of the beholder*).[6] Proceeding into the game, players move between their possible habitation in several environments. These include: the Patriarchal domain

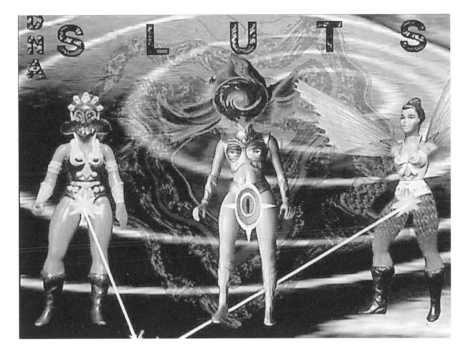

Fig. 4. VNS Matrix, "DNA Sluts." (Courtesy of the artists.)

of Big Daddy Mainframe; the Contested Zone (where the major action takes place); and the Matrix, home of ANG (the All New Gen, a nonlinear network of possibilities enmeshed in an omnipresent, intelligent mist). With their virtual partners, the DNA Sluts, players can visit the Alpha Bar, where Game Girls seduce the servile waiter-bimbots with promises of nonphallic erogenous pleasures, or they can replenish their own energy resources with G-slime by bonding with the fantastic DNA Sluts (fig. 4).

Stories, scenarios, and settings abound; sidetracks beckon. Players access phone lines where the rhetoric of technoculture meets the erotics of transgressive sexuality. Through phone lines to the Matrix, players call down the Oracle Snatch to help them detect and deactivate the drone clones of Circuit Boy; or enter the domain of the abstract, where the abject Mistress of Detestable Pleasures seduces Circuit Boy; or visit the Perfumed Garden, where "pulse poets beam their Stein lines over the ocean of messages"; or activate Gen's hostile mist and intelligent slime to "annihilate the transglobal fathernet of power and ambition" who is Big Daddy Mainframe. "Dirty work. For slimy girls."

Access:

> The name of the game is infiltration and re-mapping the possible futures outside the (chromo) phallic patriarchal code. . . . Now, with All New Gen in her role as a virus of the new world disorder, this code, like that of DNA, is interfered with and changed so that it just won't reproduce, or alternatively mutates in ways outside the binary oppositions of The Man.

The game engages players in a cheeky game of gender politics in the techno age as they, along with their countercultural cyborg-heroines, confront, with irony and tongue-in-cheek humor, a form of technologically generated, male-controlled, patriarchal politics of the late twentieth century. All New Gen invites players to take up postmodern subjectivities in which mind, body, memory, desire, and experience are combined to make possible new forms of narrative and representation, new intertextual subjectivities.

Since its inception the VNS Matrix team has toured a number of galleries and art spaces in Australia, Europe, the United States, Canada, and Japan with their multimedia installation. In 1994 Gen met with an enthusiastic audience at the International Symposium on Electronic Art in Helsinki, attracting an international cyber-art audience. In the wake of international acclaim VNS Matrix team secured an initial $100,000 grant from the Australian Film Commission to develop a prototype of an All New Gen CD-Rom game for international marketing and distribution. The New CD-Rom prototype, called Bad Code, is based on All New Gen but is enhanced with a number of sophisticated new images, 3D graphic spaces, animations, video sequences, characters, and zones. Beside these projects, members of the VNS Matrix collective operate on a number of sites on the World Wide Web. Their cyber-art experiments offer ever-expanding possibilities for imaginative, transgressive, transgendered, corporeal, libidinal, and intersubjective desires.

Background

All New Gen is the invention of VNS Matrix, a Sydney-based art collective whose members describe themselves as "cyberfeminists with attitude." Four Australian artists comprise the group: Virginia Barrett, Francesca da Rimini, Julieanne Pierce, and Josie Starrs. The two later members began some of their theoretical investigations in Adelaide while enrolled in a postgraduate women's studies course. I taught a subject in the course for which they produced a sophisticated, interactive, participatory assessment project based on readings from Lacanian psychoanalysis and French feminist theories, including Luce Irigaray's and Julia Kristeva's critiques of binary logics, sameness and difference, and investigations of the maternal body, abjection, *jouissance,* and feminine alterity. Their classroom project foreshadowed some of the inventions of the VNS Matrix collective.

The four visual artists formed a collective in 1992, united in their eclectic interests in photography, film, video, music, performance, writing, feminism, and cultural theory. They share an interest in exploring the possibilities for feminist art practice within cyberculture and enticing more girls and women into the world of cybernetics. According to the artists, "the impetus of the group is to investigate and decipher the narratives of domination and control which surround high technological culture, and explore the construction of social space, identity and sexuality in cyberspace."[7]

According to their Artists' Statement:

VNS Matrix are working primarily in the areas of computer-based technologies including graphics, animation, multimedia and, in future, virtual reality systems. Although these advanced systems hold the potential for the creation of entirely new forms of art and communication the cultural products arising from the use of new technologies are often conceptually barren. Form has rapidly become cliched as computer artists have focused on technical challenges rather than structural and conceptual possibilities such as the development of new forms of narrative and representation.

VNS Matrix believe that it is vitally important for new technologies to be used in a critical fashion, and that women have access to the production and consumption of these exciting new tools. VNS Matrix actively engages in the international cross-disciplinary debate surrounding technological development.[8]

The group takes its cues from Donna Haraway's "Manifesto for Cyborgs," utilizing computers and optical technologies to critique male-centered theories of the self. Specifically, the collective "reconstruct[s] a socialist-feminist politics . . . through theory and practice addressed to the social relations of science and technology, including crucially the systems of myth and meanings structuring our imaginations."[9] Their project seems to adopt Haraway's criteria, being "oppositional, utopian, and completely without innocence" while remaining "resolutely committed to partiality, irony, intimacy, and perversity."[10] French feminist theories of feminine desire also underlie the game girls' narratives, with particular reference to the theories of feminine alterity explored by Luce Irigaray and explorations of the Kristevan abject body as well as the Deleuzian imaginings of the body as desiring machine.

The name, VNS Matrix, carries within its signature elements from the discourses of myth, psychoanalysis, and French-influenced feminist theory, elements that register multiple and contradictory significations (*VNS*, a techno–code word, also pronounced "Venus" = the goddess of love, from the Greek, which also belongs to the word series *to venerate,* in Latin; and *Matrix* = referring to the womb in Latin, or *hystera* in Greek, with its multiple allusions to the maternal and women's bodies in myth, science, and psychoanalysis; the paranoid fantasies of men; and the generative space of feminine). The group's first work, the provocative billboard poster that announced their "cyberfeminist manifesto for the 21st century" (see fig. 3), proclaimed that "the clitoris is the direct line to the matrix . . . VNS Matrix." The billboard featured the upper torsos of three female forms, all of which displayed well-muscled arms and cropped hair. Two forms seemed to be mutating from their marinelike fossil base, their arms raised up into pseudo–iron man postures of power, their heads sprouting phallic unicorn horns borne out of popular images from science fiction fantasy. The figures signify both (and neither) masculine and feminine bodies; the products of earth, air, sky, water, and technology; aligned to the past, present, and future. The central figure, posed as an intertextual image that combines Rodin's Thinker with the Greek god Atlas, balances on her shoulders not the heavens but a celestial globe that carries the manifesto: "we are the virus of the new world disorder rupturing the symbolic from within . . . we are the future kunst." (The word *cunt* had to be altered to meet the objections of Adelaide censors.) The figures float in a dreamlike, surreal sea of mutating molecular forms. The left side of the poster features a series of vaginal cells, or cybercunts. The poster announces a new era in cyberfeminist art—one that comments ironically on masculine fantasies of domination from a new postmodern space of feminist revisioning. The poster offers a radical alternative to phallic desire. Here, as Steffensen suggests, "the 'cunt' signified scenarios are not deployed as sites for the production or reproduction of maternity or symbolically inscribed motherhood for women. They are redeployed as a site for the construction of libidinal pleasures: in sex, in horizontal rather than oedipal (vertical) relationships (i.e., collaborations), in technical production, in sexy technology—a feminized and feminist erotics of technocultural production and politics."[11]

The central Thinker/Atlas figure signals the VNS's propensity to mime and parody patriarchal myth. Students of Greek mythology will remember that Atlas was a recalcitrant Titan god who, in retribution for his inhospitality to Perseus, was shown the head of the Gorgon (or, in psychoanalytic terms, the female genitalia), whose gaze turned men into stone. He later took part in an unsuccessful war against Zeus and, as a result, was condemned to hold up the heavens. In the VNS Matrix billboard poster, the mutating feminized bodies register the contradictory elements of the Atlas myth: the god's resistance to and subversion of the patriarchal order and his threatened punishment—the masculine threat of castration. The difference in this emanation of the myth is that the Atlas figure is signified as feminine. The poster can be read from several gendered positions. From a masculine perspective the Atlas figure and its position within the VNS Matrix billboard manifesto invokes the fantasy of the phallic woman, or the monstrous power of the castrating Gorgon/Medusa, about to unleash a new world disorder. But the poster can also be read from a feminine perspective, that is, as a significant mythic revisioning of its Greek origins, one in which the full-breasted Atlas figure upholds the power of female sexuality. It is this power, the power of transgression, seduction, boundary crossing, and viral infiltration, that the All New Gens enact in order to disrupt and corrupt "Big Daddy Mainframe." The signifiers in the poster slide between masculine and feminine codings, registering "Woman" as both a threat to man (the realization of his worst fantasies) and also a conceptual space/Matrix of alterity for women *and men,* beyond phallocentric constructions.

The billboard poster, although situated within a Western Symbolic Order, is at the same time involved in a radical disruption of its sureties. It takes up Donna Haraway's call to exploit feminine otherness in order to transgress the boundaries of self and other within the contested zone of cybernetics. The manifesto announces VNS Matrix as a new voice of bad-girl feminism: "We make art with our cunt." The statement rejects the biological feminine and replaces it with new forms of cultural production. Zoë Sofoulis refers to this element in VNS Matrix as "sublimation"—the creation of a mythic feminine space, a matrix of an "omnipresent intelligence."[12] The space of desire organizes sexuality in a field other than that of the penis/phallus. The cyborg, the "illegitimate offspring of patriarchy," can be imagined as a postmodern mythological figure in a post-gendered, post-dualistic, and post-oedipal world: the world of the All New Gen.

Playing the Game

VNS Matrix engages players in a world of hybrid bodies, mutating forms with no fixed gendered identities and no fixed boundaries. In cybertalk these All New Gens are the illegitimate offspring of techno-man: unreliable and dangerous to Patriarchy. In the All New Gen game and installation the

DNA Sluts (or cyberterrorists) are named, in a playful parody of the fantasy of the phallic woman: Patina de Panties, Dentata, and the Princess of Slime. This trio act as the "mercenaries of slime." They represent, however, not Kristevan bodies of abjection but an Irigarian metaphorics of feminine alterity—a space conjured up by gaps in the narrative, holes in the social fabric. Their bodies call attention to the "slime" of eroticized female genitalia. The forms, rewritten for pleasure, are aestheticized, made abject, and turned into science fiction parodies simultaneously. They thrive on contradiction, assisting the players of the game to infiltrate and remap the future beyond patriarchal codes. The DNA Sluts guide the players through the Contested Zone of a gender politics styled by popular culture. Players refuel with G-slime when they bond with the DNA Sluts, slime that metaphorically lubricates the binary logic system in and beyond the game. Thus, the game reinvents the body, sexuality, and subjectivity beyond modernist visions.

> Instructions:
> Please monitor your levels. Bonding with the DNA Sluts will replenish your supplies. . . . Be prepared to question your gendered biological construction.

Within the Matrix there are no coded binaries of masculine/feminine. The "slime in the matrix" represents a fluid substance between liquid and gas. It slides within a feminine coded cyberspace of fluidity and mutation, an in-between world of new possibilities; a generative space of new feminist imaginings. As Sofoulis comments: "Horrific secret of the masculine sublime, slime can take on quite different connotations in female-centered myths. In proclaiming themselves 'mercenaries of slime,' VNS Matrix call attention to the phenomena of exchange, friction, lubrication, of traffic at the borders of categories, entities, and meaning systems."[13] Further, since "the clitoris is in direct line with the matrix," it appropriates the penis/phallus as a magical signifier of power and agency. The game constructs a feminine mythic space in opposition to that of Big Daddy Mainframe.

> Instructions:
> The path of infiltration is treacherous and you will encounter many obstacles. The most wicked is Circuit Boy—a dangerous techno-bimbo.

Circuit Boy is a cyberform with a detachable penis, a feminist parody of the sexy, techno/mechanical, fembot sidekicks of male science fiction fantasy (fig. 5). Read "otherwise," the cyborg figure becomes a clever digital enactment of the feminist theoretical question "penis/phallus—same difference?"[14] or: can the phallus as signifier ever be detached from the penis as referent? In this game the answer is definitely yes. As a sidekick, he is to Big

Fig. 5. VNS Matrix, "Big Daddy Mainframe and Circuit
Boy." (Courtesy of the artists.)

Daddy Mainframe what AT&T is to IBM and the military-industrial complex. His powers, however, are limited. It is the Matrix that is everywhere
and everything: an omnipresent mist of intelligence that hovers over,
around, and in the environment, threatening to infiltrate Big Daddy's
domain with the ultimate virus of a new world disorder. Circuit Boy's penis
transforms into a cellular phone that accesses the brain matter of the
Matrix, but only indirectly and with the intervention of the Cortex Crones.
He must first unscrew the phone / be detached from his penis. He has only
indirect and limited access, whereas the DNA Sluts, and players aligned
with them, have direct access to the Matrix. In addition, the Sluts are capable of independent action, whereas he must enlist the help of his Masters.
Players access the Matrix through phone lines or by bonding with the DNA
Sluts. The Matrix signifies a space of feminine alterity, a pre-oedipal, feminine sexual economy articulated beyond the Symbolic Order of language
and meaning.

The "click on" instructs players that:

> All New Gen and the DNA Sluts reveal and generate paths and mappings
> that not only work in the box, but take you beyond, into the frame, out of
> the frame, into words, into images, into new connections and allow you to
> wrap your arms around this world like radio in a web of the electronic
> and the erotic, where gender is a shuffable six letter word and power no
> longer centered in a specific organ-isation.

The game engages players in a perverse alliance between humans, machines,
and techno-organisms—into a world in which all become disloyal to (masculine) civilization.

The body here is more than the organic body, more than a textual construction. It becomes a screen onto which cultural fantasies, desires, fears,
anxieties, hopes, and utopias are projected. In a parody of cyberpunk and
chaos culture players in cyberfeminist space identify with the replicating
computer virus that is capable of infiltrating/infecting Big Daddy Mainframe (in opposition to the hacking metaphor of geek boy technological
intervention). They manipulate the body; they trade in slime. Participating
in fantasies of the fragmented body, they conjure up the blissful, the
grotesque, and the uncanny. Steffensen argues that "in VNS the matrix is re-
signified . . . as a pleasurable site for both the construction and practice of
an erotics of a female signified subject, and as a site of epistemological production and pleasure in that knowledge (informatics). . . . Within this
'futures' fantasmatic, the female subject(s) are represented as active agent(s)
of their own desires."[15]

Sadie Plant may have had them in mind when she wrote:

> Cyberpunk and chaos culture are peppered with wild women and bad girls,
> transgressions of organisation, the freaks and mutants who find their own
> languages, the non-members, the nomads, the sex that are not one; leftovers
> from history; those who have slipped past its filters too soon and accessed the
> future before its time, hybrid assemblages of what were once called human
> and machine on the run from their confinement to the world of man and
> things. Cyborgs are aliens, addicts and trippers who burn past security and
> through the ice of a culture devoted to spectacle, hacking the screens, and
> exceeding the familiar. Avatars of the matrix; downloading from cyberspace.
> They are no longer human. Perhaps they never were.[16]

Subversive Implications

Just how politically subversive can a game like All New Gen be? What are
the possibilities for and the limits of pleasure and subversion for players in

the inter(net)space of technology? Contemporary science fiction is replete with cyborgs—technological organisms that are both *and* neither human and machine. Traditionally the world of technology has been identified as a man's world, one in which he exercises his fantasies of control over cultural (re)production. But the theoretical work, performances, and writings of VNS, like that of Donna Haraway, Sadie Plant, Sandy Stone, Linda Dement, Zoë Sofoulis, and other cyberfeminists, urges new forms of cyberfeminist political engagement on the Net, forms that cyberfeminist artists like VNS Matrix turn into a playful, erotic politics within popular culture.

Linda Dement cogently comments that "the computer is the prized toy of our essentially male culture. To use technologies which are really intended for a clean slick commercial boy's world, to make personal, bodily, feminine work, and to re-inscribe this work into mainstream culture, into art discourse and into society, is a political act."[17] The "politics" to which Dement refers is one played out on the terrain of sameness and difference. Computer technology can engage its audience in this play. Within phallocratic imaginings Woman is the Other of Man. In a history of masculine narratives, women, nature, and technology stand in the place of the other, that which is passive, receptive, and under the control of masculine prerogatives. One thinks of Mary Shelley's *Frankenstein*, an investigation of the critical prototype of masculine desire: the desire to create and control human form through technology, to exert dominance over the biological processes of creation. The dream of Dr. Frankenstein, renamed and analyzed as a paranoid fantasy by Alice Jardine, is to liberate men from real women through reproductive technologies. Jardine suggests that these fantasies represent the last desperate attempt at the stage of nature's final exhaustion to drain the female human body of "the feminine."[18] She writes:

> technology always has been about the maternal body and it does seem to be about some kind of male phantasm, but, more, it perceives that the machine *is* a woman in that phantasm. According to this perception we need to find some access to this phantasm, and it seems that one of the few ways is through two particular kinds of discourses: myth and psychoanalysis.[19]

For her, feminine technoproduction through the reinvention of myth and psychoanalysis allows for a reconstruction of what it means to be female within the Symbolic Order of language.

Donna Haraway also reimagines feminine otherness with reference to technology. For her, technology is not the other of humanity but within technology otherness is brought home to coexist with the human. Technology encourages a denaturalization of the relationship between the body and cultural identity. Women can interact with technology in ways that confound humanist understandings of the unified self. Utilizing Haraway's framework, feminists can not only play a game of subversion with the unified self but also imagine new mythic spaces within which they can generate new myths, arts, and technologies.[20]

In her book *Life in the Screen: Identity in the Age of the Internet* Sherry Turkle describes the Internet as "a significant social laboratory for experimenting with the constructions and reconstructions of self that categorize postmodern life."[21] She aligns cybernetics with elements of postmodern life, including the precedence of surface over depth, of simulation over the real, of play over seriousness. Within technocultures one can image and imagine selves beyond modernist representations in which the Grand Narratives become simulacra, the unified self dissolves into fluidity, Truth gives way to situated knowledges, and multiple identities displace the search for origins.

For all of these writers, as well as their sister-practitioners on the Net, more is at stake here than the staging of new cultural myths. Cultural production is linked to a feminist politics of social and historical change. In 1987 Donna Haraway remarked, in the high feminist rhetoric of the time, that feminists must seize the tools of domination that construct the other and employ them in the service of radical revisionings: "Cyborg writing," she wrote, "is about the power to survive, not on the basis of original innocence, but on the basis of seizing the tools to mark the world that marked them as other."[22] Postmodern feminisms may be less concerned with "seizing the tools of power" than in exercising power in more strategic ways. But they remain committed to exploring reinventions of the body beyond its modernist constraints and to expanding the corporeal and libidinal possibilities of its pluralist forms. VNS Matrix aligns this exploration with a politics that directly confronts the masculine economic power of contemporary culture (Big Daddy Mainframe). The collective, through their electronic games and art practices, encourage viewers to ask not only who has control of technology (now that the girls have their hands on the tools) but how it is used, who controls it, and to what ends.

As feminists have discovered, cybernetics enables the formation of new subjectivities, of hybrid selves beyond the binary dualisms of a phallocratic culture. Within utopian versions/visions of cyberfeminism, of which the VNS Matrix posters, installations, and computer games form a part, the postmodern self can be imagined and encountered as plural and fluid. Within this techno-field, gender identifications, oedipal narratives, phallic fictions, the mind/body, nature/culture split, even the boundaries of the body can be transgressed.

Computer-generated technology, like that of All New Gen, makes possible the (virtual) realization of what Luce Irigaray calls a feminine alterity. Irigaray rehearses some of the elements of that alterity, elements that can be detected in the cyberfeminist world of the All New Gens. They include:

the construction of a feminine sexual economy, rearticulated through the Imaginary and Symbolic Order, including myths and fantasies within them;

a space of feminist imagining beyond phallocentric constraints;

the end of linear narratives and readings, not only in theory but also in practice through intertextuality (read hypertextuality);

a multiplicity of possibilities for subjectivity and post-phallic formations;

the conceptualization of a maternal genealogy, symbolizing contiguous and non-hierarchical social relationships modeled after the relationships between mothers and daughters;

a different sort of social organization based in a non-market economy;

and an alterity in which the feminine is aligned with the Maternal body, with jouissance, plurality, fluidity, and tactility: a boundless body of fluids, a body of prolific orgasmic energies, of orgasmic jouissance.[23]

For postmodern feminists like VNS Matrix, cybernetic worlds imagine Irigaray's alterity, where "woman" is reformulated through narratives and representations within a new Symbolic Order inspired by cyberspace. Utilization of the new technologies enables artists and players to engage in feminine mythic and technologically inspired spaces and struggles. New alignments and engagements follow matricicial patterns of connections where collaborations are encouraged. Cyborg bodies escape the visceral, libidinal investments of phallocratic desire. Cyberspace alters aesthetic sensibilities and offers new pleasures in a world where identities/sexualities are fluid, plural, and playful.

Many feminist theories believe that new forms of narrative and visual creation and new cultural productions of post-oedipal bodies, desires, and erotics have the potential to alter radically sexual and political practices. Catherine Waldby, one of the contributors to *Sexy Bodies*, posits an intimate relationship between fantasy, erotic practice, and the imaginary anatomy of the sexed body that, she argues, can bring about a transformation in cultural practices. She considers sexual fantasies as resources for renegotiating power relationships between men and women, male and female bodies.[24] She begins her article by analyzing how the erotics of heterosexual desire within Western phallocentric economies depend on masculine dominance, ownership of the phallus, bounded impermeable bodies, and violence against women juxtaposed against feminine subordination, lack/castration, permeable and receptive bodies, and receptivity to violence. Given this, she concludes:

> Perhaps feminism needs to develop something like a pornographic imagination in relation to masculine bodies, and bodies in general. By this I mean that it should allow itself to think through and in pleasure, in order to develop ways of fantasizing erotic surfaces and orifices, of relations between organs and parts, that depart from the monotonous imagos described earlier.[25]

Waldby considers a transgressive but familiar pornographic fantasy that defies the dominant heterosexual norm: the fantasy of the receptive heterosexual masculine body, one desirous of a receptive anal eroticism in partnership with a dominant phallic female partner. Waldby posits that such a fantasy imagines the female body imago as one not marked by castration, that is, one that severs the "natural" relation between the penis/phallus, but as one in possession of the phallus. Within the fantasy the phallus is a transferable property.

One of the scenarios in All New Gen offers such a male receptive fantasy. It is enacted in the Alpha Bar, where Dentata de Panties begins a seduction with Circuit Boy (fig. 6). She sings a Siren Song, teasing him into a seduction that involves a transgression of his bodily boundaries. She proposes a "butt fuck." He is an easy seduction. *Their boundaries merged forming new objects. She mapped his changing parameters, calculating the pleasure options. She was object-oriented desire to his subject. It was in this way that Circuit Boy learnt the rewards of willing submission* ("The Triple Temptation of Circuit Boy").[26] This scenario provides an alternative seductive fantasy for heterosexual men and women. It moves normative heterosexual desire beyond the stereotypical images of homosexual deviance. Here the VNS team present the receptive, desiring man and the phallic, sexually active woman to lure both male and female players with the temptations of a "perverse" (but not uncommonly imagined) pleasure. The game is replete with such scenarios. One is reminded of the requirement that all players bond with the DNA Sluts to refuel their G-Slime. This engagement, contrary to Freudian psychoanalytic principles, participates in a refusal to relinquish the pre-oedipal bond with the Mother/Matrix and also to imagine the abject feminine body as a body of pleasure. Similarly, the quite visibly feminine but

Fig. 6. VNS Matrix, "Dentata's Battle With Circuit Boy."
(Courtesy of the artists.)

phallic bodies of the DNA Sluts, Dentata, Patina de Panties, and the Princess of Slime, transgress the Freudian boundaries of normative sexuality and the attendant feminine body imago (see fig. 4). VNS Matrix challenges all forms of normative sexuality: it brings out the worst fantasies of a conservative, economic rationalist culture—the monstrous feminine of masculine fantasy; the phallic, desiring and desired female; the castratrice; and the receptive, submissive male—and transforms them. Their scenarios provide alternative possibilities for feminine erotic power and pleasure.

A number of VNS narratives and cyber-artworks engage with "the sexual" in ways suggestive of the erotics of Deleuze and Guattari. For example, they experiment with the principle of horizontal proliferation, of bodies as "desiring machines," and "bodies without organs" as opposed to the oedipal dynamics of hierarchical sexual and political relations. The scenarios refuse a theory of desire founded on lack. In the world of All New Gen desire is always positive and in movement. Narratives flow and break off across circuits and surfaces of desire. Neither homosexual nor straight, the scenarios occupy a third space of erotic relations. Sometimes they engage in cheeky confrontations with Freudian theory and its fears of the phallic woman, the abject body, and the like. But at other times, and in other zones of pleasure, narratives enact scenarios of Deleuzian delight. They connect bodies and machines to energies and intensities of feeling without predetermined erotogenic zones. They give rise to new forms of sexual desire.

At the end of the All New Gen installation players encounter the Bonding Booth (complete with cushions and sake), where they can link directly into networks within the Matrix, "a clitorally activated zone." The bonding booth's computer, in addition to providing a nonphallic, ungendered erotic video, enables players to create their own characters, environments, scenarios, and stories. The computer program stores, accumulates, and updates an inventory of the players' contributions, which then travel to new sites with the installation. Four nonspecific gendered, postphallic narratives, prepared by the VNS team, are available to stimulate the user's imagination. VNS rewards players' initiative by offering the possibility of unending, virtual life through the ongoing proliferation of (their) stories. Through these multiple dimensions of the game VNS Matrix articulates alternative forms of desire in the realm of public culture. In this VNS extends the erotic imaginary of theoretical feminism, providing one of Waldby's necessary resources of perversity and fantasy.

All New Gen might be defined as a "postphallic formation" in a number of ways:

it is a collaborative effort in which four women form a creative matrix to bring about new narratives, images, and representations;

those representations disrupt the modernist sureties about masculinity and femininity and the boundaries between them;

they require new linguistic codes—mutations—and new forms of text/body/technology;

they reimage/reimagine the cultural boundaries between the natural, the human, and the technological;

they give rise to new myths and new imaginings for postphallic bodies;

they invent new strategies of subversion;

they invite intersubjective interaction with new technological and intertextual bodies that presage new forms of sexuality, subjectivity, and desire;

they enable players to partake of "perverse" fantasies beyond the embodied understandings and bodily unities underwritten by psychoanalysis, patriarchal ideologies, and representations;

and their subversions take place within the largest possible political realm, Big Daddy's "transglobal fathernet of power and ambition."

The virtual space of All New Gen proliferates these possibilities endlessly.

Big claims for a computer game. Despite these new directions in theory and imaginary practice, critics of VNS Matrix question the degree to which the game is subversive to present power relations. Thom Corcoran differs from the utopian view, positing that in its plot of the All New Gen against Big Daddy Mainframe the game mirrors the operation of power and knowledge that cyberfeminism seeks to dismantle.[27] He argues that the game (at least in its initial formation) does little more than reverse the roles, giving female players access to masculine positions of power. Similarly, problems arise in the claim that the game allows players to construct a postmodern subjectivity in the "Contested Zone" where players are encouraged to question their gendered biological and cultural constructions. He claims that the game both invents a mythic, intertextual body and presents a number of scenarios that consist of fairly classic sex-role reversals. And in the final analysis All New Gen *is a game*—an experience to be encountered in the rarefied space of an experimental art gallery or on a number of websites. It does not engage the larger body politic. This perspective argues that the All New Gen project is both complicit with and subversive to present power relations at the same time.

Julieanne Pierce, one of the VNS members, agrees that the prototype developed for All New Gen in 1993 partially relied on a sex-role reversal strategy. Since that time the group has become more sophisticated in its thinking about characters, narratives, desire, and subjectivity. (Many of the references to All New Gen in this essay are taken from the more recent narratives.) Pierce explains:

> It's hard to find narratives that don't fit a genre because we are so influenced by generic types. Our present challenge is how to represent non-specific gender. We talk about gender identity and politics, constructions of identity and subjectivity and we are working on scripting these things both visually and in the narrative structure.

> This is for us the main challenge of cyber-feminism: how you incorporate a feminist language into technology, how you incorporate the body into technology, how you incorporate feminist ideology into technology and how you subvert technology for our own means and purposes. This is our prime project.[28]

Perhaps the relevant question is not whether VNS Matrix games and installations succeed in producing a postmodernist subjectivity but how the experimentations locate us in both modernist/patriarchal as well as postmodern/postphallic feminine realms. The game both opens up questions of alternate cultural identities (a form of resistance), and it also partially forecloses the questions (a recontainment). The game, as a game, has its limitations. But, more important, as Lykke claims for the Internet in general, VNS Matrix offers women (and men) a site of resistance to hegemonic discourses and the potential for interventions into the practices of sexuality, science, and technology.[29] How it will be received and what its effect will be on actual users is another matter. Its effects may be extended considerably, however, when taken as one of many experimentations that engender new virtual selves within cyberspace.

Sherry Turkle raises similar issues in her conclusion to *Life in the Screen*. She cautions that we cannot simply reject the world of cybernetics or consider the Internet as an alternative life for a minority of users. Her research leads her to concur that the Internet is an arena capable of transforming the personal and political dynamics of contemporary life. Aligning herself with the perspectives of postmodern feminism, she argues that the Net encourages us to think of ourselves and our subjectivities as "fluid, emergent, decentralized, multiplicitous, flexible, and ever in process."[30] Despite the possibilities for recontainment, our associations with the Internet and with projects like those imagined and imaged by VNS Matrix allow for new alliances, new subjectivities, and new possibilities for power relations, for desire, and for "perverse" bodily pleasures.

As Teresa de Lauretis and others have argued, myths and fantasies are not eternal truths but are structured through personal, historical, and cultural processes and practices. As such, they are open to change. When cyberfeminists reinvent the myths and fantasies that underpin masculine preoccupations with technology and technocultural production, they also make possible a revisioning of female subjectivity and feminine cultural production. It would be premature to suggest that cyberfeminist productions like those of VNS Matrix presage a new world order. They don't, at least not yet. But they do allow players to imagine the emergence of a new politics, a new erotics, and a new space for the evolution of postmodern subjectivities. They trouble the techno-terrain.

NOTES

I am grateful to Jyanni Steffensen for reading and offering helpful comments on this essay. Jyanni introduced me to a range of cyberfeminist theories and practices while writing her dissertation, which I supervised.

1. Sadie Plant, *Zeroes and Ones: Digital Women and the New Technoculture* (London: Fourth Estate, 1997), 58–59. Plant cites Donna Haraway, "A Cyborg Manifesto: Science, Technology, and Socialist Feminism in the 1980s," in *Simians, Cyborgs, and Women: The Reinvention of Nature* (London: Free Association Books, 1991). This essay first appeared in the Adelaide-based journal *Australian Feminist Studies* 4.1 (1987): 1–41.

2. I take up some of this analysis in my article "The Contested Zone: Cybernetics, Feminism and Representation," *Journal of Australian Studies* 50–51 (1996): 157–64.

3. Elizabeth Grosz and Elsbeth Probyn, intro., in *Sexy Bodies: The Strange Carnalities of Feminism,* ed. Elizabeth Grosz and Elsbeth Probyn (New York: Routledge, 1994): ix–xv.

4. VNS Matrix, All New Gen. Multi-media installation at the Experimental Art Foundation, Adelaide, South Australia, 1993.

5. "The VNS Matrix," www.next.com.au/spyfood/geekgirl/001stick/vns/vns.html, 1997.

6. "The VNS Matrix."

7. VNS Matrix, "Artist's Statement," http/www.gold.ac.uk/difference/vns.html, 1995.

8. VNS Matrix, "Artist's Statement."

9. Haraway, "Cyborg Manifesto," 163.

10. Haraway, "Cyborg Manifesto," 151.

11. Jyanni Steffensen, "Queering Freud: Textual (Re)-constructions of Lesbian Desire and Sexuality" (Ph.D. diss., University of Adelaide, Department of Women's Studies, 1996), 333.

12. Zoë Sofoulis, "Slime in the Matrix: Post-phallic Formations in Women's Art in New Media," in *Jane Gallop Seminar Papers,* ed. Jill Julius Matthews (Canberra: Australian National University, Humanities Research Centre, 1994), 100.

13. Soufoulis, "Slime in the Matrix," 102.

14. The title of an essay by Jane Gallop.

15. Steffensen, "Queering Freud," 311, 312.

16. Sophie Plant, "Cybernetic Hookers," *ANAT News* (April–May 1994): 2–8.

17. Linda Dement, "Artist's Statement about *Typhoid Mary, Working with New Imaging Technologies*" (Melbourne: National Gallery of Victoria, 1995), 30.

18. Alice Jardine, "Of Bodies and Technologies," in *Discussions in Contemporary Culture,* ed. Hal Foster (Seattle: Bay Press, 1987), 156.

19. Jardine, "Of Bodies," 156.

20. Sofoulis, "Slime in the Matrix," 105.

21. Sherry Turkle, *Life in the Screen: Identity in the Age of the Internet* (New York: Simon and Schuster, 1995), 105.

22. Haraway, "Cyborg Manifesto," 30.

23. These positions are taken up and discussed variously in Luce Irigaray, *This Sex Which Is Not One,* trans. Gillian G. Gill (Ithaca: Cornell University Press, 1985); and Margaret Whitford, *Luce Irigaray: Philosophy in the Feminine* (New York and New York: Routledge, 1991).

24. Catherine Waldby, "Destruction: Boundary Erotics and Refigurations of the Heterosexual Male Body," in Grosz and Probyn, *Sexy Bodies*, 267–68.

25. Waldby, "Destruction," 275.

26. "The VNS Matrix."

27. Thom Corcoran, " 'Lost in Cyberspace' or Remaking the Modern," *Honours* (Adelaide: University of South Australia, 1994), 55.

28. Julieanne Pierce, interview with author, 1996.

29. Nina Lykke, intro., in *Between Monsters, Goddesses, and Cyborgs: Feminist Confrontations with Science, Medicine and Cyberspace,* ed. Nina Lykke and Rosi Braidotti (London: Zed Books, 1996), 5–6.

30. Turkle, *Life in the Screen*, 263.

PART 3. Embodied Identities

Constituting Nations / Violently Excluding Women
The First Contract with America

Carroll Smith-Rosenberg

The "external frontiers of the state," eighteenth-century political theorist, Johann Fichte, argued, must become "the internal frontiers" of the citizen. Twentieth-century political theorist Etienne Balibar concurs. A nation "only reproduces itself as a nation," he writes, "to the extent that, through a network of apparatuses and daily practices, the individual is instituted as *homo nationalis*."[1] For a nation to live, that is, its heterogeneous, often contentious, inhabitants must experience themselves as integral parts of a homogeneous, collective people, organic, connected members of a national body politic. For this to happen the nation-state must assume the organic, living qualities we associate with the human body. But the body politic is not organic any more than the population of modern states is homogeneous. When we talk of a national body politic, we are talking of *virtual reality*—the willing suspension of disbelief, the projection of an image upon the screen of public discourse, the acceptance of that projection as virtual, meaning functional, meaning real in the sense of really accepted and acted upon. The more heterogeneous the population, the greater need for the acceptance of the virtual reality of the nation as a coherent body politic, especially if that population experiences itself as threatened by dangerous others either from outside or inside its national boundaries.

But to speak of bodies, real or virtual, is to open a Pandora's box of problems and questions. Which of the actual social bodies inhabiting the nation are fused and authorized as constitutive, organic parts of the nation's virtual body politic? How is that symbolic, fictive body represented? To understand the modern republic and its deployment of power, we must address these issues, for if the gendering of the body is always political, so the body politic is always engendered—and colored. In constituting the virtual body politic, to what extent do nation builders play with alternative configurations of gender and sexuality, use the liberating potential of the imagination to constitute a new, a better, nation and world? To what extent do they simply reinscribe traditional patriarchal visions of roles and hence of power?

From classical Greece through the Renaissance to the Enlightenment, the republican political body was unquestionably male. Male citizens have constituted its empowered members, women, its compromised and infirm parts. To this day women's demands to be included as full members of the national political body confuse the West's legal systems and complicate its political grammars.[2] The United States, as the first modern republic, exemplifies this engendering. The Euro-American political subject, from his origins in eighteenth-century revolutionary turmoil, has been emphatically male. Classic republican rhetoric endowed the republican subject with virile independence, martial valor, and Spartan self-control.[3] Commercial Republicanism made him an industrious producer, manly in his vigor and self-reliance.[4] Enlightenment liberalism, inscribed in both the Declaration of Independence and the Constitution, proclaimed all male citizens free and equal, sovereign members of a sovereign state. Constituting men empowered political participants in the national republican arena; these same discourses constituted women as corrupting threats to pure male political space. Classical republicanism doubly banished women from the political sphere. Not only did women lack the physical strength and martial skills to defend their own and their nation's honor; as femmes coverts they appeared the very antithesis of the independent and virtuous political actor, their bodies, wills, and earthly goods their husbands' property.[5] Commercial republicanism linked civic virtue to manly industry—at the very time that bourgeois discourses banished genteel women from the world of economic productivity—and common law denied those married women who did work the profits of their labor and their capital, thus refusing them economic independence.[6]

But what about political liberalism? Nothing logically prevents women's incorporation into the liberal vision of man as politically sovereign and endowed with natural rights to life, liberty, and property, especially property in himself. So at least modern liberal political theorists, liberal feminists, and libertarians argue.[7] Other feminists remain skeptical.[8] Still others demur. Indeed, over the past twenty years an elaborate feminist critique of liberalism has evolved, multivocal in origin and perspectives. Feminist political scientists such as Carole Pateman or Nancy

Hartsock; psychoanalytic feminists Julia Kristeva, Luce Irigaray, and Jessica Benjamin; philosopher Rosi Braidotti; historians Genevieve Fraisse and Joan Landes, while differing radically from one another, have united in formulating a feminist critique of liberalism as an epistemology and as a political system.

Carole Pateman insists that the social contract, the theoretical underpinning of liberalism and the modern republic, rests upon a sexual contract that excludes women as inferior and dangerous to the pure male republic.[9] Psychoanalytic feminists Julia Kristeva and Luce Irigaray join Pateman in attacking liberalism's exclusion of women. Indeed, their critique is far broader than Pateman's, for they see the social contract as but one example of the exclusion of women from the realm of the symbolic, that is, from language, reason, ethics, power.[10] Younger feminist theorists elaborate these criticisms. Western thought designates the masculine subject as rational, Rosi Braidotti argues in *Patterns of Dissonance,* "the counterpart of which is the symbolic sacrifice of the *feminine*. . . . This symbolic disqualification is coextensive with the material, socio-economic oppression of real-life women . . . the sacrifice of the female subject merges with the very foundations of the homosocial bond and the cultural order."[11] "Patriarchy is the practice, phallogocentricism the theory," she continues. "Both coincide . . . in producing an economy, material as well as libidinal, where the law is upheld by a phallic symbol that operates by constructing differences and organizing them hierarchically."[12]

The debate about liberalism is critically important. Feminists from Mary Wollstonecraft to Nadine Strossen have sought to wed feminism to liberalism, constituting liberal feminism, America's dominant feminist discourse. But is such a wedding in feminists' best interests? Will its resultant daughters be politically empowered members of the body politic? I am fully aware that there is no answer to these questions—easy or otherwise. Yet it remains important to raise these questions and examine these issues.

The first half of this essay explores feminist critiques of liberalism the better to create an analytic frame for examining women's uneasy, contested, and mediated inclusion as members of the modern body politic. The second half examines the very first contract with America—the Federal Constitution, ratified in 1787. Is Pateman right—does the Constitution incorporate a prior sexual contract? Can we find evidence to support a feminist critique of liberalism, if not on the austere pages of the Constitution itself, then in the welter of political rhetoric produced during the debates over the ratification of the Constitution?

Theoretical Criticism

Committed to liberty and equality, modern republics owe their theoretical legitimacy to what Carole Pateman calls "the most famous and influential political story of modern times," the social contract.[13] A band of sons, one of the original social contract stories goes, oppressed by a tyrannical father who monopolized access to all the women of the horde, killed the father and, freely contracting among themselves, established a government that recognized their freedom and equality.[14] In this way Western thought mythologized the transition from feudal to modern political forms. Contract theory was a revolutionary concept, Pateman tells us: "It was the emancipatory doctrine *par excellence,* promising . . . universal freedom." She continues:

> The assumption that individuals were born free and equal to each other meant that none of the old arguments for subordination could be accepted . . . might or force could no longer be translated into political right; appeals to custom and tradition were no longer sufficient.[15]

Liberalism's insistence that political sovereignty resides with the political citizen fueled successive political revolutions—in 1775, 1789, and 1792 with America's second revolution, Haiti's.[16]

Free and equal, by the early nineteenth century the republican subject had emerged as a liberal individualist, proud of his autonomy, renowned for his independence, his self-reliance.[17] Liberal political theory made the republican subject radically separate from and unconnected to others. Self-interest was his guiding star, self-reliance his proudest boast, self-determination his goal. Dependency upon others signaled weakness, lack of masculine fortitude and resolution. The man who depended upon others could be manipulated, his vote or sword purchased. In eighteenth-century political thought dependency signaled effeminacy and corruption. The effeminate, corrupt citizen could lay no claim to civic virtue.[18] Connectedness, dedication to the general good, concern for community traditions or family ties (characteristics of older cultures and an older republicanism), benevolence (associated with the new languages of the sentiments and romanticism), had no legitimate place within liberal contract theory. They had to be added on, associated with the sympathies, the apolitical, the private sphere—in short, with women.[19]

Julia Kristeva, in "Women's Time," introduces a psychosymbolic dimension into Pateman's political analysis, pointing to strong parallels between the symbolic and the social contract. As the social contract constituted the virtuous citizen as autonomous, and self-governing, so the symbolic contract stressed man's radical separation from others—especially from women. As the social contract condemned both dependency and women as corrupting the pure male political space, so the symbolic contract condemned connectedness as regressive, too closely associated with women's bodies, with infantile desires for the mother that must be rejected before personhood, individualization, can be achieved.[20]

Certainly, connectedness generally and women's bodies specifically threaten the Cartesian/Liberal man's sense of himself as the source, the origin of meaning. They force him to acknowledge a relation that precedes the social contract and exists outside its theory and its law. Refusing such recognition, both the social and the symbolic contract associate connectedness and interdependency with weakness. They have no place within a classical liberal world. They must be excised, sacrificed.[21] "What is our place [as women] in this order of sacrifice?" Julia Kristeva asks—and answers: "Women feel that they are the casualties, that they have been left out of the socio-symbolic contract . . . the fundamental social bond."[22]

American psychoanalyst Jessica Benjamin concurs. Standing for human connectedness, for the bond between mother and infant, women actively threaten both man's sense of separateness and his sense of radical difference from women. Women are condemned as endangering man's independence, luring him back into the helplessness and dependency of infancy. In this way, Benjamin argues, "the image of woman as the dangerous, regressive siren is born," along with its counterpart, "the wholly idealized, masterful [male] subject who can withstand or conquer her."[23] The only good woman within this scenario is the submissive, the dominated woman. The impact on women's claims to political sovereignty, to full membership in the republican body politic, is clear. As Benjamin succinctly puts the case, "The disavowal of identity with the mother is linked to the denial of [the mother's/women's] equal subjectivity."[24]

Rousseau is perhaps the quintessential liberal republican and social contract theorist. His writings exemplify Kristeva's and Benjamin's analytic arguments. For Rousseau women embodied human connectedness, interdependency, and corruption. They refused separation. Women thus threatened men's autonomy, men's Spartan dedication to the republic and public service. Unrestrained, Rousseau insisted, women's sexuality would destroy the virtuous republic and the virtuous republican man. That virtue depended on recognizing the absolute difference between men and women and consequently on the rigid exclusion of women from the body politic. If relations between women and men became "too intimate," Rousseau continued in *Discourse on Inequality,* the natural differences separating men and women would dissolve. "Women [will] make us into women," he warned. Existing outside rational male control, female heterosexual charms and desire not only threatened to effeminize men; they would undermine patterns of the male bonding necessary to the ascetic and rational life of the republic. At war with men's "morality and constitution," Rousseau warned, sexually active women would "drag . . . [men] to death without ever being able to defend themselves."[25] Only if women were excluded from the virtuous republican polis, Rousseau, the archetypal contractarian writer, insisted, could the liberal republican state emerge as a virtuous fraternal order, a band of brothers organized to resist and contain women's threatening heterosexual embraces effectively.[26]

Not only did classical liberal writers see women as the embodiment of social connectedness and a potentially effeminizing heterosexuality, but, what is perhaps even more troubling, they saw women as embodying difference itself. Contract theory, Carole Pateman points out, requires the sameness of all contracting agents.[27] Classical liberalism presumed a universal sameness: all men are created equal, that is, alike, indistinguishable from one another. All men are equal because they are alike, because they all participate in the same rights and reason. But what happens to the contractual model of sameness when difference is introduced? Can those who are different claim the same rights as those who are alike? Both contract theory and liberalism register difference as disorder and inferiority. Those who are unalike, who do not fit into the "Law of the Same," the sameness of men, are either marginalized, their needs defined as outside the legitimate concerns of the liberal state, or they are seen as deviant, inferior—and dangerous. When the latter view prevails, women are violently excluded from the polity, the body politic. Here is the crux of the dilemma feminism poses for liberalism.

When considering women's issues, political historian Genevieve Fraisse argues, liberal republican thought is explicitly exclusionary. The problem of "what is different . . . other . . . had to be solved by exclusion," Fraisse argues. Liberalism, she continues, was binary, inscribing a series of rigid distinctions between sameness and difference, reason and the irrational, science and superstition. Sexual difference constituted the ur, the primary difference, a difference so fundamental it overrode the common identity men and women shared as human beings. Because women were seen as radically unlike men, women were not considered bona fide members of the body politic. Their citizenship was at best mediated, qualified by their difference.

"It is woman's otherness [Rousseau] rejects," Fraisse continues. "Discussing the respective characteristics or merits of the two sexes is pointless. . . . [Rousseau's] reasoning is based exclusively on . . . the idea of a . . . democratic system where every individual is reflected by the whole and belongs to a [single] totality." Women would destroy the cohesiveness of that totality.[28]

Julia Kristeva agrees. She points out that neither Enlightenment humanism nor its nineteenth-century descendant, modern socialism, comfortably acknowledge difference. Rather, they turn difference into inferiority. Within both systems of thought, Kristeva argues, "sexual difference . . . translates as difference in the relation of the subject to the symbolic contract, a difference then in the relation to power, language and meaning."[29] "Difference," Jessica Benjamin adds, "is constructed as polarity; it maintains the overvaluation of one side, the denigration of the other."[30]

From Plato through Locke and Rousseau to Freud, humanist theorists have inscribed women's differences as inferiorities, representing women as hysterics, lacking the judgment, the moral capacity, the superego, to maintain social and political order. Locke states the argument most succinctly: "Only men naturally have the character of free and equal beings. Women are naturally subordinate to men and the order of nature is reflected in the structure of conjugal relations."[31] Unable to participate in orderly government, women became the emblem of disorder. "This stigmatization of woman," Braidotti continues, "turns her into an outsider. . . . Woman in the patriarchal imaginary incarnates the disquieting possibility of the absence of . . . law, of its decomposition."[32] Or as Pateman, meditating on Locke, expresses it: "In modern patriarchy, the capacity that individuals lack is politically significant because it represents all that civil order is not, all that is encapsulated in women and women's bodies. . . . Women must be subject to men because they are naturally subversive of men's political order."

The social contract banished women from the civil order, confining them within a domestic world, where men exercised a "natural" authority to govern women. Pateman points out that Locke carefully distinguished between "the new public world constituted by the universal bonds of contract between formally free and equal individuals [men / the 'law of the same'] and the private familial world constituted by natural ties and a natural order of subordination [of women]."[33] The latter must be kept separate and subordinate to the former. But even within the family man's orderly rule was not secure. Pateman reminds us of Rousseau's admonition to Emile. Men must learn to master women before they marry, Rousseau had warned; men must prepare for marriage as they would for battle with a powerful foe.[34]

Of course, much has changed since Locke and Rousseau—at least on the law books. The very words *man* and *fraternity,* we are now told, incorporate women. We have become "one of the boys." But then how do we explain women's continued marginalization within Euro-American and world political practices? One could argue that a male reinscription of the social contract to include, at least formally, all adult humans, the assumption of women into the human brotherhood simply perpetuates the social contract's inscription of "the Law of the Same," along with its inherently violent rejection of difference—and hence of women. The classic story of the social contract inscribes a violent psychosexual dynamic of male bonding and female possession that modern liberal political reforms such as suffrage and affirmative action have done little to modify.

Political cohesion is fueled by male eros, Nancy Hartsock tells us.[35] The political realm arises "from an act of generation by men that transcends and opposes physical, that is, womanly generation." Womanly generation embodies connectedness, during which the other is within the self—not in another place, that is, the place of the other. Carol Pateman concurs. In founding republics "men give birth to an 'artificial' body . . . the creation of civil society produces a social body fashioned after the image of only one of the two bodies of humankind."[36] Luce Irigaray's response is the most searing. The contracting political subject, she points out, "is father, mother and child and the relationships between them. . . . What a mockery of generation, parody of copulation and genealogy, drawing its strength from the same model, from the model of the same: the [male] subject. In whose sight everything outside remains forever a condition making possible the image and the reproduction of the self," that is, the male self.[37] Men would have women be mirrors reflecting the male republican subject's desire for an inner cohesion he does not have. It is against his representation of "woman's" weakness, "woman's" irrationality, "woman's" hysterical sexual wiles, that the republican citizen establishes his sense of his own strength, reason, and self-control.

But what if, Irigaray asks, the mirror turned into a weapon, the other "started to speak? Which also means beginning to 'see.' What disaggregation of the [male] subject would that entail? . . . a fantastic, phantasmic fragmentation. A destruc[tura]tion in which the subject is shattered, sculled, while still claiming surreptitiously that he is the reason for it all"[38]—and, let me add, deeply resentful of the other that shattered his sense of self. It is that speaking that political contract theory and the Cartesian liberal symbolic order works to prevent.

The First Contract with America:
The Constitutional Debates

Let us turn now to the first contract with America, the Federal Constitution. To flesh out the American body politic that the austere Constitution constituted, I will turn to a far more profuse body of literature, the urban and urbane political and literary magazines founded by the Constitution's principle supporters to urge ratification among the nation's influential urban elite.[39] How did these urban magazines represent women? As legitimate members of the body politic? As different from but equal to male patriot/warriors? Did the popular press extend the ringing phrases of the Declaration of Independence to include women? Or did it present women as deviations from the male norm, aberrations to be purged from a virtuous and pure body politic? Urging ratification of the new constitution, the new urban press denigrated white women and African Americans alike. It thus reaffirmed the Constitution's effacement of white women from its pages and the same Constitution's transformation of African Americans into three-fifths persons, that is, into unwhole and thus unwholesome bodies.

Polarizing gender, the new urban political magazines constituted a series of binary oppositions that constituted the virtuous republican subject virile and empowered. Representations of her physical weakness and vulnerability confirmed his valor and strength, her economic dependence affirmed his economic independence, her vanity and love of pleasure, his claims to Spartan asceticism, her whims and fancies, his reason and assiduity, her need for guidance, his right to govern himself—and her. While she sought love and protection through the arts of pleasing and serving others, he valued his independence, personal liberty, and self-reliance above life itself.[40] As in Locke's Treatises, so on the pages of the new urban press, women, the antithesis of republican strength and virtue, the embodiment of dependency, passion, and lack of self-control, were strictly confined within the domestic sphere, subject to male governance.[41]

An essay published in Boston's *Massachusetts Magazine* exemplifies the new republic's ideal vision of male/female relations. "The good husband," the essay proclaimed, treats his wife with delicacy as a woman . . . attributes her follies to her weakness, her imprudence to her inadvertence . . . pardons them with indulgence; all his care and industry are employed for her welfare; all his strength and power are executed for her support and protection; . . . the good husband . . . animate[s] her faith by his practice and enforce[s] the precepts of Christianity by his own example.[42]

The wife emerges from this homily as weak, imprudent, and totally dependent on her husband's support and protection. In contrast, we find a husband empowered with governmental powers, a husband who "pardons," "executes," "supports," "protects," "animates," and "enforces." The home, on the pages of the new nation's political magazines, as on those of *Emile,* becomes a training ground where men learn to govern wisely.

But, as Rousseau had noted, gender relations are not that simple or transparent. Even when polemically represented in the popular press, as whimsically foolish or foolishly fond, women nevertheless repeatedly endangered men's autonomy and threatened their governance. To be different, it seemed after all, was not to be without power, while the autonomous and self-reliant American man, on closer examination, turned out to be not so self-reliant after all. Although the "Founding Fathers" may not have needed women's assistance to give birth to a new republic, actual American men did report needing women. This was especially true of men who desired to cloak themselves not only in the attributes of republican virtue but in the more tangible garb of bourgeois civility. Bourgeois men depended on the gentility and social polish of their wives and daughters to establish their own claims to gentility and social respectability. But their dependence on women eroded their claims as political subjects to republican political independence and self-governance.[43] Certainly, this was the ultimate message of another magazine essay that began bravely enough by representing men as "enterprising and robust," providing for and protecting dependent women. But, the essay continued, men as well as women had needs. Men needed "female softness." Without women, it informed the urbane *Columbia Monthly Miscellany'*s new urban readers, men were often "cruel," "rough," and "barbarous." Women refined men, taught men "to please and be agreeable," to submit their wills to the wills of others. "In our sex," the essay admitted, "there is a kind of constitutional or masculine pride which hinders us from yielding in points of knowledge or honor, to each other; but we lay it entirely aside in our connection with women." We learn from women, the essayist continued, "a submission . . . which teaches us to obey where we used to command." In this essay, at least, bourgeois men desiring gentility and social polish submitted their "masculine pride" to women's guidance.

By learning to please, however, men, as Rousseau had predicted, became like women—bending, obeying "where they used to command." Sexual difference, the central truth upon which liberal political logic rested, evaporated. While ostensibly praising women's power to refine men, the essay, not surprisingly, ends on a threatened and a threatening note.

> In their forms pleasing, in their manners soft, women bend the haughty stubbornness of man . . . an insinuating word . . . even a smile . . . conquered Alexander, subdued Caesar and decided the fate of empires and kingdoms.

Fearing "the power of women to bend the stronger sex to their will," the author warned "to enjoy any pleasure in perfection, we men must never be saturated with it."[44]

Clearly, it was not enough to banish women rhetorically from the public sphere and confine them within domestic space. Essay after essay warned men to beware the wiles and deceptions of their wives. "Every woman seek[s] to please. This is the weapon conferred on her by nature to compensate for the weakness of her sex. . . . that [is how] she must establish her empire."[45]

The better to contain such feminine power, the political press deployed bitter satire, ridiculing women as foolish and vapid. Women's heads, new republican readers were told, contained nothing but "airy vapour" and snuff. Sadistically, magazine writers insisted that women's physical charms were nothing more than a compound of "cork rumps, false bums, false locks, elastic wigs . . . whitening for the neck, rouge for the cheek."[46] Women by nature were promiscuous, sexually unrestrained, excessive in their amours and reproductive capacities. Some women, the magazines continued, even boasted of their power to produce children—without the benefit of husband or state authorization, unnervingly echoing men's claims to be able to "father" states without women's assistance and authority.[47]

In a humorous effort to impose some control on women's sexual assaults, an essay entitled "SATIRE AND HUMOUR: A Plan for the Establishment of a Fair of Fairs, or Market of Matrimony," suggested that men gather four times a year in an open market to examine women wishing to marry. "All ladies desirous of disposing of their persons in wedlock [would] have liberty to repair thither and expose themselves for that purpose," the article proposed and continued that the fair grounds would be divided into "wards . . . to denote the several articles to be disposed of therein . . . viz. No. 1. VIRGINS, No. 2. WIDOWS, No. 3. DEMIREPS, No. 4. The COMMONALITY." Having reduced women's "liberty" to the right to expose themselves as "articles to be disposed of," the essay proceeded to announce that two constables would be in charge of the women. Each would carry "a red staff, as a badge of his office, made after the manner described by *ruber porrectus palus.*" These constables would be responsible for "examin[ing] and secur[ing] all counterfeits . . . enquir[ing] into the rate of exchange and giv[ing] information . . . to chapmen inclined to purchase." The essay ends with a final humiliating image—"for the amusement of the spectators, proper sack-races [would] be run by the ladies, according to the most approved practice in England and elsewhere."[48]

But did our humorous author really succeed in satirically refusing women's connection to the *Social Contract* and the proposed new contract with America, the new federal constitution? The essay contains at least one significant slippage—the inclusion of women in the category "Commonality." Common words carry many, and complex, meanings. Given the tone and sexual innuendos of the piece, one might well suppose that the meaning the author intended in choosing "commonality" as a category in which to place women as objects of examination was one in use in the early and mid-eighteenth century—that is, "the state of quality of being common to, or shared by, more than one," which, in the case of women, meant prostitutes. But the word *commonality* had a long history of political meanings as well. Chaucer used it to mean "a community, a commonwealth." In the late seventeenth-century, when Locke was writing his *Social Contract,* it carried the meaning "a free or self-governing community," which Locke contrasted to a monarchical state. Even more common was its use to describe the political "Third Estate." Certainly, this was how David Hume used it in his *History of England,* in which he wrote of "three estates, the clergy, the nobility and the commonality."[49] Intending to denigrate women sexually, had our satirist constituted them the very embodiment of the new republic?

But should we bother to take such ridicule seriously? Yes, for it formed a powerful weapon in men's struggle to allay their sense of women's power and agency and reassert their own.

Male humor sought to contain women's threats to domestic and political tranquility in two ways. First, representing women as an amalgam of cork and horsehair, powder, rouge and paint, as sexually excessive and unrestrained, by implication filled with bodily fluids, swollen orifices, made multiple through pregnancy, it constituted women corporeally grotesque. Women so depicted constituted the antithesis of the classical and contained body of civic humanism and Enlightenment liberalism. The classic body, M. M. Bakhtin argued in his study of Rabelais, was elevated, static, monumental, without openings, orifices, almost disembodied.[50] Elaborating Bakhtin, Peter Stallybrass and Allon White saw the classic body as "the radiant centre of a transcendent individualism . . . raised above the viewer and the commonality and anticipating passive admiration from below." "The classical body," they continue, "was far more than an aesthetic standard. . . . It structured . . . the characteristically 'high' discourses of philosophy, statecraft, theology and law. . . . In the classical discursive body were encoded those regulated systems which were closed, homogeneous, monumental, centered and symmetrical. . . . Gradually these protocols of the classical body came to mark out the identity of progressive rationalism itself."[51] The classical American republican could claim just such a classical body. But women, amalgams of false parts, ungoverned sexuality, and vaporous thoughts, could not. As represented in the new nation's popular press, America's women had no place within the classic halls of virtuous governance. Male humor worked on a second ideological and rhetorical level. Not only did satire denigrate and silence women (how could an eighteenth-century woman respond to the obscene reference to Horace?); it confirmed the very order it lampooned. The function of humor is to explore order but not to challenge it, symbolic anthropologist Mary Douglas argues. "The joke . . . affords the opportunity for realizing that an accepted pattern has no necessity. Its excitement lies in the suggestion that any particular ordering of experience may be arbitrary and subjective. [But] it is frivolous in that it produces *no real alternative*."[52] These satirical essays permitted men to express their fear of women's power and destructiveness, their sense that the patriarchal order had "no necessity," that it was "arbitrary and subjective," without seriously endangering that order, for there was no real alternative to marriage and common law's subjugation of women within marriage. In the end these essays merely permitted men to laugh at their own fears—and express through humor deep-seated hostilities.

To take a final look at the way humor masked male rhetorical violence, let us look at a rather odd satirical piece that eminent republican publisher Mathew Carey printed in his influential *American Museum*. This essay exemplifies both the role that humor played in veiling Federalists' hostility toward women and their use of women to delegitimize their critics, especially Western farmers who complained of hard times, shortage of specie, and heavy taxes. In this particular issue of the *American Museum*, Carey followed an article denigrating such complaints as the fears of the weak-nerved and factious, with a piece of broad and brutal political satire, "On the Fear of Mad Dogs."[53] The essay lampooned old women for spreading false alarms of dogs gone mad and consequently of disturbing the peace of "the capitol" (a word rent with multiple meanings: the seat of government, and with the slightest change of spelling, productive commercial wealth). It is not that dogs had gone mad (or that capitol, or capital, and the times had gone bad), Carey argued, but that hysterical women gossips had done both. Comparing gossiping women to old witches, scolds, and ludicrous animals, Carey not only associated the rumors of hard times with devalued women; he constituted woman as an irrational and ridiculous other to the sagacious middle-class male citizen, represented by the essay's narrative. "When epidemic terror is . . . excited, every morning comes loaded with some new disaster," the essay begins portentously. "A lady, for instance, in the country, of very weak nerves, has been frighted by the barking of a dog; the story spreads . . . grows more dismal . . . and, by the time it has arrived . . . at the capitol the lady is described . . . running mad upon all fours, barking like a dog, biting her servants, and at last smothered between two beds." As if this were not sufficient to convict women as irrational and politically dangerous, Carey's magazine repeated the story in only a slightly altered guise, now told to the male narrator, a sensible and bemused observer, by his landlady. "A mad dog . . . , she assured me," he wrote, "had bit a farmer, who soon becoming mad, bit a fine brindled cow; the cow, foaming at the mouth, went about upon her hind legs, sometimes barking like a dog, and sometimes, attempting to talk like the farmer." And so in the writings of America's most eminent Federalists man's fear of and anger against women bursts out—in ridicule that may well hide murderous rage.

Twice-told tales promise many meanings. Carey's essay associates serious economic and political complaints about the shortage of currency and the hard times that followed the Revolutionary War (complaints serious enough to threaten civil warfare from the Carolinas to Massachusetts) with the gossip of foolish and hysterical women. What better way to discredit political opponents (and to contain women politically) than to link political protests to women whose political opinions, men of all political stripes knew, could never be redeemed in the solid coin of reliable judgment and hard facts.

By way of ending, let us return momentarily to our opening series of questions: How is the national body politic represented? Whose bodies are authorized as legitimate powerful members of that body politic? In magazine issue after magazine issue the new American is represented as a genteel, self-reliant, rational, successful man of European origins. And women? We have seen how they are represented—as "airy vaporous" heads, covered with powder, painted with rouge, adorned with false locks, filled with fancies, fears, and superstition, as cork rumps, as foolish gossips, running on all fours or attempting to stand on their hind legs and talk like a (politically protesting) farmer.

The Euro-American political subject who appeared on the pages of the new nation's urban press was a composite figure, a patchwork of contradictory political and economic discourses who shared but one common characteristic, their insistence that the political subject was male. His political cohesion depended on the press's construction of all women (Euro-American, African American, and American Indian) as the political subject's negative others and, consequently, as unfit, flawed members of the body politic.

NOTES

1. For Johann Fichte's statement in *Redenandie deutsche Nation* (Address to the German People), 1808, see Etienne Balibar, "The National Forum: History and Ideology," trans. Immanuel Wallerstein and Chris Turner, *Review, Fernand Braudel Center* 13 (1990): 329–61, 347–48, and 345–51, esp. 345, 349.

2. Feminist political theorists and critical legal theorists have explored this issue at length. The literature is extensive. For a few examples, see: Nancy Fraser, *Justice Interruptus: Critical Reflections on the "Postsocialist" Condition* (New York: Routledge, 1997); Iris Marion Young, "Mothers, Citizenship and Independence: A Critique of Pure Family Values," *Ethics* 105 (1995): 535–56; Mary Lyndon Shanley and Martha Minow, "Relational Rights and Responsibilities: Revising the Family in Liberal Political Theory and Law," *Hypatia* 11.1 (1996): 4–29; Deborah L. Rhode, "Feminism and the State," *Harvard Law Review* 107.6 (1994): 1181–1209; Robin West, "Jurisprudence and Gender," *University of Chicago Law Review* 55.1 (1988): 1–72.

3. For a definitive analysis of classical republican thought and imagery, see J. G. A. Pocock's *Machiavellian Moment: Florentine Political Thought and the Atlantic Republican Tradition* (Princeton: Princeton University Press, 1975).

4. See, for example, Isaac Kramnick, *Republicanism and Bourgeois Radicalism: Political Ideology in Late Eighteenth-Century England and America* (Ithaca: Cornell University Press, 1990).

5. For various examples, see Pocock, *Machiavellian Moment,* esp. 465 and 475. See also discussions in Rogers M. Smith, "'One United People': Second-Class Female Citizenship and the American Quest for Community," *Yale Journal of Law and the Humanities* 1.2 (1989): 229–93, esp. 241–48. For a comparison with European political thought, see Joan B. Landes, *Women and the Public Sphere in the Age of the French Revolution* (Ithaca: Cornell University Press, 1988); and Lynn Hunt, "The Many Bodies of Marie Antoinette: Political Pornography and the Problem of the

Feminine in the French Revolution," in *Eroticism and the Body Politic,* ed. Lynn Hunt (Baltimore: Johns Hopkins University Press, 1991), 108–30.

6. See Linda Kerber's pathbreaking *Women of the Republic: Intellect and Ideology in Revolutionary America,* published for the Institute of Early American History and Culture, Williamsburg, Va. (Chapel Hill: University of North Carolina Press, 1980), esp. chap. 5. See also Mary Lynn Salmon and Mary Beth Norton.

7. Nadine Strossen; I would also include Peggy Watson in this category. See her essay "Civil Society and the Politicisation of Difference in Eastern Europe," in *Transitions, Environments, Translations: The Meanings of Feminism in Contemporary Politics,* ed. Joan Scott, Cora Kaplan, and Debra Keates (New York: Routledge, 1997).

8. A number of feminist theorists are working to create a middle ground. While recognizing the difficulties that liberalism poses for a feminist legal/political agenda, they fear relinquishing arguments based on an insistence on universal human rights. They insist that feminists must therefore continue to work within a liberal frame. For examples of efforts to constitute such a middle ground, see Seyla Benhabib, *Situating the Self: Gender, Community and Postmodernism in Contemporary Ethics* (New York: Routledge, 1992); Seyla Benhaib and Drucilla Cornell, eds., *Feminism as Critique: On the Politics of Gender* (Minneapolis: University of Minnesota Press, 1986); Drucilla Cornell, *The Imaginary Domain: Abortion, Pornography and Sexual Harassment* (New York: Routledge, 1991); Christine A. Littleton, "Equality across Difference: A Place for Rights Discourse?" *Wisconsin Women's Law Journal* 3 (1987): 189–212.

9. Carole Pateman, *The Sexual Contract* (Stanford: Stanford University Press, 1988); Carole Pateman and Elizabeth Grosz, eds., *Feminist Challenges: Social and Political Theory* (Boston: Northeastern University Press, 1986); Zillah R. Eisenstein, *The Radical Future of Liberal Feminism* (Boston: Northeastern University Press, 1993). For historical analyses of liberalism, see Joan B. Landes, *Women and the Public Sphere in the Age of the French Revolution* (Ithaca: Cornell University Press, 1988); and Genevieve Fraisse, *Reason's Muse: Sexual Difference and the Birth of Democracy,* trans. by Jane Marie Todd (Chicago: University of Chicago Press, 1989).

10. Luce Irigaray, *Speculum of the Other Woman,* trans. Gillian C. Gill (Ithaca: Cornell University Press, 1985); *This Sex Which Is Not One* (Ithaca: Cornell University Press, 1985); and "Cosi Fan Tutti," *Vel* 2 (1975). For a selection of Julia Kristeva's essays, see *The Kristeva Reader,* ed. Toril Moi (New York: Columbia University Press, 1980). For critical analyses of French psychoanalytic feminism, see "Body/Text," in Julia Kristeva, *Religion, Women and Psychoanalyses,* ed. David Crownfield (Albany: State University of New York, 1992); and Naomi Schor, "This Essentialism Which Is Not One: Coming to Grips with Irigaray," in *The Essential Difference,* ed. Naomi Schor and Elizabeth Weed (Bloomington and Indianapolis: Indiana University Press, 1994). For a different French feminist voice, see Antoinette Fouque, especially an interview with her in *differences:* Antoinette Fouque, Marcel Gauchet, and Pierre Nora, "Women in Movements: Yesterday, Today and Tomorrow. An Interview," ed. Anne Berger, trans. Arthur Denner, *differences: A Journal of Feminist Cultural Studies* 3.3 (1991): 1–25.

11. Rosi Braidotti, *Patterns of Dissonance* (New York and London: Routledge, 1991), 215.

12. Braidotti, *Patterns of Dissonance,* 213.

13. Pateman, *Sexual Contract,* 1.

14. Pateman, *Sexual Contract,* 2.

15. Pateman, *Sexual Contract,* 39.

16. C. L. R. James, *Black Jacobins: Toussaint L'Ouverture and the San Domingo Revolution,* 2d rev. ed. (New York: Vintage Books, 1989).

17. See Pateman's discussion, *Sexual Contract,* 38.

18. For a discussion of the role dependency played in eighteenth-century republican understandings of political corruption, see Pocock, *Machiavellian Moment,* 407–8, 484–86, and chap. 14.

19. For suggestive, though quite disparate, discussions of the sympathies, see Julie Ellison, *Delicate Subjects: Romanticism, Gender and the Ethics of Understanding* (Ithaca: Cornell University Press, 1990); Robert A. Erickson, *The Language of the Heart, 1600–1750* (Philadelphia: University of Pennsylvania Press, 1997); Adela Pinch, *Strange Fits of Passion: Epistemologies of Emotion, Hume to Austen* (Stanford: Stanford University Press, 1996).

20. Kristeva, "Women's Time," *Kristeva Reader,* 187–213, esp. 188–93.

21. In contrast, it must be noted, Kristeva sees motherhood and pregnancy as literal embodiments of the fluid intersection of self and other. She deploys them as powerful metaphors to symbolize the embrace of difference, the refusal of hierarchicalization.

22. Kristeva, "Women's Time," 199.

23. Jessica Benjamin, *The Bonds of Love: Psychoanalysis, Feminism and the Problem of Domination* (New York: Pantheon Books, 1988), 164; see also 167, 175–76.

24. Benjamin, *Bonds of Love,* 165.

25. Jean Jacques Rousseau, *Emile; or, On Education,* trans. A. Bloom (New York: Basic Books, 1979), 358–59.

26. See Genevieve Fraisse's citations from and discussion of Rousseau in *Reason's Muse,* 167 and chap. 6, generally. See also Joan B. Landes's citations and discussion of Rousseau's sexual attitudes in *Women and the Public Sphere,* 87, 86–88, and chap. 3 generally.

27. Pateman, *Sexual Contract,* 56; Fraisse, *Reason's Muse,* 167–68.

28. Fraisse, *Reason's Muse,* 167–68.

29. Kristeva, "Women's Time," 196.

30. Benjamin, *Bonds of Love,* 167.

31. Locke, quoted by Pateman, *Sexual Contract,* 52.

32. Braidotti, *Patterns of Dissonance,* 213.

33. Pateman, *Sexual Contract,* 96.

34. Rousseau, *Emile,* 445. See also Pateman's discussion, *Sexual Contract,* 98.

35. Nancy C. M. Hartsock, *Money, Sex and Power: Toward a Feminist Historical Materialism* (New York: Longman, 1983), see chap. 8 in particular. For Pateman's discussion of Hartsock's argument, see *Sexual Contract,* 89.

36. Pateman, *Sexual Contract,* 102.

37. Luce Irigaray, "Any Theory of the 'Subject' Has Always Been Appropriated by the 'Masculine,'" *Irigaray Reader,* 133–46, 136.

38. Irigaray, "Any Theory of the 'Subject,'" 135.

39. The end of the Revolutionary War and demands to reform or rewrite the Articles of Confederation led publisher/politicians in Philadelphia, Boston, and New York to found political magazines addressed to the new nation's emerging commercial and professional middle class. Five political/literary magazines were published during the years surrounding the ratification debates. Philadelphia boasted of two magazines: Mathew Carey's *American Museum,* and the urbane *Columbian Magazine and Monthly Miscellany.* In New York arch Federalist Noah Webster edited and published the *American Magazine.* In Massachusetts Isaiah Thomas first transformed his newspaper, the *Massachusetts Spy,* into a magazine, the *Worcester Magazine.* In 1788 Thomas began a second magazine, the *Massachusetts Magazine.* New Brunswick, New Jersey, on the route between Philadelphia and New York and near the College of New Jersey (aka Princeton University) also boasted of a political/literary journal, albeit a short-lived one, the *New Jersey Magazine.* This essay is based on a close reading of the essays published in these magazines.

40. See, for example: "A Short Enquiry How Far the Democratic Governments of America Have Sprung from an Affirmation for Democracy," *Columbian Magazine and Monthly Miscellany* (hereafter cited as *Columbian Magazine*) 1 (Sept. 1787): 631–32; John Quincy Adams, "An Oration, Delivered at the Public Commencement in the University of Cambridge, in New England on July 18, 1787," *Columbian Magazine* 1 (Sept. 1787): 625–28; "The Loves of Artho and Colval: A Fragment," *Columbian Magazine* 1 (Sept. 1787): 30; "Maxims for Republics," *American Museum* 2 (July 1787): 80–82; Francis Walsh Jr., "A Gothic Story," *American Magazine* 1 (Oct. 1788): 779–82. Polarizing its representations of gender, the urban press constituted Americans' embrace of political independence as masculine, as in Doctor Plainsense's comment in the *Columbian Magazine,* "the plain masculine independent genius of enlightened America," and effaced women from the body politic, as in the comment "the people of Pennsylvania, in general, are composed of men of three occupations, the farmer, the merchant and the mechanic." Doctor Plainsense, "The Pedantry of Technical Phraseology Condemned," *Columbian Magazine* 1 (Nov. 1787): 805–8, 805; and One of the People, "To the Freemen of Pennsylvania," *American Museum* 2 (Oct. 1787): 371–75, 373. The press also made it clear that men aspiring to civic virtue should live a celibate life. Supplement of the *Pennsylvania Packet and General Advertiser,* Feb. 15, 1770.

41. Women who sought to make a public role for themselves were roundly criticized for endangering the public order. See criticisms of women religious figures Mother Ann Lee of the Shakers and Jemimah Wilkinson of the Universal Friends. "Some Account of the Tenets and Practice of the Religious Sect call Shakers," and "Account of Jemimah Wilkinson, Styled the Universal Friend, also of Her Doctrines and Followers, Philadelphia, Feb. 14, 1787," in *American Museum* 1 (Feb. 1787): 163–65, 165–69; (Apr. 1787): 333–38; and (May 1787): 462–67.

42. "Character of a GOOD HUSBAND," *Massachusetts Magazine* 1 (Mar. 1789): 177.

43. For a discussion of the role women played in late-eighteenth-century Euro-American bourgeois discourses, see Carroll Smith-Rosenberg, "Domesticating Virtue," in *Literature and the Body: Essays on Populations and Persons,* ed. Elaine Scarry (Baltimore: Johns Hopkins University Press, 1988). See also Ruth Bloch, "The Gendered Meanings of Virtue in Revolutionary America," *Signs* 13 (1987): 34–58.

44. "SENTIMENTAL AND MORAL ESSAYS: On the Happy Influence of Female Society," *American Museum* 1 (Jan. 1787): 72–78.

45. "Thoughts on the Dress of American Ladies," *Columbian Magazine* 1 (Sept. 1787): 638–39, 638.

46. *Pennsylvania Packet and Daily Advertiser,* May 13, 1788, n.p.

47. "MISCELLANIES: Speech of Miss Polly Baker, before the Court of Judicature, in Connecticut, where she was Presented for the Fifth Time for having a Bastard Child," *American Museum* 1 (Mar. 1787): 243–45.

48. "SATIRE AND HUMOUR: A Plan for the Establishment of a Fair of Fairs, or Market of Matrimony," *American Museum* 1 (Feb. 1787): 152–54.

49. Compact Edition of the *Oxford English Dictionary* (Oxford: Oxford University Press, 1979): 1:483.

50. M. M. Bakhtin, *Rabelais and His World,* trans. H. Iswolsky (Cambridge: Massachusetts Institute of Technology Press, 1968).

51. Peter Stallybrass and Allon White, *Politics and Poetics of Transgression* (Ithaca: Cornell University Press, 1986), 21–22.

52. Mary Douglas, "The Social Control of Cognition: Some Factors in Joke Perception" *Man* 3 (1968): 361–76, esp. 364, 368–69.

53. "HUMOUR: On the Fear of Mad Dogs," *American Museum* 1 (Mar. 1787): 262–64.

Virtual Sex, Real Gender
Body and Identity in Transgender Discourse

Bernice L. Hausman

Transsexual discourses first appeared in the late 1940s and early 1950s. Produced in dialogues between transsexuals and their doctors, they reached a level of public attention in the late 1960s and after with the publication of the most famous transsexual autobiographies.[1] Transsexual autobiographies share similar narrative strategies, including: (1) the production of a seamless story about gender identity that obscures the significance of technology to the transsexual phenomenon; and (2) a recurrent reference to the physiology of the body as the cause of transsexual identity. These autobiographies are also intended to be educational documents, as each author not only represents the development of his or her own experience as a transsexual subject but explains clinical theories of transsexualism to the reader. In this way the authors hoped to educate the reading public about transsexualism, which is most often portrayed as an unfortunate condition necessitating medical intervention.[2]

Most recently, transsexual authors and others who may have undergone partial "sex change" procedures have begun to produce a different kind of discourse about gender.[3] More overtly political, and less obviously autobiographical, this discourse is more appropriately called "transgender theory," since it not only attempts to question many of the assumptions about the gender system that transsexualism relies on but also tries to provoke its readers to political and social activism. *Transgender* in this context means a revision of the transsexual position that came about as many would-be transsexuals began to acknowledge that changing from one sex to another did not necessarily alleviate the core social issues involved in the transsexual phenomenon, most prominently, the social requirement that males be masculine and females feminine. *Transgender* is also a more inclusive term, as it groups under its purview transsexuals, those individuals who undergo partial physical sex change, and those who engage in any behavior that "crosses" or transgresses established gender codes. Specific definitions of *transgender* depend, of course, on the author's political intents and affiliations.[4]

Transsexual discourses both assume and assert that the body ("sex") reflects, expresses, and signifies according to the mind ("gender"). Sex must be the same as gender; the body is a mirror of identity. In transgender discourse the body does not have to match the mind or have any predetermined meaning. In fact, a radical discontinuity between the sexed body and gendered experience is celebrated in much transgender theory. Transgender theorists tend to continue the presumption, however, that those who want to should be able to change their sex to be comfortable with themselves. This is more than a logical contradiction in their work. It belies a crucial set of beliefs about mind/body dualism, beliefs that replicate transsexual theory's insistence that the body can be the mind's double. In transgender theory the idea that one's body can and should be a willed phenomenon and the idea that bodies are voluntary husks for individual experience are linked to the assertion that changing sex is a radical act of gender activism—the release of the repressed other inside—rather than a capitulation to gender discourses and norms.

In this way transgender theory pretends to reverse the "transsexual position" in relation to gender norms but, instead, only replicates that position. Significantly, transgender discourses argue that sex itself is insignificant to the being of the subject. The bodies legible in many transgenderist writings signify only as representational problems—they inhibit the expression of the subject and are therefore distinct from the "true being" of that subject. (This scenario partially reverses transsexualism's tendency to assert physiological intersexuality as a probable cause of cross-sex identification, an assertion that suggests the body as the real origin of social behavior.) Changing the body's sex becomes, then, a viable project for reordering expectations of gender performance or for reordering social norms of gender. Sex, in transgender theory, is a virtual system, the reorganization of which will produce reality effects in the "real world" of gender.

This essay concerns the tensions inherent in transgenderism as an idea and as a subject position from which emanates a political discourse about gender. These tensions are linked, as I will show, to representations of and arguments about what constitutes sex and what constitutes gender. These, in turn, are linked to ideas about the person (specifically about identity and its constituents) and the role of technology in relieving modern individuals of the constraints of the body. One intriguing aspect of transgender discourses is how they utilize and manipulate feminist discourses on sex and gender. In a sense transgender discourses can demonstrate to feminism problems that exist in its own theoretical frameworks, as these are stretched to their breaking point by transgender theorists. Ultimately, thinking about sex as virtual and gender as real will keep us—a collective, inclusive us—from tackling systematic discrimination of women and of those persons whose gender presentation is at odds with cultural norms. To understand *gender* as a virtual system, then, is to see that it manipulates representations of the real but does not change the foundational perceptions of bodies upon which the "real" depends.

Degendering to Regendering

In "A Critique of the Sex/Gender Distinction," the first chapter of her book *Imaginary Bodies: Ethics, Power and Corporeality,* Australian feminist Moira Gatens argues that one significant effect of feminists' "use of the sex/gender distinction is to encourage or engender a neutralization of sexual difference and sexual politics."[5] Gatens connects this neutralization directly to the idea of a passive, inscribed-on (as opposed to an active, inscribing) body. In Gatens's account feminists who took up the sex/gender distinction that was originally articulated by psychoanalyst Robert Stoller in the 1960s and 1970s—and here Gatens includes Kate Millett, Germaine Greer, Ann Oakley, Nancy Chodorow, Dorothy Dinnerstein, and Michèle Barrett—argued for "degendering" as the strategy and goal of feminism. Gatens critiques this account of sexed experience by arguing against it as a "socialization theory, which posits the social acquisition of a particular gender by a particular sex" in a rationalist, ahistorical account that "posits a spurious neutrality of both body and consciousness" (7).

For Gatens bodily sex is not insignificant to the gender presentation of the subject. She writes, "The orthodox account of the gender/sex distinction claims that the social determination of personal identity operates at the level of ideas, the level of 'the mind.'" In the context of the (historical) sexedness of the subject, however, "what this account fails to note is the obvious divergence between feminine behaviour or experience that is lived out by a female subject and feminine behaviour or experience that is lived out by a male subject (and vice versa with masculine behaviour)" (Gatens 9). *Female subject* and *male subject* are terms that for Gatens signify the "situated" bodies of men and women—bodies, that is, that signify sex in a culture that only recognizes two sexed positions, male or female. Her argument against "degendering" as a strategy—and one way to understand degendering is to think of it as a removal or destruction of gender as a behavior that regulates the bodily performances of male and female subjects—is thus an argument against the notion that the body passively receives ideational categories of personality and consciousness.

Gatens's account of some feminist attempts to define and destroy the sex/gender distinction suggests that gender as a conceptual tool gained hegemony within feminist theory precisely because it relegated sex to "the biological, anatomical or physiological body" (Gatens 11). Feminist analysis could, in this scenario, concentrate on what was really important, the mind, and, what's more, what could be changed, ideological constructs. The body, it seemed, was fixed: immutable, stable, without history. Gatens counters this view by elaborating a concept of the "imaginary body," a body "necessary in order for us to have motility in the world, without which we could not be intentional subjects. The imaginary body is developed, learnt, connected to the body image of others, and is not static" (12). In other words, the imaginary body is historical.

In addition, the imaginary body is the ideational construct through which the real body signifies and is interpreted by others. In this sense the imaginary body constitutes the set of images and ideas through which, as subjects, we experience our embodiment. Crucial to that embodiment is, of course, sex. Gatens argues that the concept of the imaginary body allows us to understand a relation between sex and gender that while not determined—is not entirely coincidental: "Masculinity and femininity as forms of sex-appropriate behaviours are manifestations of a historically based, culturally shared phantasy about male and female biologies, and as such sex and gender are not arbitrarily connected. The connection between the female body and femininity is not arbitrary in the same way that the symptom is not arbitrarily related to its etiology." Feminist attention to gender as the category through which patriarchal authority maintains its power is thus a mistake, because "to treat gender, the 'symptom,' as the problem is to misread its genesis" (13).

Transgender theorists borrow some of the central categories and arguments from those Gatens calls the degendering feminists, although the degree and the spin of these borrowings differs in each case. Martine Rothblatt's book The Apartheid of Sex: A Manifesto on the Freedom of Gender argues for abolishing the notion of sexual difference altogether. Her general idea is that sexual status (and usually she specifies genital status)[6] offers society no information about the mental or emotional traits of any given individual; thus, sexual difference (or genital difference) has no social value as a classificatory system—it doesn't describe or predict anything. She makes an analogy between sex and race, the latter of which, she accurately points out, has been discredited as a significant biological category. Where sexual difference does seem to make some difference—conception, gestation, lactation—she argues that technology makes these differences moot: sperm banks make heterosexual conception obsolete, men can (or soon will be able to) gestate, and formula exists for feeding infants. The technology that ultimately does away with sexual difference is, of course, sex change: as long as humans can change sex through technological intervention, "natural" sexual difference has no meaning.[7] In Rothblatt's view sexual morphology should depend only on the will of the subject.

Rothblatt argues that the problem with the "apartheid of sex" is the idea that a particular type of body determines specific social behaviors. (Here we see her in conflict with Gatens's claims concerning the nonarbitrary relation between sex and gender.) In claiming that sex has no predictive value, Rothblatt suggests that gender based on sex is nonsensical, and to get rid of a useless system of classification we need to get rid of it at the level of the initial labeling—that is, what happens when a baby is born and the birth attendant calls it a boy or a girl. In many ways this is a bold move, because, in concentrating her analysis on sex, Rothblatt accurately highlights the problem with gender—that as a signifying system it depends upon a spurious, determining referential relation to the sexed body. That is, femininity operates culturally as the understood natural and only normal outcome of the female body (and vice versa for masculinity and the male body).

The difficulty with Rothblatt's terminology shows through, however, in her slippage between sex and gender as analytic categories: at points she argues that sex should be a "freely choosable human behavior and not a necessary consequence of chromosomal or genital configuration" (20). This slippage—from sex as a spurious biological category to sex as gender—demonstrates that Rothblatt wants to make sex into gender; that is, she wants sex not to refer to a description of bodily physiology and anatomy but to refer to a description of behaviors and activities. Gatens observes that Nancy Chodorow similarly "slides from notions of sex to notions of gender" without marking the slippage as problematic, and she suggests that this slippage from "biological terminology" to "psychological terminology" indicates an overall lack of attention to the body as a historical category (10–11). That Rothblatt uses the category of sex as a way to subsume the body within a psychologized concept of gender is evident in the following: "People should explore genders. When they settle on a set of gender behaviors, the name for that set describes their sex. . . . The important point is that gender exploration should come first, through free choice, and that sex is just the label for one's chosen gender" (Rothblatt 21). Compare the implications of this position to one prevalent in transsexual discourse: "people should be allowed to be the sex they feel they are as a gender." In fact, these are the same statement.

Kate Bornstein, on the other hand, uses *gender* as a universal term for both physical and social sexual differences. The problem with this usage is that it results in rather problematic terminology—for example, "biological gender." Bornstein's use of the phrase *biological gender* constitutes part of her argument against the idea that biology has any priority over what constitutes gender—in this sense her argument is the same as Rothblatt's. Bornstein's view, which she develops from Kessler and McKenna's *Gender: An Ethnomethodological Approach,* argues that all representations of sex (biological ones included) are gender, since they emanate from culture. Using the term *biological gender* is a way of highlighting the cultural construction of the body within the concept of sexual dimorphism; it is a way of making legible the body's inscription as a sexed cultural body.[8]

Rothblatt's usage is more successful as a subversion of the "sex/gender system," however, since it does a better job of demonstrating how scientific ideas about a determining biological sexual difference support ideas of social sexual difference. In a fundamental way the gender system reproduces itself each time a birth attendant says "boy" or "girl"—assigning sex is a way of setting up expectations of what we call gender. To call for an end to the "apartheid of sex" is therefore to do more than just argue for a plurality of gender presentations—it is a recognition of the way in which a system of gender polarization depends upon "biological essentialism," which is another way to signify a belief in the socially determining power of sexual biology.[9]

Rothblatt and Bornstein have the same goal, ultimately: they both want to end the linkage between perceptions of the body's sex and expectations about behavior and social performance as that sex. In addition, both are in agreement about the voluntary relation each subject should have to what Rothblatt calls sex and Bornstein calls gender. If Rothblatt's *The Apartheid of Sex* is utopian and impassioned in its argumentative plea to end the gender system, Bornstein's *Gender Outlaw* is postmodern and ironic in its self-reflexive, "pastiche" style and its suggestive (but not always sustained) discussion. In a characteristic "aside," indicated in the text by a different typeface and format, Bornstein asks the following questions:

>>What's your gender?
>>When did you decide that?
>>How much say do you have in your gender?
>>Is there anything about your gender or gender role that you don't
   like, or that gets in your way?
>>Are there one or two qualities about another gender that are
   appealing to you, enough so that you'd like to incorporate those
   qualities into your daily life?
>>What would happen to your life if you did that?
>>What would your gender be then?
>>How do you think people would respond to you?
>>How would you feel if they did that?

(79)

The implication of these questions is clear: it isn't right that we don't have "choice" in our gender: this lack of choice cramps our style, gets in our way, and makes changing to another gender dangerous. This same kind of voluntarism is evident in *The Apartheid of Sex* as well: Rothblatt foresees a world in which "manhood and womanhood can be lifestyle choices open to anyone, regardless of genitals" (3). What is interesting about this view of gender (or sex) as a voluntary status or set of behaviors is that it is based on the idea that the subject has a voluntary or entirely self-willed *identity*. Rothblatt writes, "When society understands that the mind dictates sex roles, it is possible to think that one's sex role is easily alterable—after all, we all change our minds" (144), suggesting that identity—as expressed in sex role behavior—is about the mind; is, in fact, the mind.

Rothblatt comes to argue for a new "system" that would, in her eyes, have greater predictive value than the current gender system. Her system would classify people according to erotic pleasures and levels of desire and would label people with different colors.[10] In a sense she wants to replace a binary system with one that has more classificatory slots—but she believes in classification all the same. Indeed, in Rothblatt's view once a person defines him- or herself according to this paradigm, the paradigm will better predict his or her behavior; this is what makes her system superior to what she calls apartheid of sex. Notice, however, Rothblatt's dependence on prediction, the idea that we should be able to label and know people through classifications; notice, in other words, the desire to order social behavior. This idea would seem to conflict with Rothblatt's other claim that there are as many sexual identities as people in the world, given that each is unique, since such radical diversity obviates against predictive classification.

Bornstein has no such desire—if anything, she would like to see greater chaos in the world of gender. Certainly, she presents herself as having experienced such chaos both before and since her sex change surgery (which she refers to as "gender conversion"). But she maintains, although her argument logically points in the opposite direction, that some people need technological sex change for their "comfort level," even though the rest of us should shake ourselves up and become much *less* comfortable with our gender.[11]

For Bornstein, as for Rothblatt, fighting against gender means reconceptualizing what gender is—or, rather, understanding its "true nature" in a way that redefines it:

> If ambiguity is a refusal to fall within a prescribed gender code, then fluidity is the refusal to remain one gender or another. Gender fluidity is the ability to freely and knowingly become one or many of a limitless number of genders, for any length of time, at any rate of change. Gender fluidity recognizes no borders or rules of gender. (51–52)

Rothblatt, in her book, uses the idea of a gender continuum (21). What is unclear in Bornstein's quote is what relation this new "gender fluidity" has to the idea of gender as a code of behavior linked conceptually to perceptions of the body's sex. There are not limitless numbers of genders precisely because gender is a system that refers back to the body as its a priori counterpart. Even if, as Judith Butler has shown, gender precedes sex,[12] sex is still necessary to gender as its mythic "natural origin." That's why we link up gender to the body in the way that we do; the linkage may be spurious and after-the-fact (putative rather than determining), but it exists all the same. For Moira Gatens the relation between the two terms is not entirely spurious; in her analysis bodily sex itself suggests limits to gender signification: "the body can and does intervene to confirm or to deny various social significances in a way that lends an air of inevitability to patriarchal social relations" (10). Representations of sex define the imaginary body and naturalize our understanding of gender; in the context of a society founded on sexual dimorphism, genders come in twos.

I don't know what it means to propose proliferating or fluid genders—or even to suggest a "continuum" of gender. What we can do, it seems to me, is demonstrate the radical discontinuities possible between bodies and behaviors. To expand on Gatens, this would mean driving a representational wedge between imaginary sexed bodies and gender performances. It would also mean imagining the body differently by questioning those images and paradigms that define the sexed body as we know it now. To herald "fluidity" as a new gender paradigm, however, is to suggest a movement between existing positions that will somehow "deconstruct" the structure within which those positions make sense. That structure is about identity and how it is constituted.

Gender is fluid in Bornstein's sense only if we believe that people knowingly take on identities and thus gender identities—take them on, shuck them off, deform and reformulate them. Yet that kind of willful identity play is impossible. When Butler talks about the performative constitution of gender identity, she is talking about the repetitive quality of performances that add up, over the course of a lifetime, to the production of a certain representation that is taken to be the identity core from which those performances emanate (144–49). Changing those performances, through the parodic play she calls subversive repetition, can affect the larger social system but only through the slow accrual of their limited local effects. When Bornstein talks about this kind of subversion, which she calls fluid gender, it happens in about an hour. Make a new gender, make a new self: no one has to play by the rules. The problem is that gender as a system doesn't work that way. One can't simply alter "identity" at will; Bornstein is talking about a willful playing with self-presentation, a kind of willful playing that may be fun and may make others think about the gender system and its hold on their behaviors and their expectations of others, but she isn't talking about fundamental change in a system that organizes behavior and classifies people according to rules of propriety and proper representation.

This problem is also evident in the following:

> I love the idea of being without an identity, it gives me a lot of room to play around; but it makes me dizzy, having nowhere to hang my hat. When I get too tired of not having an identity, I take one on: it doesn't really matter what identity I take on, as long as it's recognizable. I can be a writer, a lover, a confidante, a femme, a top, or a woman. I retreat into definition as a way of demarcating my space, a way of saying "Step back, I'm getting crowded here." . . . Gender identity is a form of self-definition: something into which we can withdraw, from which we can glean a degree of privacy from time to time, and with which we can, to a limited degree, manipulate desire. (Bornstein 39–40)

Gender identity here is a good thing, when constructed by the individual as a "private" thing. It is something produced actively by the subject as an escape from social pressure.

This seems an odd comment in a book dedicated to (in her words) deconstructing the gender system. The problem with gender identity as a concept is that it retroactively proposes that individuals who act a certain way do so as an expression of an inner, fixed self. What Bornstein is really writing about here is taking on a role as a way of defining herself in the moment; her discussion really isn't about producing new and different identities. But, I want to ask, if identity is essentially a performative effect, then doesn't taking on a role have a larger social impact? Gender identity isn't, in this theory, private at all—as a mode of self-expression and self-definition, it is linked to the public presentation of self. We cannot take refuge in identity because it exists as part of a larger social system of regulation, control, and the circulation of power. Bornstein and Rothblatt both argue that recreating gender identities is a valid form of gender resistance and subversion, yet these arguments show a studied blindness to (or denial of) the regulative power of such identity positions and labels.

This is where Bornstein and Rothblatt are clearly writing outside of the degendering framework that Gatens critiques. While aspects of the transgender analysis replicate aspects of the feminist arguments concerning the "destruction" of gender through "resocialization," Bornstein's use of the term *deconstruction* with reference to the gender system is significant. Her use of Butler's notion of the subversive power of "proliferating" gender performances is also important in this regard. Both Rothblatt and Bornstein argue, albeit implicitly, for *regendering* as a strategy of gender subversion. In this sense they perceive that producing *more genders* will disrupt a social system based on the recognition of only two genders. They utilize the notion that gender is absolutely arbitrarily connected to bodily sex in order to promote a multiplicity of gendered identities and performances. This plurality of genders, they believe, will make it impossible to regulate individuals into the confining gendered positions that are based on binary sexual difference. Thus, they deconstruct gender by forcing the sex/gender system to exceed its own logical boundaries.

Other transgender theorists work within a "regendering" framework, although differently. Minnie Bruce Pratt's *S/He* and Leslie Feinberg's *Stone Butch Blues* are both fictionalized autobiographical accounts of transgendered experience.[13] Both Pratt and Feinberg produce arguments about the relation of sex to gender as a way of theoretically grounding their presentations of transgendered self, and in these arguments we can trace another transgender theory of regendering as a strategy of gender subversion.

Transgendering Butch and Femme

Both Pratt and Feinberg situate their stories within lesbian communities. Pratt's *S/He* constitutes a series of short narratives about her coming to a "femme" identity from the androgyny of 1970s lesbian feminism.

Feinberg's novel, *Stone Butch Blues,* narrates the story of a transgendered woman who comes to that identity after experiencing the working-class butch/femme bar scene of the 1960s and a stint "passing" as a man during the recessions of the 1970s. For each author feminism provided an impetus for political understanding as well as a constraint against authentic self-representation. In both *S/He* and *Stone Butch Blues* feminism as a movement draws boundaries around "woman" as a category—boundaries that are understood as restrictive, oppressive, and counter to the goal of gender liberation. Both texts also attempt to demonstrate that butch/femme pairings can provide precisely that gender liberation, which is linked narratively to a sense of authentic, personal identity.

This "personal identity" is a gendered identity that is understood to be absolutely separate from one's bodily sex, as in the degender feminist theory discussed by Gatens. Minnie Bruce Pratt writes that transgender theory

> explores the infinities, the fluidities of sex and gender. The African-American woman eating sushi at the next table may be a woman lovely in her bones, gestures, tone of voice, but this does not mean that her genitals are female. If the handsome Filipino man in the upstairs apartment is straight-appearing, this does not mean his erotic preference is the "opposite sex." . . . The person on the subway you perceive as a white man in a business suit may have been born female, may consider herself a butch lesbian, or may identify himself as a gay man. The M and F on the questionnaire are useless. (22)

Yet in both *S/He* and *Stone Butch Blues* butchness and femmeness are presented as physical realities, truths about the embodied subject that cannot be masked or otherwise obscured. Pratt writes, "You point out a photograph, me in a wool plaid jacket and camouflage pants, in animated talk with another woman at a demonstration. I was wearing the disguise in which I attempted escape from the country of cornered women. You say, 'No matter what you wear you still move like a femme'" (125). In *Stone Butch Blues* the protagonist, Jess, and her butch friends attempt to make themselves up as women when they cannot find factory jobs: Jess says, "Look Grant, if it works for you then do it. But nobody's gonna hire me with that fucking wig on. And makeup's not gonna do it either. I need a bushel basket to hide who I am" (144).

In these texts butch and femme are categories of masculine and feminine identity that are apparent in the subject's bodily self-presentation. In this sense butch and femme are gendered categories that subsume the body as a representation of the psychological reality of the subject. Yet not all theorists involved in the "butch/femme debates" understand butch/femme identity as, essentially, a reflection of an inner gender identity expressed through the body. Other proponents of the radical subversiveness of butch/femme lesbian identity argue that, for example, "we labeled ourselves as part of our cultural ritual,"[14] suggesting a knowing performativity of gender. In addition, Joan Nestle understands that "butch-femme was an erotic partnership serving both as a conspicuous flag of rebellion and as an intimate exploration of women's sexuality" (101). In this sense butch/femme is the name for a style of sexual relationship and identity that was historically situated and experientially flexible (103–5).

I don't have the space here to explore the wide-ranging discussion that has come to be called the butch/femme debate. A comprehensive analysis of *S/He* and *Stone Butch Blues* would necessarily traverse that discursive terrain. What I want to do, however, is to suggest the ways in which Pratt and Feinberg interpret and present butch/femme identities as part of a strategy of transgender regendering; how, in other words, these authors take the categories of butch and femme from the context of lesbian experience and theory and rearticulate them in the context of transgender experience and theory. This displacement and replacement of the categories of butch and femme constitutes the central motif of Pratt and Feinberg's regendering strategy; it is also what distinguishes their work from that of Bornstein and Rothblatt, whose "transgender regendering" emerges from transsexual experience and theory.

In her essay "Identity and Seduction: Lesbians in the Mainstream" Linda Hart argues that "within the terms of the specular economy only the butch is the 'real' lesbian. . . . If sighting the butch produces a recognition of the instability of gender, this seeing nonetheless retains, indeed depends upon, the facticity of sex. *As the figure who makes possible the entry of lesbians into the visible, the butch balances uneasily on the divide between disruption of rigid heterosexual sign systems and assimilation or reification of the heterosexual dyad.*"[15] Hart's essay concerns the performance art of Split Britches, a lesbian couple who often perform butch/femme. While some lesbian performance theorists have faulted Split Britches for producing assimilationist theater—that is, butch/femme representations that can be understood by the audience to have no specifically lesbian content—Hart argues that, "if some spectators did not *see* lesbians in this performance, it is because these lesbians resist and mock the permissible visibility of dominant sexual discourse" (132).

The relation of this "visibility" of the butch/femme couple as lesbian (or queer) and the potential subversiveness of the butch/femme couple as a transgendered representation is central to the narratives of *S/He*. In "Jellyfish" Pratt writes of walking through a hotel lobby: "On the towering merry-go-round of a lobby couch, a circle of white men sit staring at us, hostile, cheated of grabbing at me like a gold ring, cheated of their ride at the amusement park by the sea. Their stares kill us with each step we take across the crowded floor. They know what they see: No real man, and no real woman, but a couple of queers" (135). Yet in "Kisses," when she and her lover go to the latter's gym, she writes, "It's a gay gym, but a few heterosexual couples insist they can do it anywhere they please, the man and woman who rolled writhing on the mats—while the infrequent men caught at it with each other in the bathroom are always kicked out. *Though we are two women, here we'd be seen as heterosexual, and resented.* No, no kissing here" (146). The potential subversiveness of the performance is always determined by its context as well as, Linda Hart might add, whether or not the audience is capable of *seeing* that context and *reading* it in relation to the performance. As Hart suggests, the figure of the butch is both what constitutes the visible lesbian *and* that which is most likely to be assimilated as a copy of heterosexuality.

This is precisely the point at which a butch/femme regendering strategy of gender subversion can falter. The risks of replicating existing gender norms are very high. As Pratt points out in "Kissing," there are scenarios in which a butch/femme lesbian couple can stand in for oppressive, public heterosexuality. In addition, in order for the butch/femme regendering strategy to work as a subversion of traditional gender norms, sex must be conventionally legible as a truth of the body, and the butch/femme couple must be seen as parodically subverting the norm, not as trying to attain it. In order to operate safely in the world, however, the lovers in *S/He* are constantly watchful of their reception by others—how those others perceive them; whether those others can, in fact, correctly "read" their sex in relation to their gender presentation. To be read correctly is to be physically at risk; to be read incorrectly is to pass as normatively heterosexual but to be safe.

In the context of such an ambivalent challenge to an oppressive "gender system," it is instructive to consider the envisioned effect of dismantling that system. In much transgender theory gender is dispersed through multiplicity and the achievement of authentic identity: people are allowed to "be themselves." Both *Stone Butch Blues* and *S/He* end with the protagonist-narrators coming to terms with their identities in the context of their political histories. Both protagonists embrace identities that are more complex than those they started with. For Pratt this means complicating the idea of sexual difference (man/woman) with a notion of multiple genders (186–87). For Feinberg it means refusing to pass as a man: "I fought long and hard to be included as a woman among women, but I always felt so excluded by my differences. I hadn't just believed that passing would hide me. I hoped that it would allow me to express the part of myself that didn't seem to be a woman. I didn't get to explore being a he-she though. I simply became a he—a man without a past" (*Stone*, 222). Both make peace with past experiences and conclude by looking toward a future of change.

Significantly, in both texts there is a fundamental move toward comfort with the self—and this is a point of connection between the regendering strategies of Pratt and Feinberg and those of Bornstein and Rothblatt. Yet, while all four seem bent on producing identities that provide "comfort" for the subject as a body, Rothblatt and Bornstein are more positive in their assessment of the possibility of such a goal. These latter theorists believe in a radical pluralism of sex identity and a community of impeccable tolerance—acceptance and personal growth are hallmarks of the communities they envision. Both Rothblatt and Bornstein are unrepentant new age utopianists, seeing a certain kind of freedom from social constraints upon behavior not only possible but probable in the near future. Their work idealizes a model of open-ended gender play in which everyone examines and has fun with the different aspects of their gendered personas, and they believe, fundamentally, that this kind of play will result in a saner, more livable, and just world. Yet, while Pratt and Feinberg might authorize such gender play as politically subversive, they both produce graphic representations of the very real, physical costs of such "play." In *S/He* and *Stone Butch Blues* representations of public violence against those who transgress the norms of gender behavior, as well as the very difficult social relationship carved out by the protagonists in *S/He*, work to unsettle the optimism of the texts' endings.

At the end of *Stone Butch Blues* the narrator has spoken publicly at a rally for gay rights and is considering a job as a union organizer. The text ends with her remembering "Duffy's challenge. *Imagine a world worth living in, a world worth fighting for.* I closed my eyes and allowed my hopes to soar. . . . A young man on a nearby roof released his pigeons, like dreams, into the dawn" (Feinberg, *Stone*, 301). Pratt finishes *S/He* with these words: "We walk home talking again of fundamental change, of the edifice of power, of what is to be done. We are the obscure stones at whose shift the walls will crack from bottom to top, dirt to wind, so that all can be built again for all. If the lowest stones move, those who scrape and sell even the sky will crash down in a scatter of glittering rock" (189). Yet for both authors the public display of butch/femme identity—being queer together as a couple, being visibly butch and femme *and* woman and woman—is dangerous. There is always a threat of external violence, of physical conflict.

The optimistic portrayals at each text's ending must be read against the implication that such optimism necessitates face-to-face political struggle with others who refuse to grant personhood to those who do not produce conventional representations of gendered selfhood.

The "comfort" in these texts admits of no technological "fix"; if anything, it is the result of decades of personal and political struggle. If Jess, in *Stone Butch Blues*, states that "I didn't regret the decision to take hormones. . . . And the surgery [mastectomy] was a gift to myself, a coming home to my body" (224), she also stops taking hormones and passing as a man because she feels uncomfortable with the male presence she seems to create: "My face no longer revealed the contrasts of my gender. I could see my passing self, but even I could no longer see the more complicated me beneath my surface" (222). For Jess the technology of passing allows her to "survive," in a narrow economic sense, but not to produce a comfortable identity. Her comfort comes, as I suggested earlier, from accepting the complications of an identity that, at least in conventional terms, contradicts sexed embodiment at a number of levels.

This is not to argue for butch/femme regendering as a more successful transgender strategy than Bornstein and Rothblatt's regendering strategies. I am not convinced that Minnie Bruce Pratt and Leslie Feinberg do more than reify notions of masculinity and femininity as idealized—if stylized— aspects of self that exist in a Platonic formality and express themselves through human subjects. In this sense their texts do little more than reconceptualize the lesbian butch and femme within the context of what Pratt calls "the emerging thought of transgender liberation—a movement that embraces drag queens and kings, transsexuals, cross-dressers, he-shes and she-males, intersexed people, transgenderists, and people of ambiguous, androgynous, or contradictory sex and gender" (21). With so many constituencies to "cover," such a movement is bound to produce vague goals and tenets—or to make problematic connections between identity groups— for Pratt is not arguing for an articulated, forged, theoretical connection but an overarching theory that "embraces" all. In a similar way Feinberg argues, in a short pamphlet entitled "Trangender Liberation: A Movement Whose Time Has Come," that, while transgendered people and gay people constitute two distinct groups whose membership only partially overlaps, "we face a common enemy. Gender-phobia—like racism, sexism, and bigotry against lesbians and gay men—is meant to keep us divided" (2, 6). That is, the category of gender is what connects groups whose experiences and embodied subjectivities might otherwise be considered distinct.

Gender can only do that if, as Feinberg writes in "Transgender Libera-

see previous page

tion," it is understood as "self-expression, not anatomy" (2, 5). Indeed, what seems to unite all the groups listed by Pratt is a desire to promote identity as authorized by the self rather than the social. Yet what seems to me to be the most interesting aspect of *S/He* and *Stone Butch Blues* is left out of this notion of an individual, self-authorizing identity—that is, the difficult negotiation of an embodied self in a social context to come to terms with a complex identity that is produced precisely through that negotiation. In this sense gender can never be "self-expression" but is always one product (among many) of the experiences of embodied, situated, subjectivity—in Gatens's terms, one effect of living in relation to an imaginary body. To the extent that both Minnie Bruce Pratt and Leslie Feinberg offer the materials for such an analysis, their "transgender" texts participate in a theoretical struggle to redefine the conventional relation between sex and gender that does not relegate sex to virtuality—or insignificance.[16]

Virtual Gender

Kate Bornstein and Martine Rothblatt's optimism about the future and their belief in what Teresa Ebert might call "ludic politics"—"a textual practice that seeks open access to the free play of signification in order to disassemble the dominant cultural policy (totality), which tries to restrict and stabilize meaning"[17]—is evident in the way that each celebrates the "cyber world" and its possibilities for gender re-creation. Rothblatt writes:

> Computers and telecommunication are likely to play an important role in dismantling the apartheid of sex. It is much easier to disconnect ourselves from thousands of years of rigidly fixed notions about sex and gender when we telecommunicate than when we are face to face. (149)

chpt 4 link

This communication is "easier" because "cyberspace readily allows people to transcend their known sexual identity" (149). And in the future, "when cyberspace is enhanced by virtual reality, there [will be] innumerable opportunities to 'try on' genders as part of cybersexual explorations" (152). In Rothblatt's view, in cyberspace people can really act on the continuum of gendered behaviors that she argues is the true reality of humanity. Virtual reality (VR) will be the model from which the real world of gender will take its cues. VR will certainly make it easier to make the gender shift, since in Rothblatt's scenario the presence of the body is a constraint upon social change.

For her part Bornstein writes that the "future of gender" is "already here today, alive and thriving within the structures of our primitive virtual realities." She defines VR more broadly than most, including "the written word, the telephone, electronic bulletin boards, and . . . theater" within its purview. VR transforms gender because VR is "a method of making partitions obsolete. We have the opportunity to play with gender in much the same way that we get to play with other forms of identity—through performance in any virtual medium" (Bornstein 138). Significantly, Bornstein believes that what we do in VR, how we play with gender and reenvision it, will model gender for us in the real. As in Rothblatt's argument, to rethink gender we need to be in a space where our bodies do not matter.

For most humans, however, bodies matter in daily life. They do not necessarily matter all the time—witness Denise Riley's astute observation that "perhaps the power of complaints about 'being treated as a sexual object' comes in part from experiences of the sudden violence of being pulled back into 'being a woman' by, say, shouts on the street you walk down, your thoughts 'elsewhere.'"[18] "Being treated as a sexual object" here is tantamount to being reminded of one's body, of the sex of that body, whatever identity position one might generally inhabit. Thus, while using VR as a tool to reimagine and reconfigure relations between people, we need to remember that those relations need to be changed in the real, where people's bodies come into contact—visual, physical—every day. If we don't account for the stresses and difficulties of that very contact, we will never find a way to change the social realities that refer back to the sexed body as their origin.

We need to address the idea of sex itself so as not to forget that normative expectations of gender performance are so powerful precisely because they link social behaviors with specific body morphologies. As Judith Butler has so persuasively shown, sex (as body, biology) does not underlie or determine gender presentation: that presentation itself constructs the body it is said to represent. In this sense gender is a simulation—self-perpetuating and without a referential relation to the real. Rather, its relation to the real is one of attribution. But norms of gender work *because* they are linked by attribution to perceived biological differences between what are designated as "the sexes"—that is, gender norms depend upon sexual difference as a recognizable and predictable perceptual system. Disrupting this linkage— making it impossible to use *sex* as the after-the-fact referent for gender by disrupting received wisdom about sex itself—constitutes, I believe, a significant challenge to the gender system precisely because it demonstrates that gender (and not sex) is virtual. By this I mean that, like VR, gender describes a simulated set of experiences that produce and maintain reality effects, while as an experience it is fictive—in Robert Markley's words, "a narrative that creates a coherence it would like to imagine 'really' exists."[19]

This does not mean that we ignore Moira Gatens's argument that the relationship of sex to gender is not entirely arbitrary. An interrogation of sex as a biological category that will not sustain gender as its determined social product should involve an examination of the ways in which physiology and anatomy do put constraints upon what counts as a sexed body or a gendered performance. Only by demonstrating the impossibility of a determining relation between sex and gender can we begin to suggest linkages between the two terms that do not uphold the status quo. For example, Gatens argues,

> To insist on two bodies is strategically important given that we live in a patriarchal society that organizes itself around pure sexual difference, that is male or female, and will not tolerate sexual ambiguity, for example, hermaphrodites, but forces a definite either/or sex on each person. . . . However, even the *biological* determination of sex is not so straightforwardly clear and we must acknowledge sex as a continuum and bodies as multiple. (19n. 30)

If sex is not virtual, what does it mean to say it is real? Does that mean that it is not discursive, or socially constructed? Can it be real and not determinative of social behavior? I want to explore these questions by examining Kate Hayles's discussion of *embodiment* as a category of experience that is crucial to postmodernism, even as it is a category most obviously evacuated of significance by postmodern theory. As she analyzes—and argues for—embodiment in relation to VR, Hayles provides some critical concepts for elaborating the tensions between sex and gender that I am examining here.

Hayles writes that "the dematerialization of embodiment . . . is one of the characteristic features of postmodern ideology" and one that will "likely stupefy future generations."[20] She defines *embodiment* as distinct from "the body," the latter of which she understands as "normative relative to some set of criteria" and as "an idealized form that gestures toward a Platonic reality" (Hayles, "Materiality," 154–55). The body in this sense is an abstraction, a representation held to be, or attempting to be, universal in its scope. The body is also what "is naturalized within culture; embodiment becomes naturalized only secondarily through its interactions with concepts of the body" (156). "Embodiment," in Hayles's scenario, is "contextual, enwebbed within the specifics of place, time, physiology and culture that together comprise enactment." It also "individually articulates" (thus is not universal) and, because of this, is "inherently destabilizing with respect to the body, for at any time this tension can widen into a perceived disparity" (154–55). Embodiment is also performative (156).

With this set of distinctions between the body and embodiment—the former abstract and universal, although naturalized; the latter instantiated and particular—it would be easy to make a corresponding distinction between sex (as an abstraction, a universal representation of bodily difference) and gender (as the instantiated, sedimented incorporations of bodily difference). After all, haven't I been trying to argue for sex as having a special relation to the body? Isn't gender performative? Such a distinction would eventually fail to convince, however, since the body as I have been trying to represent it is far from abstract; indeed, it is the product of the sedimented reality of living as a sex. What I think Hayles is getting at—and what I want to theorize—is a distinction between scientific representations of the body and the experience of living as a sexed body; a body, that is, defined by sexual dimorphism, but experiencing the inventedness and partiality of its designations. Thus, in my analysis talking about the body and about embodiment in her terms is always within the category "sex." The sexed body—the sexually dimorphic body of science—is a representation that all real bodies—that is, embodied persons—are said to experience and ascribe to, but it is a body that is indeed an abstraction, a normative construct, an idea. Gatens's "imaginary body" represents this idealized abstraction of scientific discourse as it is incorporated by individuals into embodied experience. Our experiences as embodied persons consistently refer to the notion that the body is the source (and not partial outcome) of sexually differentiated behaviors. This is especially true, as Hayles describes it, in the inscribing experiences that attempt to enforce "nonverbal lessons" about performing as a sex—"boys don't walk like that," etc.—even as they demonstrate that that performance is an achieved phenomenon (157).

In my analysis Hayles's comment that the "dematerialization of embodiment" is a "characteristic feature of postmodern ideology" describes postmodernism's embrace of gender over sex. Gender is a category of experience and classification that emerged in the post–World War II period as a way to distinguish biology (sex) from psychosocial identity (gender).[21] Gender is a way to talk about sexual experiences and classifications without reference to the body. Feminists appropriated the concept from medicine in the 1960s and 1970s precisely because it seemed to promise a discourse about the historicity and social embeddedness of women's subordination. Gender theory suggested that the problem couldn't be assimilated to "biology," which was perceived as monolithic, unchangeable, and true. Since the mid-1970s sex discrimination has become gender discrimination and thus does not describe perceptions of women per se but concerns behaviors, experiences, representations, and identifications available to either sex. The way that gender has developed as a category of analysis—within and without feminist theory—has enhanced the idea that as a concept it isn't about bodies at all. Thus, the body is a problem that gender theory can't solve, or even approach, even as postmodernism circles around it endlessly.

To say that the abstract body is sex and that embodiment is gender is to replicate the problem of postmodernism's refusal of the material exigencies of physical life. To argue that sex as a category encompasses both the body and embodiment is to emphasize a shift away from the popular notion of social construction as discursive inscription. Lived bodies are not "blank slates" onto which culture writes its codes, nor are they empty shells into which culture pours its significations. As helpful as gender has been to develop feminist theories of women's subordination, we now need to return to and complicate sex in an effort to rethink embodiment during an era bent on watching it (virtually) disappear.

Denaturalizing the body and demonstrating its discursivity, the classic postmodern move, does not address those nasty problems of embodiment that still live with us, even in postmodernity. Whether or not we really live in bodies defined by sexual dimorphism is a question begging for scientific and social analysis. One way to stretch the boundaries of such an inquiry would be to exploit the "tension" between embodiment and the body that Hayles remarks on, that is, the discontinuities between abstract conceptions of sexual difference and the lived experiences of being a sexed subject. The problem that Hayles points out, and which I agree with her on, is that denaturalizing the body ends up making it seem as if embodiment doesn't matter in the postmodern world at all. Indeed, Hayles deconstructs the postmodern blindness to bodily significance by demonstrating how embodiment is crucial to the production of that oh-so-postmodern of products, information—which in the rhetoric of cyberspace has no matter at all. She writes, "virtual reality (VR) is a sophisticated computer technology that puts the body into an intense and direct feedback loop with a simulation." In a sense VR depends upon the subject's embodiment because it takes over some of the characteristics of embodiment: "Virtual technologies modify the body's proprioceptive sense at the same time that they extend and reinforce it." Proprioception, in Hayles's words, is "conveyed through the inner ear and internal nerve endings, defines body boundaries and gives us the sense that we inhabit our bodies" (167).[22]

Virtual reality is a technology, then, that relies on a rhetoric of bodily insignificance even as it depends upon the subject's embodiment for its reality-effects. And, moving back to consider the transgender discourses discussed earlier, we remember that both Bornstein and Rothblatt value cyberspace and virtual reality as "sites" for gender play and gender transgression precisely because in them embodiment does not matter. There, subjects can be an identity without a body, which is a concept implicit in the central trope of transsexualism ("a man/woman trapped in a woman/man's body"). As Hayles writes, "cyberspace [is] conceptualized as a disembodied realm of information that humans enter by leaving their bodies behind. In this realm, so the story goes, we are transformed into information ourselves and thus freed from the constraints of embodiment. We can take whatever form we wish, including no form at all."[23] Yet, as she reminds us in a question, "Is it necessary to insist, once again, that embodiment is not an option but a necessity in order for life to exist?" (Hayles, "Boundary Disputes," 466). Indeed, representations of personal decisions made by these two prominent transgender theorists suggest that not only is embodiment not inconsequential to the subject's identity but that they perceive embodiment necessarily to correspond to the body of sexual dimorphism.

In the afterword to *The Apartheid of Sex* Rothblatt writes:

> For most of my life I lived as a man. I went to school as a man and became a lawyer. I launched satellite systems as a man and became an entrepreneur. I got married as a man and started a family. Then, a few years ago, I decided to convert and become a kind of transgendered woman. Why? *Because there was a lot more to my soul than the masculine persona I had become. There was a woman who needed to be expressed.* (159; emph. added)

And in the "International Bill of Gender Rights" that appends *The Apartheid of Sex* Rothblatt includes "The Right to Control and Change One's Own Body": "All human beings have the right to control their bodies, which includes the right to change their bodies cosmetically, chemically, or surgically, *so as to express a self-defined gender identity*" (168; emph. added).

Similarly, in *Gender Outlaw* Bornstein writes:

> I never hated my penis; I hated that it made me a man—in my own eyes, and in the eyes of others. *For my comfort, I needed a vagina—I was convinced that the only way I could live out what I thought to be my true gender was to have genital surgery to construct a vagina from my penis.* Fortunately, I don't regret having done this. (47; emph. added)

She also writes:

I had my genital surgery partially as a result of cultural pressure: I couldn't be a "real woman" as long as I had a penis. Knowing what I know now, I'm real glad I had my surgery, and I'd do it again, just for the comfort I now feel with a constructed vagina. I *like* that thang [*sic*]! (119)

These statements suggest that, at least for these writers, sexed embodiment is a central component to ideas about the self—in other words, a central component to identity. They argue, however, that when the subject perceives his or her sexed body to be an inaccurate representation of the self, the subject should have the right to change that body—specifically, to the "other body," understood as the opposite body of sexual dimorphism. Thus, the body of science and the embodied experiences of material life come together in the calls for individual self-determination of bodily habitus.

Subjectivity, in this sense, is a product of the mind, and one's body is its apt reflection. But that body is also a *necessary* reflection of identity—that is why there is such stress on "comfort" in both texts. This suggests that, like VR discourses, these transgender discourses discount the significance of embodiment yet depend on it as a ground for human experience. They assert that gender can be a disembodied experience—all "mind" and cyberplay— yet maintain that gender needs an appropriately sexed body to "express itself."[24]

Taking Hayles's ideas about embodiment seriously means thinking about what Jacquelyn Zita suggests is the "historical weight of the body": "This body is not only a thing in the world, subject to physical gravity, but a thing that carries its own historical gravity, and this *collected weight* bears down on the 'sexedness' of the body and the possibilities of experience. Postmodernism is right in revealing the 'inventedness' of this body but wrong in supposing that this implies a protean self ambulating between 'positionalities.'"[25] Notice that Zita links history with the physical: "collectively" they provide the body with its sexual "weight," together they create and sustain sexed embodiment. This "protean self," the real of identity *as* gender, surfaces throughout transgender discourse, over and against the virtuality, the infinite mutability of the sexed body. And yet, in their discussion of VR, Bornstein and Rothblatt show that in this opposition between sex and gender, it is truly *gender* that is virtual—that which exists without a body, that which is centrally not embodied, and thus that which exists as pure simulation. Rather than argue *for* virtual gender, we must, it seems to me, advocate a return to embodiment and its problems as a central component of feminism's analysis of women's situation and as the name for a complex of issues that transsexualism and transgenderism bring into bold relief.[26]

Most transgender discourses, like transsexual discourses, end up promoting the sexed body as representative of gendered identity. In both discursive scenarios embodiment is acknowledged as a problem, but the problem is quickly "solved" through recourse to a "technological fix." As should be clear from my preceding comments, I am critical of this notion that technology solves—or even addresses—the tensions of sexed embodiment. Discursive solutions, such as Judith Halberstam's claim that "we are all transsexuals. . . . [F]or some of us our costumes are made of fabric or material, while for others they are made of skin; for some an outfit can be changed; for others, skin must be resewn. There are no transsexuals,"[27] deny the material limits of the human body and its resistance to tissue alteration. Skin is only a fabric enclosing the body in a metaphoric sense—and, while we cannot stop using metaphors to represent the body, we should be able to recognize them as such and avoid the category mistakes that allow us to elide the differences between the two terms fused in the figure.

In "Organs without Bodies" Rosi Braidotti suggests that there currently exists a "paradoxical mixture of simultaneous discursive overexposure and absence" concerning the body.[28] Transgender theory contributes to this overexposure and this absence by simultaneously demonstrating contradictions inherent in sexed embodiment and denying the significance of embodiment to gendered subjectivity. I would suggest that one way to rectify this problem of the body's ubiquitous presence and seeming invisibility is to begin to examine it as a material entity, beginning with an interrogation of those categories, like gender, that have contributed to the body's contradictory status by serving as an alibi for a notion of identity that exists as pure information.

NOTES

1. See, for example, Christine Jorgensen, *Christine Jorgensen: A Personal Autobiography* (New York: Paul Eriksson, 1967); Jan Morris, *Conundrum* (New York: Harcourt Brace Jovanovich, 1974); Mario Martino, *Emergence* (New York: Crown Publishers, 1977); Renée Richards, *Second Serve: The Renée Richards Story,* with John Ames (New York: Stein and Day, 1983); and Nancy Hunt, *Mirror Image* (New York: Holt, Rinehart, and Winston, 1978).

2. See chapter 5 of my book, *Changing Sex: Transsexualism, Technology, and the Idea of Gender* (Durham: Duke University Press, 1995), for a detailed discussion of transsexual autobiographies.

3. Since writing this essay, a number of books and essays on transsexualism and

transgenderism have been published. This piece is thus only a part of a conversation that is currently heated and detailed and which has taken off in directions unanticipated by my thoughts in 1996. In addition, I overlooked at least one consideration of virtual reality and transgender theory (see Stone below). Please see Riki Anne Wilchins, *Read My Lips: Sexual Subversion and the End of Gender* (Ithaca: Firebrand, 1997); Richard Ekins, *Male Femaling: A Grounded Theory Approach to Cross-Dressing and Sex-Changing* (New York: Routledge, 1997); Richard Ekins and Dave King, eds., *Blending Genders: Social Aspects of Cross-Dressing and Sex-Changing* (New York: Routledge, 1996); Holly Devor, *FTM: Female-to-Male Transsexuals in Society* (Bloomington: Indiana University Press, 1997); Kate Bornstein, *My Gender Workbook* (New York: Routledge, 1998); Allucquère Rosanne Stone, *The War of Desire and Technology at the Close of the Mechanical Age* (Cambridge: MIT Press, 1995); and Jay Prosser, *Second Skins: The Body Narratives of Transsexuality* (New York: Columbia University Press, 1998). See also Susan Stryker, ed., *GLQ* 4.2 (1998), for a special transgender issue.

4. For example, the following definitions of *transgendered* appeared on the "alt.transgendered" newsgroup on the Internet: "Transgendered refers to people who possess the qualities of both male and female in the way they think act and live. There are various degrees of transgenderism. Ranging from simple cross-dressing (periodically dressing as or wearing articles of clothing of the opposite sex) to post-op transsexualism (surgically changing one's sex to the opposite" (Kelly Ann, <kstiles@ix.netcom.com> <alt.transgendered> [25 Sept. 1995]); "Transgendered generally means that we look down, note that we have genitals, note that we feel grief that they aren't the right ones, and set about resolving the problems which arise from those feelings" (Joan Tine, <jott@snugbug.cts.com> <alt.transgendered> [25 Sept. 1995]); "Trangendered has TWO uses: 1. A general term referring to those who are not satisfied by remaining full time in the appearance of their genital sex. This includes transvestites, transgenderists (who live full time as women), transsexuals who are in one stage or another of a rather lengthy transition, and post-op TSs. . . . 2. A specific term used for transgenderists. . . . Those who crossdress full time are, of course, living as women to the best of their ability and want to be recognized as women. . . . The thing that separates Transgenderists from Transsexuals is that Transgenderists do not have, and usually don't want, genital surgery" (Allison Marsh, <goodl@mail.halcyon.com> <alt.transgendered> [19 Sept. 1995]); "Trans is short for trangender, or, as I prefer to think of it (following author Kate Bornstein), transgressively gendered" (Dallas Denny, <aegis@mindspring.com> <alt.transgendered> [11 Oct. 1995]).

Transgender theorist Leslie Feinberg writes, "There are other words [other than 'he-shes'] used to express the wide range of 'gender outlaws': transvestites, transsexuals, drag queens and drag kings, cross-dressers, bulldaggers, stone butches, androgynes, diesel dykes or berdaches—a European colonialist term. We didn't choose these words. They don't fit all of us. It's hard to fight an oppression without a name connoting pride, a language that honors us. In recent years a community has begun to emerge that is sometimes referred to as the gender or transgender community.

Within our community is a diverse group of people who define ourselves in many different ways. Transgendered people are demanding the right to choose our own self-definitions." Leslie Feinberg, *Transgender Liberation: A Movement Whose Time Has Come* (New York: World View Forum, 1992), 5–6. Hereafter all references will appear parenthetically in the text.

5. Moira Gatens, *Imaginary Bodies: Ethics, Power and Corporeality* (New York: Routledge, 1996), 4. Hereafter all references will appear parenthetically in the text.

6. Indeed, Rothblatt's consistent reference to sexual difference *as genital difference* demonstrates an unconscious tendency to think of sex as genitalia, a common tendency in transsexual discourses in which genitals are the focus of anatomical sex change.

7. Martine Rothblatt, *The Apartheid of Sex: A Manifesto on the Freedom of Gender* (New York: Crown, 1995), 17. Hereafter all references will appear parenthetically in the text.

8. Kate Bornstein, *Gender Outlaw: On Men, Women, and the Rest of Us* (New York: Routledge, 1994), 30. Hereafter all references will appear parenthetically in the text. Suzanne Kessler and Wendy McKenna, *Gender: An Ethnomethodological Approach* (Chicago: University of Chicago Press, 1985).

9. For an excellent discussion of biological essentialism from a feminist perspective, see Sandra Bem, *The Lenses of Gender* (New Haven: Yale University Press, 1993), 6–38.

10. Literally. Some of Rothblatt's examples of "Chromatic Sexual Identity" follow: "Green: An equally aggressive/nurturing person who does not try to appear sexy; Pine Green: A slightly (about one-third) aggressive but mostly nourishing (about two-thirds) person who does not try to appear sexy; Lime Green: A slightly (about one-third) nourishing but mostly aggressive (about two-thirds) person who does not try to appear sexy; Purple: A nonaggressive person, self-described as equally nourishing and erotic" (114). She also describes orange, brown, white, and black.

11. I have not seen Kate Bornstein in performance. Ann Kilkelly, a performance artist and theorist, tells me that in performance Bornstein puts in play the very discomfort with gender and body that is subordinated in *Gender Outlaw*. Kilkelly emphasizes that it is precisely Bornstein's evident discomfort within her own body and performance space that puts into play questions about gender. Kilkelly argues that texts like *Gender Outlaw* don't adequately account for the radical effect of Bornstein's theater (pers. comm., April 19, 1996, Blacksburg, Va.).

Not having seen Bornstein on stage, I cannot argue with Kilkelly's account and interpretation. On the other hand, I am interested here in analyzing written texts whose circulation, I believe, is greater than the number of people privy to a Kate Bornstein performance. Texts like *Gender Outlaw* and *The Apartheid of Sex* represent important discursive evidence of the way in which transgender theorists choose to utilize accepted gender narratives to promote their political interests. Certainly, a fuller treatment of this topic would have to take into account the diverse sites, discursivities, and textualizations through which and within which transgender narratives take shape.

12. Judith Butler, *Gender Trouble: Feminism and the Subversion of Identity* (New York: Routledge, 1990). Hereafter all references will appear parenthetically in the text.

13. Minnie Bruce Pratt, *S/He* (Ithaca: Firebrand, 1995); Leslie Feinberg, *Stone Butch Blues* (Ithaca: Firebrand, 1993). Hereafter all references will appear parenthetically in the text.

Feinberg's book is generally understood to be fictionalized autobiography. *S/He* is more appropriately defined as "creative nonfiction." In "Gender Quiz," the first essay in the volume, Pratt writes that "we cannot move theory into action unless we can find it in the eccentric and wandering ways of our daily life. I have written the *stories* that follow to give the theory flesh and breath" (22; emph. added). This emphasis on "story" suggests that Pratt values narrativity over "fact."

It is perhaps significant to note here that Leslie Feinberg and Minnie Bruce Pratt are partners. Thus, the masculine lesbian lover in *S/He* is Feinberg.

14. Joan Nestle, *A Restricted Country* (Ithaca: Firebrand, 1987), 103. Hereafter all references will appear parenthetically in the text.

15. Lynda Hart, "Identity and Seduction: Lesbians in the Mainstream," in *Acting Out: Feminist Performances,* ed. Lynda Hart and Peggy Phelan (Ann Arbor: University of Michigan Press, 1993), 125. Hereafter all references will appear parenthetically in the text.

16. I find it disheartening, then, that Minnie Bruce Pratt writes, "The *M* and the *F* on the questionnaire are useless" (22). I want to ask, useless in terms of what? In terms of determining or predicting the gender identity of the subject so labeled? Yes, and here Pratt would agree with Rothblatt that the "apartheid of sex" has little value as a predictive system. But "M" and "F" are ways—paltry, insufficient, undertheorized ways—to understand the physical body and its functions. Rather than condemning them as "useless," and thus relegating the sexed body to insignificance, I would like to see an interrogation of those categories and their insufficiencies, their partialities, their room for improvement.

17. Teresa L. Ebert, "The 'Difference' of Postmodern Feminism," *College English* 53 (1991): 887. For an extended discussion of these issues, see Teresa L. Ebert, *Ludic Feminism and After* (Ann Arbor: University of Michigan Press, 1996).

18. Denise Riley, "Does Sex Have a History?: 'Women' and Feminism," *New Formations* 1 (1987): 38.

19. Robert Markley, "Introduction: Shreds and Patches: The Morphogenesis of Cyberspace," *Configurations* 2 (1994): 435.

20. N. Katherine Hayles, "The Materiality of Informatics," *Configurations* 1 (1993): 147. Hereafter all references will appear parenthetically in the text.

21. See Hausman, *Changing Sex,* esp. chap. 3 ("Managing Intersexuality and Producing Gender"), for a discussion of this development.

22. Anne Balsamo concurs with Hayles. In "The Virtual Body in Cyberspace" Balsamo writes that, "although the body may disappear representationally in virtual worlds—indeed, we may go to great lengths to repress it and erase its referential traces—it does not disappear materially in the interface with the VR apparatus or, for that matter, in the phenomenological frame of the user" (126). She adds that

"what these VR encounters really provide is an illusion of control over reality, nature, and especially over the unruly, gender- and race-marked, essentially mortal body. . . . With virtual reality we are offered the vision of a body-free universe" (127). Significantly, Balsamo connects these discourses of disembodiment with "at least one very traditional cultural narrative: the possibility of transcendence, whereby the physical body and its social meanings can be technologically neutralized. . . . [T]he applications that include a representation of the body project a utopian desire for control over the *form* of personal embodiment." Anne Balsamo, *Technologies of the Gendered Body: Reading Cyborg Women* (Durham: Duke University Press, 1996), 128; emphasis added.

23. N. Katherine Hayles, "Boundary Disputes: Homeostasis, Reflexivity, and the Foundations of Cybernetics," *Configurations* 2 (1994): 464. Hereafter all references will appear parenthetically in the text.

24. Feinberg's experience is more complex, but she nevertheless produces a similar rhetoric about the body in *Stone Butch Blues*. After Jess undergoes a mastectomy, Feinberg writes: "There it was—the body I'd wanted. I wondered why it had to have been so hard" (177). Later Feinberg writes that "the surgery was a gift to myself, a coming home to my body" (224).

25. Jacquelyn N. Zita, "Male Lesbians and the Postmodern Body," *Hypatia* 7.4 (1992): 126; emphasis added.

26. For this reason I am especially interested in reading Jay Prosser's book *Second Skins: The Body Narratives of Transsexuality* (see n. 3).

27. Judith Halberstam, "F2M: The Making of Female Masculinity," in *The Lesbian Postmodern*, ed. Laura Doan, Between Men–Between Women: Lesbian and Gay Studies Series (New York: Columbia University Press, 1994), 212.

28. Rosi Braidotti, "Organs without Bodies," *differences* 1.1 (1989): 151.

Sexual Difference and Collective Identities
The New Constellation

Seyla Benhabib

Postmodernism and Globalization

In retrospect, the term *postmodernism,* which dominated discussions in the humanities and the social sciences in the 1980s and which announced a new spirit of the epoch, appears to have captured a play at the level of surfaces only. Postmodernism heralded the end of history, understood as a cumulative, progressive, coherent sequence; postmodernism announced the end of man and reduced the anthropological subject to a vanishing face in the sand, a disappearing signifier, a fractured, centerless creature. Postmodernism trumpeted the end of philosophy and of master-narratives of justification and legitimation. Certainly, there were distinctions between postmodernism and poststructuralism. While the former designates a movement with wide currency in many different fields, the latter refers to a specific moment in the evolution of theory in the European but particularly French context, at which point Marxist and psychoanalytic paradigms, as well as the models of Claude Lévi-Strauss and Ferdinand de Saussure, which had dominated French theory construction from the early 1960s onward, came to an end. Judith Butler and Chantal Mouffe were correct in remarking that one should not lump together Michel Foucault, Jean-François Lyotard, Jacques Derrida, as if they all represented the same philosophical traditions.[1] Nonetheless, each of these thinkers, in different ways, contributed to the set of cultural sensibilities that we associated in the 1980s with the term *postmodernism.*

Frederic Jameson was one of the few social and cultural critics to point out that postmodernism's fixation upon incommensurabilities, conflicts, and antagonisms at the level of surfaces was failing to account for processes of uniformization and homogenization occurring at deeper levels. Jameson sought to establish links between late capitalism's developmental stage and postmodernism. Contingency at the surface is necessity at a deeper level, he argued; antagonism at one level is subservience to the same forces at another, less visible level.[2] Jameson was right: there is little question that the surface antagonisms, conflicts, and agonistics noted by postmodernists were accompanied by deeper forces of economic, military, technological, communications, and information integration, in short, by what we have come to call "globalization" in the 1990s. If *fragmentation* was the code word of the 1980s, *hybridity* is the code word of the 1990s; if *incommensurability* was a master term for the 1980s, *interstitiality* is the one for the 1990s; if the "clash of cultures" was the horizon of the 1980s, *multiculturalism* and *polyglotism* are the framework of the 1990s.[3]

It is my thesis that the new constellation formed by the coming together of global integration and apparent cultural fragmentation is the contemporary horizon against the backdrop of which we must rethink the project of contemporary feminism. Our contemporary condition is marked by the melting down of all naturalistic signifiers in the political and cultural realm and a desperate attempt to recreate them. The decline of superpower polarism and the end of the Cold War have brought with them a dizzying reconfiguration in the map of Europe. But not only in Europe, elsewhere in the world as well, one senses contradictory pulls at work: as globalization proceeds at a dizzying rate, as a material global civilization encompasses the earth from Hong Kong to Lima, from Pretoria to Helsinki, worldwide integration is accompanied by cultural and collective disintegration. India and Turkey, among the earliest and oldest democracies of the Third World, are in the throes of religious struggles and ethnic strife that at times call into question the very project of a secular representative democracy. Need one mention the civil war in the former Yugoslavia, the ethnic massacres in Bosnia and Kosovo, or the simmering nationality conflicts in Chechneya, Azerbaidjan, Macedonia, and Rwanda? As the markers of certainty at the economic, geopolitical, and technological spheres decline, and such differentials can no longer be used to create hierarchies among nations and cultures, new signifiers are generated to fill their place—signifiers that seek to renaturalize historical and cultural identities by presenting them as if they were racially and anthropologically deep-seated distinctions.[4] The worldwide resurgence of ethnic and nationalist movements, at a time of the decline and weakness of nation-states everywhere, is a further testimony to this process. What does this mean for contemporary feminism? How can we think of sexual difference in the context of new struggles around collective identities?

Debates around identity, which have always played a crucial role in the women's movement, are now dominating nationalist, separatist aspirations worldwide. The purpose of this contribution is to engage in a retrospective analysis of identity debates within feminism of the last two decades while keeping in mind the insights and dangers inaugurated by the new global constellation. The "paradigm wars" of feminist theory, which raged among critical and poststructuralist theorists in particular, lead me to draw some general analytical conclusions about identities, be they personal, gender, or national ones. I will propose a narrative model for conceptualizing identity at all these levels, and, by toggling back and forth between global political considerations and the concerns of feminist theory, I hope to outline a viable model for thinking about identities in the context of radical democratic politics.

The Problem of the Subject Revisited

In my view the most important theoretical issue to emerge out of the feminism/postmodernism debates of the 1980s remains the problem of the subject. This problem comprises several others: first, how do we reconceptualize subjectivity in the light of the philosophical contributions of feminism? How does feminism alter our understanding of the traditional epistemological or moral subject of Western philosophy—the *cogito ergo sum* of Descartes or the Kantian rational moral agent who is free only insofar as he can act in accordance with a universal law that as a rational being he legislates to himself? Has the feminist emphasis on embodiedness, intersubjectivity, caring and empathy, sexuality and desire, subverted the categories of the tradition? In doing so, what has it brought in their place?[5]

Second, what is the relation between subjectivity and political agency? Can we think of political/moral/cultural agency only insofar as we retain a robust conception of the autonomous, rational, and accountable subject, or is a concept of the subject as fragmentary and riveted by heterogeneous forces, more conducive to understanding varieties of resistance and cultural struggles of the present?[6] These issues were at the heart of my disagreement with Judith Butler.

My position was that in *Gender Trouble,* at least, Butler subscribed to an overly constructivist view of selfhood and agency that left little room for explaining the possibilities of creativity and resistance. I objected that the term *performativity* appeared to reduce individuals to masks without an actor or to a series of disjointed gender enactments without a center. Butler clarified subsequently that she had meant by "performativity" not a dramaturgical but a linguistic model. She writes in *Bodies That Matter: On the*

Discursive Limits of "Sex": "Performativity is thus not a singular 'act,' for it is always a reiteration of a norm or a set of norms, and to the extent that it acquires an act-like status in the present, it conceals or dissimulates the conventions of which it is a repetition."[7] Relying on Derrida's appropriation of speech-act theory, Butler sees performativity as a reenactment, as an iteration, that in the process of enunciation also transforms what it iterates or enunciates. Repetition and innovation, necessity and contingency, are brought together in an interesting fashion here. I have little quarrel with this view of linguistic agency; however, I think that one needs a stronger concept of human intentionality and a more developed view of those communicative-pragmatic abilities of everyday life in order to explain how speech acts are not only iterations but also innovations and reinterpretations, be it of old linguistic codes, of communicative, or behavioral ones. One needs to supplement Derrida's and Austin's views with Jürgen Habermas's theory of communicative action and speech pragmatics.

This philosophical disagreement concerning the nature of language and human intentionality was not always at the forefront of our earlier exchanges. Butler's most recent work in *Excitable Speech* helps articulate these differences more sharply. In this work Butler explores, among other issues, Derrida's critique of J. L. Austin's theory of speech acts.[8] What she fails to note, and what is of crucial importance in our dispute, is that Derrida and Habermas agree that the Austinian theory of speech acts is too conventionalist, that is, that it identifies performativity with the fulfillment or satisfaction of a given social code or norm.[9] Derrida and Habermas concur that the most interesting aspects of language-in-use occur in those situations when there are no stipulated social rules or codes. Such situational understanding is quite distinct from fulfilling a norm or following a convention. In his critique of John Searle, Derrida complains that Searle's "speech act" theory cannot account for the "surfeit of meaning" that transcends the boundaries of mere conventionality. There is always "more" in language. Derrida writes:

> I do not believe that iterability is necessarily tied to convention, and even less, that it is limited by it. Iterability is precisely that which—once its consequences have been unfolded—can no longer be dominated by the opposition nature/convention. It dislocates, subverts, and constantly displaces the dividing line between the two terms. It has an essential rapport with the force (theoretical and practical, "effective," "historical," "psychic," "political," etc.) deconstructing these oppositional limits.[10]

For Habermas this more in language comes about through the communicative competence of social actors in generating situational interpretations of their life-world through communicative acts oriented to validity claims. For Derrida the surfeit of meaning, the subversions that transform iterations, are part of the bounty of language itself. For Habermas this surfeit is part of the bounty of communication, not merely of language but of language-in-use. The crucial issue is this: Can there be resignification without communication among members of a language game? If, as Derrida argues and Habermas concurs, speech acts are acts not only, or primarily, because they reproduce a set of established norms and conventions but because they reinterpret and resignify, modify, and discursively challenge such norms and conventions, then how does one know, how does anyone know, that such resignification and reinterpretation has taken place?[11] In the Derridian model of speech as enunciation the surplus of meaning seems to reside in the almost oracular quality of utterances themselves. In the model of communicative pragmatics, by contrast, the same proposition, let us say "The moon is made of green cheese," can be treated as incorporating different speech acts, depending on the validity claims raised by the speaker and accepted or rejected by the hearers. For example, is this statement to be understood as a scientific claim about the material composition of the moon or as an expressive-poetic claim about one's emotions concerning the moon? Or is it a normative statement, exhorting us to accept as correct—that is, right—that we should view the moon as if it were made of green cheese? In communicative pragmatics the intentions of the speaker and the negotiations between speaker and hearer about these intentions are articulated through the various validity claims that one and the same proposition can embody. These are the claims to truth or falsehood; rightness or wrongness; sincerity and deception; and intelligibility or the lack thereof. The validity claims of propositions cannot be identified independently of the intentions of their speakers.

As *Excitable Speech* makes admirably clear, views of political agency and legal accountability are inextricably bound up with our philosophical understanding of linguistic activity. Nevertheless, there is still no explication in this account of how regimes of discourse/power, or normative regimes of language and sexuality, both circumscribe and enable the subject. As Allison Weir observes:

> What's lost here is any recognition of the perspectives of the participants in these performances, and hence, any meaningful differentiation among unreflective, deliberative, dogmatic, defensive, anxious, ironic, playful, and parodic performances of gender, and any understanding of the ways in which these interact and conflict in specific performances and particular subjects. What's lost then, is any meaningful concept of agency, and any meaningful concept of subversion.[12]

I would like to suggest a narrative model of subjectivity and identity constitution instead of the performativity model.[13] My contention is that the narrative model has the virtue of accounting for that "surfeit of meaning, creativity and spontaneity," which is said to accompany iteration in the performativity model as well but the mechanisms of which cannot be explained by performativity.

I will introduce the narrative model, first, by an excursus into Virginia Woolf's novel *Orlando* and, in the second place, through a detailed examination of Charles Taylor's views on the constitution of identities through "webs of narratives." There is an interesting convergence of literary and philosophical perspectives here: both Woolf and Taylor outline a notion of a "core" self, the constitution of which Woolf leaves mysterious, and Taylor tries to account for in several ways. My own views of narrativity develop in interlocution with their writings.

The Narrative Model of Identity Constitution I: Virginia Woolf's *Orlando*

Narrativity and identity, or the manner in which the telling of the story of the self reinforces or undermines a particular understanding of self, is a major preoccupation of high modernist literature from Marcel Proust to James Joyce, from Robert Musil to Virginia Woolf. Due to her incisive entanglement of the confluence of one's sense of self with fantasies and expectations about one's sex/gender, Virginia Woolf's work remains a beacon guiding us when we start navigating the stormy waters of identities.

In October 1928, the month during which Virginia Woolf delivered the two lectures that were to form the basis of *A Room of One's Own* (1929), her novel *Orlando* appeared.[14] An exuberant, fantastic, lyrical, satirical novel, *Orlando,* in the words of one critic, "stages the mobility of fantasy and desire; it is a narrative of boundary crossings—of time, space, gender, and sex."[15] This biography begins in the late 1500s in the Elizabethan age as the story of a beautiful and talented young man, of noble descent, good fortune, and great promise—so bright is the future held in store for this young man that the Queen Elizabeth takes a fancy to him and showers him with amorous advances. After falling madly in love with a mysterious and fickle Russian princess, Sasha, Orlando accepts to be sent to Constantinople as the Crown's ambassador; there, falling into a deep trance that lasts several days, he awakens to find himself a woman. "Orlando had become a woman—there is no denying it," writes Woolf.

But in every other respect, Orlando remained precisely as he had been. The change of sex, though it altered their future, did nothing whatever to alter their identity. Their faces remained, as their portraits prove, practically the same. His memory—but in future we must, for convention's sake, say "her" for "his," and "she" for "he"—her memory then, went back through all the events of her past life without encountering any obstacle. Some slight haziness there may have been, as if a few dark drops had fallen into the clear pool of memory; certain things had become a little dimmed; but that was all. (107)

The last phrase—"that was all"—conceals the extent to which the entire novel is a meditation upon the complex themes of personal identity, sexual difference, the construction of gender, and the quest of the artist to discover the innermost sources from which creativity, art, imagination, and fantasy spring. "Orlando was man till the age of thirty; when he became a woman and has remained so ever since" (107). Virginia Woolf's narrative defies easy categorization in terms of androgyny, bisexuality, or the polymorphous perversity of all sexual desire. It is "an exuberant and fantastic sexual ideal,"[16] a story of multiple and transgressional sexuality. Dedicated to Woolf's lover, Vita Sackville-West, and composed during Sackville-West's travels to the Near East, *Orlando* is both "public and private, directed to an audience of one and many."[17]

Having survived the sarcasm, hypocrisy, and baseness of the savants of the eighteenth century, personified by Pope, Addison, and Dryden, Orlando faces the repressive gender roles of the nineteenth century. "One might see the spirit of the age blowing, now hot, now cold, upon her cheeks. And if the spirit of the age blew a little unequally . . . her ambiguous position must excuse her (even her sex was still in dispute) and the irregular life she had lived before." Fixed sexual identity, as defined by rigid gender roles and categories, is not central to the core identity of the self, Woolf intimates. The sources of the self as a unified being, if there are any at all, suggests Woolf, lie deeper. Looking through her shirt pockets, Orlando discovers a "sea-stained, blood-stained, travel-stained," manuscript of her poem "The Oak Tree." She had started working on it back in 1586, close to "three hundred years" ago from the point at which the narrator finds her/himself in the second half of the nineteenth century. Meanwhile, as she looks through the pages of the manuscript, she realizes:

how very little she had changed all these years. She had been a gloomy boy, in love with death, as boys are; and then she had been amorous and florid; and then she had been sprightly and satirical; and sometimes she had tried prose and sometimes she had tried drama. Yet through all these changes she had remained, she reflected, fundamentally the same. She had the same brooding meditative temper, the same love of animals and nature, the same passion for the country and the seasons. (181)

"Yet through all these changes she had remained, she reflected, fundamentally the same." What is the meaning of this "sameness" of the self? Through what sets of characteristics or activities, patterns of consciousness or behavior, do we say of someone that they are the "same"? In philosophical language, how is the identity of the self that remains self-same to be thought of?

Virginia Woolf gives no unequivocal answer to this question—perhaps it allows none. Sometimes she suggests that the core identity of the self is formed by a set of gender-transcending characteristics that in old-fashioned language we would refer to as "character"—Orlando had the "same brooding meditative temper, the same love of animals and nature, the same passion for the country and the seasons." And it is these moral, cognitive, and aesthetic dispositions, Woolf intimates, that constitute her as "fundamentally the same."

The Narrative Model of Identity Constitution II: Charles Taylor's *Sources of the Self*

Charles Taylor's *Sources of the Self* is an attempt to disentangle philosophically the relationships between a sense of core identity and a set of dispositional attitudes, or "strong evaluative commitments," also cherished by the self. Two metaphors dominate Taylor's lucid analysis of self-identity: that of "horizons," on the one hand, and "webs of interlocution," on the other. Of horizons Taylor writes: "My identity is defined by the commitments and identifications which provide the frame or horizon within which I can try to determine from case to case what is good, or valuable, or what ought to be done, or what I endorse or oppose." "To know who I am," he emphasizes, "is a species of knowing where I stand."[18] A horizon of strong evaluations or of strong evaluative commitments is for Taylor "integral" to human personhood.[19]

The metaphor of webs of interlocution suggests a different approach, one more in consonance with a narrative view. "This is the sense in which," Taylor writes,

one cannot be a self on one's own. I am a self only in relation to certain interlocutors: in one way in relation to those conversation partners who were essential to my achieving self-definition; in another in relation to those who are now crucial to my continuing grasp of languages of self-understanding—and, of course, these classes may overlap. A self exists only within what I call "webs of interlocution."[20]

The answer to the question of who I am always involves reference to "where" I am speaking from and to whom or with whom.

The dialogic narrative view, which I share with Taylor and which I shall distinguish from the more essentialist model of "strong evaluative commitments," is the following: To be and to become a self is to insert oneself into webs of interlocution: it is to know how to answer when one is addressed; in turn, it is learning how to address others. Of course, we never really "insert" ourselves but, rather, are thrown into these webs of interlocution, in the Heideggerian sense of *Geworfenheit*. We are born into webs of interlocution, or into webs of narratives—from the familial narrative to the linguistic one to the gender narrative and to the macronarrative of one's collective identity. We become who we are by learning to become a conversation partner in these narratives. Although we do not choose the webs in whose nets we are initially caught or select those with whom we wish to converse, our agency consists in our capacity to weave out of those narratives and fragments of narratives a life-story that makes sense for us, as this unique individual self. Certainly, the codes of established narratives in a culture define our capacity to tell the story in very different ways; they limit our freedom "to vary the code."[21] But, just as in a conversation it is always possible to drop the last remark and let it crash upon the floor in silence or to carry on and keep the dialogue alive and going or to become whimsical, ironic, and critical and to turn the conversation upon itself, so, too, in telling the tale of a life-story that makes sense to us we always have options. These options are not ahistorical; they are culturally and historically specific; furthermore, for each individual there is the master-narrative of the family structure and of gender roles into which he or she is thrown. Nonetheless, just as the grammatical rules of language, once acquired, do not exhaust our capacity to build an infinite number of well-formed sentences in a language, so, too, socialization and accumulation processes do not determine the life-story of this unique individual and his or her capacity to initiate new actions and new sentences in a conversation. Donald Spence, a psychoanalyst, formulates the link between the self and narration perspicaciously:

> It is by means of a continuous dialogue with ourselves—in daydreams, partial thoughts, and full-fledged plans—that we search for ways to interact with our environment and turn happenings into meanings, and we organize these

interactions by putting our reactions into words. . . . Language offers a mechanism for putting myself into the world, as Heidegger might phrase it, and for making the world part of me; and language very likely determines the way in which experience will be registered and later recalled.[22]

Are there really significant distinctions between the dialogic and narrative understanding of the self and the view of strong evaluations that Taylor also adumbrates? Indeed, there are, and spelling them out will give one a firmer grasp of the postmodernist objection that any conception of a "core identity" is essentialist, ahistorical, and implausible.

Consider some postmodern objections to the concept of strong evaluations: certainly, the experiences of fragmentation, collage, the senseless being-next-to-each-other in space and time of individuals, and cultural fragments are authentic. They express and articulate a material and lived reality of our social and cultural world. Particularly postmodern selves seem to suffer from the inability to make strong evaluative commitments. What implications does this have for Taylor's theory? In the face of cultural forms of possible selfhood that contradict his theory, Taylor can say two things: one response could be that individuals do have strong evaluative and constitutive commitments, although they may not be known to them. It is only the standpoint of the observer or the philosophical analyst or the psychotherapist who could disclose them. A second response could be that individuals whose lives lack such strong evaluative commitments also lack the essential conditions of what Taylor refers to as "integral, that is, undamaged human personhood."[23] Taylor entertains both options; it is the second claim that I find particularly problematic and that I would like to focus upon.

How plausible is it to argue that such strong evaluative commitments are essential to human personhood, as essential—let us say—as the capacity to be a conversation partner in a web of interlocution? I think there is a confusion of levels in Taylor's argument at this point: Taylor confuses the *conditions of possible human agency* with a *strong concept of moral integrity*. But it is possible to think of the first without the second. Consider two human types: the seducer and the ironist. The one goes through life accumulating conquests, love affairs, and broken hearts; is unable to make strong commitments or even state where or for what he stands. Or take the ironist: vigilant and self-reflective, self-critical and whimsical, she retains a distance from all commitments; she thrives on not making strong evaluations or strong evaluative commitments.

Of course, Taylor could respond that in the case of the seducer the horizon of strong evaluations out of which he acts are those of narcissistic self-gratification in having others fall for him, whereas in the case of the ironist a certain sense of sovereign control and not giving oneself to any one thing too much is the secret horizon of strong evaluation. If the philosopher were the psychotherapist for these individuals, her task would consist in showing to them what they implicitly presuppose. One could shift from the language of self-description and self-identification to the language of observational assessment to sustain Taylor's view of strong evaluations.

Undoubtedly, in many instances in human life and interaction such a shift in perspective from the standpoint of the agent to that of the observer is justifiable and valid. Nonetheless, it cannot be that there is always and necessarily a disjunction between the language of self-evaluation and description and that of the third-person observer's point of view. I think we can entertain the possibility that there are human lives that lack a horizon of strong evaluations and evaluative commitments. Such lives may lack a certain depth, a certain integrity, a certain vibrancy and vitality, but we know that they can be lived, and we know they are led by some. It just seems wrong to say of a life-story that lacks this core of strong evaluations that it is not a human life-story at all; should we, rather, not say that it is not a very desirable, deep, or worthwhile one? What is at stake here?

We have to think of the continuity of the self in time not through a commitment *to a specific set of evaluative goods* but through the *capacity to take and adopt an attitude* toward such goods, even if, and particularly if, this attitude means one of noncommitment. There can be *self-identity* without *moral integrity;* the core identity of a self is better defined through the second-order attitudes and beliefs that this self has toward making first-order commitments. Put in the language of narration: it is not what the story is about that matters but one's ability to keep telling a story that makes sense to oneself and to others about who one is. Strong evaluative commitments may or may not be a part of such narratives or fragments of narratives. Donald Spence writes of the self as a "signature," a "fingerprint." "The way a life is conceived or described tells us something important about the teller that he very likely does not know himself. . . . The concept of self reminds us that a certain structured constellation of attitudes, principles, and values contributes to our view of everyday happenings and affects the way these happenings are represented in memory and recovered in time."[24] This "certain structured constellation of attitudes" may or may not entail strong evaluations or evaluative commitments. It is the signature that matters, not the document that is signed, or, to remain at the level of metaphor, what matters are the marks left by the fingerprint, not the ink nor what the marks are imprinted upon. Taylor's view of the self is not about the signature but about the document that is signed, and it is not about the imprint but the ink and the pad on which they are left. And this, I am arguing, is a confusion of levels of analysis.

Ironically, objections that consider views like Taylor's concept of strong evaluations essentialist also succumb to the same confusion: they assume that any conception of identity suggests the fiction of a stable, frozen, and fixed subject, preceding in time the multifarious performatives of gender and language, social roles and individual postures, through which we become who we are. The language of strong evaluative commitments suggests a "doer who precedes the deed" (Nietzsche). Yet, if we think of the identity of the self in time not in terms of a set of strong evaluative commitments but, rather, in terms of an ability to make sense, to render coherent, meaningful, and viable for oneself one's shifting commitments as well as changing attachments, then the postmodernist objection loses its target. The issue then becomes whether it is possible to be a self at all without some such ability to continue to generate meaningful and viable narratives over time. My view is that, hard as we try, we cannot "stop making sense," as the Talking Heads urge us to do. We will try to make sense out of nonsense.

Are there constraints, then, on what makes sense? Put differently: what if strong assumptions about narrative with their inevitable overtones of beginning, unfolding, and resolution—the classical model of a tragedy from which we can draw lessons for life—find their way into this model and thus push the illusions of coherence, continuity, and fixity from one level unto the next? I would like to suggest that "making sense" does not involve an Aristotelian or Victorian model of narrative, with a coherent beginning, unfolding, and end. It involves, rather, the psychodynamic capacity to go on, to retell, to re-member, to reconfigure. This retelling, re-membering, and reconfiguring always entail more than one narrative; they occur in a web of interlocution, which is also a conversation with the other(s). Others are not just the subject matters of my story; they are also tellers of their own stories that compete with my own, which unsettle my self-understanding, and which spoil my attempts to "master-mind" my own narrative. Narratives cannot have closure precisely because they are always aspects of the narratives of others; the sense that I create for myself is always immersed in a fragile "web of stories," which I as well as others spin.[25] Psychoanalytic feminism both challenges and supplements the narrative model. "The shadow cast by the other subject," in Jessica Benjamin's words, is permanent.

Psychoanalytic Feminism: The Limits of Narrativity

If we view the human child as a fragile, dependent creature whose body needs to be cared for, sustained, and nurtured and whose various needs have to be satisfied, we have to take seriously the psychoanalytic insight that there is a corporal, somatic memory, that is, the unconscious. This is the point at which the insights of psychoanalytically inspired feminism aid in developing the narrative model further. Every story we tell of ourselves will also contain another of which we may not even be aware, and, in ways that are usually very obscure to us, we are determined by these subtexts and memories in our unconscious. The self is not sovereign, or, in Freud's famous line, "Das Ich ist nicht Herr im eigenen Haus," "the ego is not master in its own house."[26] Poststructuralist/discourse feminists, alert to the oppressive language of *Herrschaft/Knechtschaft,* in Freud's formulation, follow Nietzsche and Foucault in arguing that the *Ich,* the Ego, is an instance that we must get rid of altogether. The psychoanalytic insight that the sovereignty of the "I" is never unlimited but always dependent upon contexts, conscious and unconscious, that the I cannot master, is translated by them into the call to get rid of the I as an instance of coherent mastery and ordering altogether. The I becomes an instance of repression; the sovereignty of the I is viewed as the striving after a form of repressive and illusory unity. Hence, identity is viewed as a suspect category. Perhaps, however, we can think of the phrase "Das Ich ist nicht Herr im eigenen Haus" in quite a different way.

The I can never be master in his house because a household is composed of other beings whose needs, desires, and concrete identities always make claims upon one and remind one of the inevitable perspectivality and limitedness of one's own point of view. Only the male subject could consider itself "the master of the household." All others, women, children, domestics, other dependents like the elderly, always knew that there were limits to mastery and agency. The view that only one perspective dominated could only be the view of the master; they knew how to view themselves as they appeared to the master, as they appeared to one another, and to themselves. A household consists of multiple, complex perspectives and voices often contesting with one another, arguing with one another. Webs of interlocution are often family brawls, and only some family brawls succeed in making good conversations. More often than not they fail. The individual is thus always already situated in a psychosomatic context that we can define as the psychic economy of the household it is born into and grows up in as a child.

Although we can never extricate ourselves from the material and spiritual webs that these beginnings implicate us in, we nonetheless can weave them together into a narrative of the many voices within us and the many perspectives that have constituted our field of vision.

This, however, is an interminable task; for narration is also a project of recollection and retrieval. We can only retrieve more or less, retell more or less, those memories ingrained upon the body, those somatic impressions of touch, tone, and odor that have defined our early being-in-the-world. They can only be relived in the present, as meaningful within our present narrative. They are only "for us," our access to them can never be "in itself," or *an sich*. The attempt to relive these memories outside the temporal horizon of the present would put the self in danger of regression, dissipation, and loss of ego boundaries. For those whose childhood was one of abuse and systematic mistreatment, the present may be a constant process of warding against being overwhelmed by such memories and by the pull of the past. Yet there may also be ways of recouping these memories in the present such as to generate new and future horizons of meaning. Personal identity is the ever fragile achievement of needy and dependent creatures whose capacity to develop a coherent life-story out of the multiple, competing, and often irreconcilable voices and perspectives of childhood must be cherished and protected. Furthering one's capacity for autonomous agency is only possible within a solidaristic community that sustains one's identity through listening to one and allowing one to listen to others with respect within the many webs of interlocution that constitute our lives.

Complex Subjectivities, the Politics of Difference, and the New Constellation

The intuition that there is a close link between certain views of identity/subjectivity and collective politics is an old one. At least since the work of the Frankfurt School, which attempted to explain the rise of fascism in Europe through a mix of Marxist and psychoanalytic theory, we can hold onto the following insight: the inability of an individual at the psychic level to acknowledge the otherness within herself will, more often than not, manifest itself in the urge to split the other off and project it unto an external figuration outside oneself.[27] This projected or "abjected" other is thus excised from oneself; by placing it outside itself, the self feels secure in maintaining the boundaries of its own identity without being threatened by dissolution into otherness. The other is the stranger, the foreigner, the one who is "alien" and "unlike" us. All authoritarian and fascist movements of our century, and not only of ours, manipulate this fear of losing ego boundaries and self-identity by making a group of collective others the bearers and carriers of certain naturalistic traits that are said to be different from and a threat to one's own identity. Already in the sixteenth century, during and after the Spanish Inquisition against the Jews of Spain, the doctrine of *la limpeaza de la sangre* (i.e., the cleanliness of blood) was practiced.[28] Not doctrinal belief or religious practices but a biological category, itself only a phantasmagoric figment of the imagination, became the divider between the Jews and the Catholics. How does one prove "cleanliness of the blood"? In the case of the Spanish Inquisition this meant not only that those who had intermarried but all others who had some Jewish descendants had to be gotten rid of. It is hard to imagine, but this is historically documented, what mechanisms of state control and persecution had to be mobilized in a sixteenth-century society in order to establish, first, the fact of Jewish blood in one's lineage and, second, to carry out the extermination or forced conversion of those so identified.

Think now of a more recent example. During the war in Bosnia Herzogovina it was reported that Bosnian Serb soldiers in several instances not only raped Bosnian Muslim women but detained them in special camps where they were subject to continuous rapes such that they would become pregnant. To view women as the booty of war is an ancient human practice. Yet reflect for a moment on the ethnic genocide behind this act of impregnation. The reasoning of Bosnian Serbs appears to have been the following: since they refuse to acknowledge a separate Muslim Bosnian identity, since in the eyes of the Serbs the Bosnian Muslims are an insignificant and bastard category, a people who should never have been granted official recognition, by impregnating their women, the Serbs took themselves to be ending this group's identity. Muslim women would now bear Bosnian Serb offspring. Yet the bizarre blindness in this act is not recognizing that this offspring would be half-Serb and half-Muslim.[29] Paradoxically, then, the attempt to eliminate ethnic otherness results in the creation of more "ethnic bastardization" or "hybridization." These children of war will become the purest examples of collective impurity and hybridity.

The narrative view of identity regards individual as well as collective identities as woven out of tales and fragments both one's own and those of others. While narrativity stresses otherness and the fluidity of the boundaries between the self and others, authoritarian and repressive movements respond to the search for certainty, for rigid definitions, for boundaries and markers.

"The Shadow of the Other Subject":
Jessica Benjamin's Intervention

In an impressive contribution to these discussions entitled "The Shadow of the Other (Subject): Intersubjectivity and Feminist Theory,"[30] Jessica Benjamin deepens our understanding of the homologies as well as disanalogies between processes of interpsychic and intrapsychic recognition. "The question whether a subject can relate to the other without assimilating the other to the self through identification corresponds to the political question whether a community can admit the Other without her/him having to already be the same, or become the same. What psychoanalysis refers to as omnipotence is thus always linked to the ethical (respect) and the political (non-violence)" (240). Omnipotence is the name for the fantasy that I can mold the world and the others to fit my desires, that I can control them so completely that I will never be rendered vulnerable, dependent, frustrated, and needy. Classical political philosophy named the fantasy of omnipotence the "regime of tyranny."

Yet, despite this homology between accepting the other within and respecting the other without, intrasubjectivity in the psyche and intersubjectivity in the political world cannot be mapped onto each other. "The psychological relations that constitute the self" cannot be collapsed "into the epistemological and political positions that constitute the subject of knowledge or history" (234). For each individual the process of "splitting," as an ongoing active process of idealization and defense performed with respect to the other, has a unique trajectory and logic. The other is significant in this story only insofar as he or she is introjected by the self in a particular manner and imbued with certain meanings. Whether the political other is conceived as the enemy or as the liberator, as the oppressor or the redeemer, as the purifier or the seducer—to play only with some permutations—will depend not only on the cultural codes of the public world but primarily on the individual psychic history of the self.

Benjamin makes the important observation that "the opposition recognition/negation is therefore not precisely the same opposition as mutual recognition/breakdown. All negotiation of difference involves negation, partial breakdowns. Breakdown is only catastrophic when the possibility of reestablishing the tension between negation and recognition is foreclosed, when the survival of the other self, of self for other, is definitely over" (241). An individual may become incapable of establishing and sustaining this tension because she or he is delusional and violent or completely rigid and fragmented. In either case the ability to "narrate" proximity and distance, intimacy and alienation, gets lost or impaired.

Using the analogy advisedly, one can say that, politically, a regime of recognition without negation would correspond to despotism. In the eyes of the despot all are one and equal, but there is no democratic sphere of jostling and collaborating, competing and cooperating. That is why despotism is like the death of the political body: it eliminates the possibility of negation.

What is surprising in Jessica Benjamin's illuminating contribution is her insistence that "identity is not self. To include without assimilating or reducing requires us to think beyond the binary alternatives of self-enclosed identity and fragmented dispersal to a notion of multiplicity. What kind of self can sustain multiplicity, indeed, the opposition to identity that the relation with the different other brings?" (247). Benjamin understands identity as sameness, indeed as the compulsory recreation of sameness. As I have sought to argue, however, precisely because the self cannot be viewed as a substrate that remains self-same over time, other models of identity have been suggested in the Western philosophical tradition. The narrative model of identity is developed precisely in order to counteract this difficulty. According to this model, identity does not mean "sameness in time" but, rather, the capacity to generate meaning over time such as to hold past, present, and future together. In arguing that "inclusion thus calls for difference, not synthesis," Benjamin repeats some of the postmodernist prejudices against the narrative search for coherence. Inclusion, I would argue, does not call for *symbiosis,* but it does call for some kind of *synthesis.*[31] In order to retain the degree of separateness and otherness that the permanent struggle for recognition pushes selves into, a strong sense of respect for the autonomy of the other and for his or her equal right to retain such difference is required.[32] When some such synthetic narrative is not available, then recognition can indeed break down altogether and result in violence and civil war, armed conflict or silent confrontation. As Benjamin succinctly observes, "Owning the other within diminishes the threat of the other without, so that the stranger outside is no longer identical with the strange within us" (250). This capacity to own up to the "strange" within and the "stranger" without presupposes the capacity for narrative synthesis: the capacity to generate individual and collective stories of the many voices within us, reflecting the fragility as well as the complexity of the webs of interlocution that constitute us.

The Vocation of the Feminist Theorist:
A Cultural Broker?

During historical periods such as ours, when economic-technological and political changes are leading to restructuring of millions of lives, the search for certainty grows. The more fluid the environment becomes, the more unpredictable and opaque it grows, the more we retreat into the walls of our certainties, into the markers of the familiar. Hence, globalization is accompanied by demands for isolationism, for protectionism, for raising the walls that divide us and them even higher, for making them sturdier.

Theories of fragmentary and dispersed subjectivity, which were so fashionable at the height of postmodernism, ignored these demands for stability and understanding. The dispersal of the subject, yes, indeed the "death" of the subject, was thought to be a good thing. Yet the search for coherence in an increasingly fragmentary material and cultural world, the attempt to generate meaning out of the complexities of life stories, is neither wrong nor unjust nor meaningless. The challenge in the new constellation is the following: Can there be coherent accounts of individual and collective identity that do not fall into xenophobia, intolerance, paranoia, and aggression toward others? Can the search for coherence be made compatible with the maintenance of fluid ego boundaries? Can the attempt to generate meaning be made compatible with an appreciation of the meaningless, the absurd, and the limits of discursivity? And, finally, can we establish justice and solidarity at home without turning in upon ourselves, without closing our borders to the needs and cries of others? What will democratic collective identities look like in the century of globalization?

One consequence of the new constellation among issues of sexual difference and collective identity is a renewed respect for the universal. The feminist movement in the 1980s lived through a "hermeneutics of suspicion." Every claim to generalization was suspected of hiding a claim to power on the part of a specific group; every attempt to speak in the name of "women" was countered by myriad differences of race, class, culture, and sexual orientation that were said to divide us. The category "woman" became itself suspect, and feminist theorizing that spoke about woman or the female of the species was dubbed the hegemonic discourse of white, middle-class, professional, heterosexual women. We are still reeling from the many divisions and splinterings, the amoebalike splittings, of the women's movements.

I sense, however, a new awareness afoot—a recognition of interdependence among women of different classes, cultures, and sexual orientations;[33] more significantly, I sense a renewed respect for the moral and political legacy of universalism out of which the women's movements first grew in the eighteenth and nineteenth centuries. Consider the remarkable issue on Universalism of the journal *differences*. In "French Feminism Is a Universalism" Naomi Schor writes:

> And yet just as some women have resisted the critique of universalism, so too, universalism has clung to life. This refusal simply to fade away gracefully is indicated by the recent return of the universal among some of the feminist and postmodernist theorists who at other times and in other situations wholeheartedly embraced the critique of universalism. I count myself among them. . . . If Auschwitz dealt the Enlightenment ideal of universalism—a notion rejected by fascism—a death blow, what may pass for the repetition of Auschwitz, the ongoing ethnic cleansing in Bosnia-Herzegovina, has if not revived universalism then called into question the celebration of particularisms, at least in their regressive ethnic form.[34]

A further consequence of the new constellation is a reconceptualization of the position of the feminist theorist as a critical intellectual. In *Situating the Self,* in order to explicate the possibility of social and cultural criticism, which, while being situated and contextbound, nonetheless aspired to transcend its own parish walls, I used the metaphor of exile. I argued that "the social critic who is in exile does not adopt the 'view from nowhere' but the 'view from outside the walls of the city,' wherever those walls and those boundaries might be. It may indeed be no coincidence that from Hypatia to Diotima to Olympe de Gouges and to Rosa Luxembourg, the vocation of the feminist thinker and critic has led her to leave home and the city walls."[35] The metaphor of the exile to describe the vocation of the feminist critic has received a spirited objection from Rosi Braidotti in her provocative work *Nomadic Subjects.*[36] Braidotti agrees with me that we must empower women's political agency without falling "back on a substantialist vision of the subject," but she objects to the emphasis on exile:

> the central figuration for postmodern subjectivity is not that of a marginalized exile but rather that of an active nomadism. The critical intellectual camping at the city gates is not seeking readmission but rather taking a rest before crossing the next stretch of desert. Critical thinking is not a diaspora of the elected few but a massive abandonment of the logocentric "polis," the alleged "center" of the empire, on the part of critical and resisting thinking beings. Whereas for Benhabib the normativity of the phallogocentric regime is negotiable and reparable, for me it is beyond repair. Nomadism is therefore also a gesture of nonconfidence in the capacity of the "polis" to undo the power foundations on which it rests.[37]

This is an eloquent characterization of some fundamental differences. Only Braidotti has an unrealistic conception of identity. For her matters of identity seem infinitely deconstructable figurations. She defines nomadic consciousness as "not taking any kind of identity as permanent." The nomad "is only passing through; s/he makes those necessarily situated connections that can help her/him to survive, but s/he never takes on fully the limits of one, national fixed identity. The nomad has no passport—or has too many of them."[38]

Yet there is an enormous difference between having no passport or having too many. The refugee, the illegal immigrant, the asylum seeker, who have no passport also have no protection from the collective and organized power of their fellow human beings. She or he is at the mercy of border patrols, emigration officials, international relief organizations.[39] She has lost, in Hannah Arendt's famous words, "the right to have rights," that is, the right to be recognized as a moral and political equal in a human community.[40] In a century that has made statelessness and the condition of being a refugee a global phenomenon, this is not a matter to be taken lightly.

To have too many passports is the privilege usually of the few. Nation-states are still loathe to recognize the status of dual citizenship: it is only rare circumstances of family, work, and political history that place one in these situations. I would agree with Braidotti that the complexity of our cultural, ethnic, racial, and linguistic identities and heritages are not reflected in our passports, in our identity as nationals of this or that state. We must have the right, however, to become a member of a polity; the rules of entry into a polity must be fair and in accordance with human dignity. And to achieve this we must indeed renegotiate the normativity of the "logocentric polis." The feminist theorist at the present is one of the brokers in this complex renegotiation of sexual difference and new collective identities.

Having started with Virginia Woolf, let me end by returning to *Orlando* once more. It is now Thursday, October 11, 1928, and Orlando is driving past Old Kent Road to the family estate that they have possessed for four hundred years. Orlando, now a mother and writer, calls Orlando at the turn by the barn, but Orlando did not come. But she had many other selves to choose from: "A biography is considered complete if it merely accounts for six or seven selves, whereas a person may well have as many thousand" (235). For some unaccountable reason, complains Virginia Woolf, sometimes the conscious self wishes to be but one self. "This," she observes, "is what some people call the true self, and it is, they say, compact of all the selves we have it in us to be; commanded and locked up by the Captain self, the Key self, which amalgamates and controls them all" (236). Having winked in the direction of the Nietzschean-Freudian critique of the unitary self as the captain self with the master key, Woolf now bows toward Taylor's theory of strong evaluative commitments.

> And it was at this moment, when she had ceased to call "Orlando" and was deep in thoughts of something else that the Orlando whom she had called came of its own accord. . . . The whole of her darkened and settled, as when some foil whose addition makes the round and solidity of a surface is added to it, and the shallow becomes deep and the near distant; and all is contained as water is contained by the sides of a well. So she was now darkened, stilled, and become, with the addition of this Orlando, what is called, rightly or wrongly, a single self, a real self. (249)

These are not the last lines of the novel and I do not want to leave the impression that they may be. In the last pages of the book Orlando experiences moments of intense recollection and ultimate reconciliation, uttering, "Ecstasy," as she catches a vision of her seafaring captain husband, now returned, Shelmerdine. A quaint, romantic, we might even say regressively traditional female ending to a novel so daring! But I shall resist the temptation to draw a single, coherent philosophical conclusion from Woolf's complex narrative, for I frankly do not know that there is a single conclusion to be drawn. The mark of a great work of art is to hold together in a single intuition those complex conceptual relationships that it is the task of philosophical reflection to disentangle.

NOTES

This essay has been a long time in the making. Versions of it were delivered at the NEH Seminar on Ethics and Aesthetics organized by Anthony Cascardi and Charles Altieri at the University of California at Berkeley in the summer of 1993. The discussion of Virginia Woolf and Charles Taylor formed part of a lecture delivered at the Northwestern Humanities Institute Series that took place in the spring of 1994 and entitled "Sources of the Self in Contemporary Feminist Theory." Versions were read as a plenary address to the conference on "Virtual Gender: Past Projections, Future Histories," organized by the Interdisciplinary Group for Historical Literary Study and the Women's Studies Program at Texas A&M University in April 1996, at the New School for Social Research Graduate Faculty Women in Philosophy Colloquium in the spring of 1996, and in March 1998 at the Cambridge University Interdisciplinary Feminist Philosophy Colloquium. It will also be published in SIGNS 24.2 (winter 1999): 335–63. Copyright © 1999 by the University of Chicago. All rights reserved. My thanks go to participants on all those occasions for their criticisms and comments. I owe special thanks to Bonnie Honig, Lynn Layton, Doris Sommer, Jill Frank, and Melissa Lane for commenting on versions of this essay at various stages of its evolution.

1. See Judith Butler, "Contingent Foundations: Feminism and the Question of 'Postmodernism'"; and Chantal Mouffe, "Feminism, Citizenship, and Radical Democratic Politics," both in *Feminists Theorize the Political,* ed. Judith Butler and Joan W. Scott (New York: Routledge, 1992), 3–22; 369–85.

2. Frederic Jameson, *Postmodernism; or, The Cultural Logic of Late Capitalism* (Durham: Duke University Press, 1991), 37–38, 48ff.

3. "Political empowerment," writes Homi Bahba, "and the enlargement of the multiculturalist cause, come from posing questions of solidarity and community from the interstitial perspective." *The Location of Cultures* (New York: Routledge, 1994), 3.

4. The new literature on Islamic movements, and in particular the use of terms like *Jihad* to designate all aspirations in the contemporary world for ethnic, religious, and cultural particularisms, even if well intentioned, unfortunately contribute to the portrayal of "Islam" as the enemy of the West. After the end of the Cold War Islam becomes the new arch enemy. The title, when not the substance, of Benjamin Barber's well-known book *Jihad vs. McWorld: How Globalism and Tribalism Are Reshaping the World* (New York: Ballantine Books, 1995) succumbs to these tendencies.

5. See the important new collection by feminist philosophers of a more analytical orientation, Louise M. Anthony and Charlotte Witt, eds., *A Mind of One's Own: Feminist Essays on Reason and Objectivity* (Boulder: Westview, 1993).

6. One of the more exciting and incisive contributions to our exchange, collected as *Feminist Contentions: A Philosophical Exchange* (New York: Routledge, 1995), is the recent article by Amanda Anderson entitled, "Debatable Performances: Restaging Contentious Feminisms" (*Social Text* 16 [1998]: 1–24). Anderson passes some unfortunate judgments about the motives as well as the context of the publication of this work, naming us "an elite 'gang of four'" (1). Despite some unwarranted rhetorical side-flourishes, Anderson defends a "more capacious model of dialogue, one that can accommodate different forms of political practice, particularly disruptions of spectacle, performance" (2). Defending Habermas against me, or my earlier work against exchanges with Butler, Anderson attempts to show how communicative ethics can be made compatible with processes "of radical *disidentification*" (2). I find this an interesting argument; however, I remain skeptical on two counts: first, as I argue in the body of this article, "disidentification" only works against a background of identification constituted through narrative. Otherwise, disidentification may not be in the service of the self, but it can further the dissolution of a strong sense of self. Second, I also remain skeptical about the "transformative-political" potential of such performative disidentifications. As Anderson notes (19), I am a civil-libertarian on a whole range of issues relating to pornography, sadomasochism, etc., but I do not share the optimism of the artistic avant-garde of the modern period, since the Dadaist movement of this century, that the performa-

tive disruptions of artistic life must also produce good politics. The *politics of culture* must always be judged against the background of the *culture of politics* in any given country. The United States, since the 1960s, has managed to produce an avant-garde artistic culture in arts, theater, dance, music, and literature, which is the envy of the world, without managing to solve the problems of corrupt campaign financing, blockages in legislative processes, misguided foreign policy, lack of universal healthcare coverage, parental leave, decent housing and education, for all who live in this polity. It is my sense of these discontinuities and contradictions between culture and politics, and not some "cultural purism," that leads me to be skeptical about the "cultural politics of the performative."

7. Judith Butler, *Bodies That Matter: On the Discursive Limits of "Sex"* (New York: Routledge, 1993), 12.

8. Judith Butler, *Excitable Speech* (New York: Routledge, 1997), 146–55.

9. Jürgen Habermas, "Excursus: On Leveling the Genre Distinction between Philosophy and Literature," in *The Philosophical Discourse of Modernity,* trans. Frederick Lawrence (Cambridge: MIT Press, 1987), 194–99.

10. Jacques Derrida, "Limited Inc a b c . . . ," in *Limited Inc.,* trans. Samuel Weber (Evanston: Northwestern University Press, 1988), 102.

11. Martin Jay had seen these different orientations to language to be the central issue of contention among critical theorists and poststructuralists in his essay "The Debate over Performative Contradiction: Habermas versus the Poststructuralists," in *Philosophical Interventions in the Unfinished Project of Enlightenment,* ed. by A. Honneth, Thomas McCarthy, Claus Offe, and Albrecht Wellmer (Cambridge: MIT Press, 1992), 261–80.

For an exploration of the complex issues of understanding (*Verstaendigung*), reaching understanding (*Einverstaendnis*), and consensus (*Konsens*) in universal pragmatics, see the exchange between myself and David Hoy on Habermas's theory of universal pragmatics: Seyla Benhabib, "The Local, the Contextual and/or Critical," and David Hoy, "Debating Critical Theory," *Constellations: An International Journal of Critical and Democratic Theory* 3.1 (1996): 83–95, 104–15.

12. Allison Weir, *Sacrificial Logics: Feminist Theory and the Critique of Identity* (New York: Routledge, 1996), 127.

13. I would like to caution that I am using these terms in the specific sense that they have acquired in this debate. At some level all narratives are performatives, and many performatives involve a narrative dimension. Nonetheless, at the level of identity constitution these terms suggest distinct theoretical options. Also, the term *performativity* has been used to refer to a theory of individual identity constitution as well as to a theory of sexual identity formation. In this essay I am dealing with individual and collective identities and not with sexual identity per se. I thank Doris Sommer for alerting me to possible misunderstandings in the uses of these terms.

14. Virginia Woolf, *Orlando: A Biography,* 9th ed. (Glasgow: Triad Grafton, 1977), 106–7. All references in parentheses in the text are to this edition.

15. Karen R. Lawrence, "Orlando's Voyage Out," *Modern Fiction Studies* 38. 1 (1992): 253.

16. Kari Elise Lokke, "Orlando and Incandescence: Virginia Woolf's Comic Sublime," *Modern Fiction Studies* 38.1 (1992): 236.

17. Lawrence, "Orlando's Voyage Out," 257.

18. Charles Taylor, *Sources of the Self: The Making of Modern Identity* (Cambridge: Harvard University Press, 1989), 27.

19. Surely, however, this claim is far too specific to a certain ethos of modernity to be generalizable backward and forward in the history of culture. The language of strong evaluations and strong evaluative commitments implies an ethics of autonomy and an ethos of disenchantment. Since our moral and value universes have become disenchanted in characteristically modern ways, we are thrust into the position of making strong evaluations and strong evaluative commitments. In an enchanted universe these evaluations are not "mine"; they simply are "part" of my being in virtue of the constitutive identity that I share with others. They are mine because they are a part of my value universe. The language of strong evaluative commitments with its Kantian and Weberian overtones would be curiously out of place here. Joel Anderson analyzes the tensions between Taylor's "expressivism and his moral realism" in "The Personal Lives of Strong Evaluators," *Constellations: An International Journal of Critical and Democratic Theory* 3.1 (1996): 17–39.

20. Taylor, *Sources of the Self,* 36.

21. Thanks to Toni Morrison's contributions in giving voice to black Americans, and in particular African American women, we have learned the variability of "narratives and codes" across groups and cultures. The comparative study of narrative voices and codes would contribute to a philosophical understanding of the constitution of selfhood across racial and gender divides. Morrison's work also shows us the indispensability of narrative for the *empowerment* of oppressed and marginal groups.

22. Donald Spence, "Turning Happenings into Meanings: The Central Role of the Self," in *The Book of the Self: Person, Pretext and Process,* ed. Polly Young-Eisendrath and James Hall (New York: New York University Press, 1987), 134.

23. Taylor, *Sources of the Self,* 27.

24. Donald Spence, "Turning Happenings into Meanings," 132–33.

25. Margaret R. Somers and Gloria D. Gibson write: "Above all, narratives are *constellations of relationships* (connected parts) embedded in *time and space,* constituted by *causal emplotment*" in "Reclaiming the Epistemological 'Other': Narrative and the Social Constitution of Identity," in *Social Theory and the Politics of Identity,* ed. by Craig Calhoun (Cambridge: Basil Blackwell, 1994), 37–99, esp. 59. Emphasizing that the narratives within which social actions are embedded can only be intelligible against a background, Somers and Gibson attempt to connect views of social structure and social agency through the narrative paradigm. "Narrative identities are constituted by a person's temporally and spatially variable 'place' in culturally constructed stories comprised of (breakable) rules, (variable) practices, binding (and unbinding) institutions, and the multiple plots of family, nation, or economic life" (67).

This view of narrative is metatheoretical, or second order, in that it does not prejudge the content of the culturally constructed stories, practices, and institutions and should not be confused with theories of relationality and the "relational self" (Carol Gilligan). Relationality is *one form* of narrative emplotment. Furthermore, in that culturally constructed stories are comprised of rules, this view is also compatible with universal pragmatics, which seeks to analyze such rules as they would undergird all cultural constructions insofar as they are only reproduced by the communicative competence of ordinary actors. Equally significantly, practices and institutions are not narratives themselves; they constrain narratives; they limit the agent's abilities to vary the code although they are lived through and experienced by social agents through narrative emplotment. As Somers and Gibson write, "Although we argue that social action is intelligible only through the construction, enactment, and appropriation of narratives, this does not mean that actions are free to fabricate narratives at will; rather, they must 'choose' from a repertoire of available representations and stories. Which kinds of narratives will socially predominate is contested politically and will depend in large part on the distribution of power" ("Narrative and Social Identity," 73).

The pitfalls of moving too quickly from a metatheoretical perspective on narratively constituted actions and identities to prescribing social science methodologies is incisively analyzed by Sayres S. Rudy in "Global Books and Local Stories: Theory and Anti-Theory in Social Research," in *Proceedings of the Junior Fellow's Conference,* vol. 3 (Vienna: 1998), 61–111. Institut fuer die Wissenschaften vom Menschen.

In this essay I am developing a metatheoretical, or second-order, perspective for conceptualizing narratively constituted identities. The social-theoretical implications of this perspective would need to be worked out in future work. My thesis is that narrativity and critical social theory based on the communicative action paradigm are mutually compatible.

26. Sigmund Freud, "A Difficulty in the Path of Psychoanalysis," in *Standard Edition of the Complete Psychological Works,* ed. and trans. James Strachey (London: Hogarth, 1953ff.), 17: 143.

27. Julia Kristeva has also explored these links in *Nations without Nationalism,* trans. Leon S. Roudiez (New York: Columbia University Press, 1993).

28. Benzion Netanyahu, *The Marranos of Spain, from the late XIVth to the XVIIIth Century* (Millwood, N.Y.: Kraus Reprint Co., 1973).

29. I thank Professor Michael Herzfeld for pointing out that, according to kinship practices of these groups, it would be the father's rather than the mother's ethnic identity that would determine ethnic lineage!

30. Jessica Benjamin, "The Shadow of the Other (Subject)," *Constellations: An International Journal of Critical and Democratic Theory* 1.2 (1994): 231–55. Hereafter all references will appear parenthetically in the text.

31. The question of "synthesis," whether in psychology or epistemology—that is, whether all attempts at unity and the search for some general rule that particulars share are inherently oppressive and repressive—has been at the center of recent debates in critical theory. Formulated very generally, while critical theorists seek to

defend the possibility of "synthesis without violence," most poststructuralists, beginning with Jacques Lacan in his work on the ego, deny this possibility. For a general statement of the epistemological problem, see Albrecht Wellmer, "The Dialectic of Modernism and Postmodernism: The Critique of Reason since Adorno," *The Persistence of Modernity: Essays on Aesthetics, Ethics, and Postmodernism*, trans. David Midgley (Cambridge: MIT Press, 1991); Joel Whitebook gives an incisive and extensive discussion of different ideals of the ego and of synthesis prevalent in critical theory and poststructuralism while exploring the ambiguities of Adorno's position, in *Perversion and Utopia: A Study in Psychoanalysis and Critical Theory* (Cambridge: MIT Press, 1995), esp. 119–65. Philosophically, we are dealing with the same issue of how to understand activity, be it linguistic or epistemological, psychic or social, that is rule governed without being at the same time dogmatically subservient to the rules but creative, innovative, and playful in contextually implementing them.

32. Benjamin misunderstands my use of the term *autonomy* in the debate with Judith Butler. She writes: "The autonomy and intact reflexivity that Benhabib wants to rescue have been revealed to be an illusion, based on the denial of the subject's social production, on a break that conceals and represses what constitutes it" (233). She also claims that there is a contradiction between the conception of autonomy I use in the debate with Butler and my position in the "Generalized and Concrete Other." See Benjamin, "The Shadow of the Other (Subject)," 251n. 5.

Benjamin confuses autonomy with autarchy—only an autarchical conception of autonomy would deny the "subject's social production." Since *Critique, Norm and Utopia* I have subscribed to the notion that autonomy is not autarchy and that the ability to distance oneself from one's social roles, traditions, history, and even deepest commitments and to take a universalistic attitude of hypothetical questioning toward them is what constitutes autonomy. This is the salvageable and still valid kernel of the Kantian injunction to consider ourselves as beings who, through their actions, could legislate a universally valid moral law. Indeed, the "intersubjective" turn of Kantian ethics, initiated by Karl Otto-Apel and Jürgen Habermas, has been at the center of my concerns for the last decade. In this discourse ethics model we understand "universalizability" in procedural terms as the ability to take the standpoint of the other in an actual and idealized moral dialogue through a process of reversing perspectives. As Thomas McCarthy has observed, "The emphasis shifts from what each can will without contradiction to be a general law, to what all can will in universal agreement to be a universal norm." *The Critical Theory of Jürgen Habermas* (Cambridge: MIT Press, 1978), 326.

My contribution to this general program has been the insistence, thoroughly inspired by feminist moral theory and psychoanalysis, that taking the "standpoint of the other" in real and virtual moral discourse be understood so as to include the "concrete," and not only the "generalized," other. This conception of autonomy requires no denial of the heteronomy of the subject, that is, of the fundamental dependence of the self on webs of narrative interlocution that constitute it. Only to be "constituted" by narrative is not to be "determined" by it; situatedness does not preclude critical distantiation and reflexivity. As I wrote in *Critique, Norm and Utopia,* "The ideal community of communication corresponds to an ego identity which allows the unfolding of the relation to the concrete other on the basis of *autonomous* action." Seyla Benhabib, *Critique, Norm and Utopia: A Study of the Normative Foundations of Critical Theory* (New York: Columbia University Press, 1986), 342. I see no reason to retract this claim. In these post-utopian times we have become more sensitive to the breakdown of recognition and communication. We have come to see the recalcitrance of alterity, the violence always lurking in human relationships, the potential for breakdown of communication, and the disappointment and hurt that accompany unrequited recognition and love. But in these hard times as well the task of critical philosophy is to think through beyond the given to the regulative limits of our concepts. "Autonomy" in action, conduct, and thought that is generated through critical reflection and a principled moral stance is one such limit-concept of modern philosophy. It must not be confused with the fantasy of "autarchy," which also inhabits the early bourgeois male imagination and which I have discussed in "The Generalized and the Concrete Other," included in *Situating the Self: Gender, Community and Postmodernism in Contemporary Ethics* (New York and London: Routledge and Polity, 1986).

33. The work of María Lugones on "mestizaje" ("Purity, Impurity and Separation," *Signs* 19.2 [1994]: 458–80) and Gloria Anzaldúa and Norma Alarcón on cultural interstitiality (*Making Face, Making Soul/Haciendo Caras: Creative and Critical Perspectives by Women of Color* [San Francisco: Aunt Lute Books, 1990], 361) deal with parallel themes. I would like to thank my student Edwina Barvosa for drawing my attention to Chicana women's writing and multiplex identities in her dissertation "Multiple Identity and Citizenship: The Political Skills of Multiplex Identities," (Ph.D. diss., Harvard University, 1998).

34. Naomi Schor, "French Feminism Is a Universalism," *differences: A Journal of Feminist and Critical Studies* 7.1 (1995): 15–48, esp. 28.

35. Benhabib, "Feminism and the Question of Postmodernism," in *Situating the Self,* 228.

36. Rosi Braidotti, *Nomadic Subjects: Embodiment and Sexual Difference in Contemporary Feminist Theory* (New York: Columbia University Press, 1994).

37. Braidotti, *Nomadic Subjects,* 32.

38. Braidotti, *Nomadic Subjects,* 32.

39. Benhabib, "Democracy and Identity: Dilemmas of Citizenship in Contemporary Europe," in *Democracy—A Culture of the West? Proceedings of the German Political Science Association* (Leverkusen: Leske and Budrich, 1998).

40. Hannah Arendt, *The Origins of Totalitarianism* (1951; rpt., New York: Harcourt, Brace and Jovanovich, 1979), 290ff. See also Seyla Benhabib, *The Reluctant Modernism of Hannah Arendt* (London: Sage Publications, 1996).

Contributors

Harriette Andreadis is Associate Professor of English at Texas A&M University. Her classic article "The Sapphic-Platonics of Katherine Phillips (1631–1664)," which originally appeared in *Signs: A Journal of Women in Culture and Society,* has been reprinted in *Literature Criticism from 1400 to 1800,* vol. 30 (Gale Research Inc., 1996). She is completing a book-length study of the history of early modern female same-sex relations *Sappho in Early Modern England: Constructions of a Female Erotics, 1550–1700.*

Seyla Benhabib is Professor of political theory in the Government Department at Harvard University. She is the author of *Critique, Norm and Utopia: The Normative Foundations of Critical Theory* (Columbia University Press, 1986), *Situating the Self: Gender, Community, and Postmodernism in Contemporary Ethics* (Routledge and Polity, 1992), and *The Reluctant Modernism of Hannah Arendt* (Sage, 1996) and coeditor of *Feminist Contentions: A Philosophical Exchange* (Routledge, 1994). She currently chairs the Committee for the Degree on Social Studies.

Charlotte Canning is Associate Professor of theater history, criticism, and theory in the Department of Theater and Dance at the University of Texas at Austin. She is the author of *Feminist Theaters in the U.S.A.: Staging Women's Experience* (Routledge, 1996).

Bernice L. Hausman is Assistant Professor of English at Virginia Polytechnic Institute and State University. She is author of *Changing Sex: Transsexualism, Technology, and the Idea of Gender* (Duke University Press, 1995) and has published in *Journal of the History of Sexuality, Journal of Medical Humanities,* and *Feminist Studies.* Her current research concerns contemporary practices of infant feeding and maternal embodiment.

Janel Mueller is William Rainey Harper Professor in the Humanities and the editor of *Modern Philology.* She is the author of *The Native Tongue and the*

Word: Developments in English Prose Style, 1380–1580 (University of Chicago Press, 1984) as well as numerous articles and books on Renaissance and seventeenth-century literature.

Mary Ann O'Farrell is Associate Professor of English at Texas A&M University. She is the author of *Telling Complexions: The Nineteenth-Century English Novel and the Blush* (Duke University Press, 1997). She is currently at work on a project about representations of blindness in literature and film.

Kay Schaffer is Associate Professor in the Department of Social Inquiry at the University of Adelaide. She is most recently coeditor (with Sidonie Smith and Jennifer Sabbioni) of *Indigenous Australian Voices: A Reader* (Rutgers University Press, 1998) and *Constructions of Colonialism: Eliza Fraser's Shipwreck* (Cassell, 1998); she is also the author of *In the Wake of First Contact: The Eliza Fraser Stories* (Cambridge University Press, 1995) as well as numerous articles in literary and feminist journals.

Sidonie Smith is Professor of English and Women's Studies and Director of Women's Studies at the University of Michigan. Her most recent publications include: *Women, Autobiography, Theory: A Reader,* coedited with Julia Watson (University of Wisconsin Press, 1998); *Indigenous Australian Voices: A Reader,* coedited with Kay Schaffer and Jennifer Sabbioni (Rutgers University Press, 1998). She is also the author of *Subjectivity, Identity, and the Body: Women's Autobiographical Practices in the Twentieth Century* (Indiana University Press, 1993). She has just completed a book on women's travel narratives called *Women on the Move: Twentieth-Century Travel Narratives and Technologies of Motion* (University of Minnesota Press, forthcoming).

Carroll Smith-Rosenberg is Professor of History and Women's Studies at the University of Michigan; she is also graduate chair of the American Culture Program. She is the author of *Disorderly Conduct: Visions of Gender in Victorian America* (Oxford University Press, 1985) and editor of *Women in Culture and Politics: A Century of Change* (Indiana University Press, 1986). She has also written numerous articles on women, gender, and sexuality.

Helen Thompson is Assistant Professor of English at Arizona State University. She has published an essay on Frances Burney's *Evelina* and is presently working on a study of misrecognition, disguise, and the category of the self in the early English novel.

Lynne Vallone is Associate Professor of English at Texas A&M University. She is the author of *Disciplines of Virtue: Girls' Culture in the Eighteenth and Nineteenth Centuries* (Yale University Press, 1995) and the coeditor (with Claudia Nelson) of *The Girls' Own: Cultural Histories of the Anglo-American Girl, 1850–1915* (University of Georgia Press, 1994). She is completing a book-length study of Queen Victoria's girlhood.

Robyn R. Warhol is Professor of English and Director of Women's Studies at the University of Vermont. She is the author of *Gendered Interventions: Narrative Discourse in the Victorian Novel* (Rutgers University Press, 1989) and the coeditor (with Diane Price Herndl) of *Feminisms: An Anthology of Literary Theory and Criticism,* now in a revised second edition (1997). She is currently completing a book entitled *Having a Good Cry: Feelings and Popular Cultural Forms.*

Index